Fictions Inc.

FICTIONS INC.

The Corporation in Postmodern Fiction,
Film, and Popular Culture

RALPH CLARE

Rutgers University Press
NEW BRUNSWICK, NEW JERSEY, AND LONDON

LIBRARY OF CONGRESS CATALOGING-IN-PUBLICATION DATA

Clare, Ralph, 1975–
 Fictions Inc. : the corporation in postmodern fiction, film, and popular culture / Ralph Clare.
  pages cm
  Includes bibliographical references and index.
  ISBN 978-0-8135-6588-0 (hardcover : alk. paper)
  ISBN 978-0-8135-6587-3 (pbk. : alk. paper)
  ISBN 978-0-8135-6589-7 (e-book)
 1. American fiction—20th century—History and criticism. 2. Capitalism in literature. 3. Corporations in literature. 4. Industries in literature. 5. Motion pictures—Social aspects—United States—History—20th century. 6. Motion pictures—United States—Plots, themes, etc. 7. Postmodernism—United States—History—20th century. I. Title. II. Title: Corporation in postmodern fiction, film, and popular culture.
 PS374.C36C53 2014
 813'.5093553—dc23   2014000068

A British Cataloging-in-Publication record for this book is available from the British Library.

A version of chapter 5 originally appeared in *Studies in the Novel* 45.1 (2013): 102–122, and a version of chapter 6 appeared in *Critique: Studies in Contemporary Fiction* 54.1 (2012): 28–45. The author wishes to thank both journals for the permission to reprint the essays in modified form here. The Hal Leonard Corporation has granted permission to use the lyrics from Stereolab's "Wow and Flutter," written by Tim Gane and Laetitia Sadler, from the album *Mars Audio Quintet* (Elektra, 1994). The University of California Press has given permission to use several lines from Rainer Maria Rilke's "The Swan" from *Rilke: Selected Poems*. Trans. C.F. MacIntyre. U of California P, 1940.

Copyright © 2014 by Ralph Clare. All rights reserved

No part of this book may be reproduced or utilized in any form or by any means, electronic or mechanical, or by any information storage and retrieval system, without written permission from the publisher. Please contact Rutgers University Press, 106 Somerset Street, New Brunswick, NJ 08901. The only exception to this prohibition is "fair use" as defined by U.S. copyright law.

Visit our website: http://rutgerspress.rutgers.edu

Manufactured in the United States of America

A book in the American Literatures Initiative (ALI), a collaborative publishing project of NYU Press, Fordham University Press, Rutgers University Press, Temple University Press, and the University of Virginia Press. The Initiative is supported by The Andrew W. Mellon Foundation. For more information, please visit www.americanliteratures.org.

For my parents

*The first thing I did was make a mistake. I thought
I had understood capitalism, but what I had done
was assume an attitude—melancholy sadness—
toward it. This attitude is not correct.*

—DONALD BARTHELME, "THE RISE OF CAPITALISM"

Contents

	Acknowledgments	xi
	Introduction: From Manchuria to Manchuria Inc.	1
1	California Dreaming: Twentieth-Century Corporate Fictions at the End of the Frontier	18
2	"Domo Arigato, Mr. Sakamoto, for the New Non-Union Contract!": (Multi)national Threats and the Decline of the American Auto Industry in Ron Howard's *Gung Ho*	50
3	Good Times, Bad Times . . . You Know I Had My Share(s): The Corporation in Five Popular Films	74
4	A Capital Death: Medicine, Technology, and the Care of the Self in Don DeLillo's *White Noise*	115
5	Family Incorporated: William Gaddis's *J R* and the Embodiment of Capitalism	136
6	Your Loss Is Their Gain: The Corporate Body and the Corporeal Body in Richard Powers's *Gain*	158
	Conclusion: Corporate Hegemony, Cubed	180
	Notes	207
	Works Cited	221
	Index	235

Acknowledgments

I would like to thank those who have been instrumental to my personal and intellectual development over the years and without whose teaching and encouragement I would not be writing these very lines. I would also like to acknowledge the California State University system, which granted me three degrees and which provides such important services and opportunities for so many. Despite all the state and university brass do to compromise higher education at the CSUs, the faculty and staff of those institutions still find ways to put the students first. Here are just a few of those therein who fight the good fight: Ray Zepeda with his pipe, in a bar, or on his boat, but Ray Zepeda; Stephen Cooper; Suzanne Greenberg; Fred Wegener; Elyse Blankley, whose razor-sharp intellect and wit are equally as impressive as her *Women in Love* Gudrun-inspired hula dance; Roland Bush, whose late-night courses spilled from the classroom and into Hoff's Hut as inevitably as the wine that filled our glasses there; and Bill Nericcio, diabolical lit critic at large, who taught me how the study of literature could be infused with a kind of mischievous intent. It is perhaps no accident that his books rest on my shelves touching spines with Nietzsche.

As to the specific development and production of this book, much appreciation goes to Adrienne Munich and Celia Marshik for being such careful and thorough readers of the manuscript in its earliest formations. There were kind words and deeds that went along with this as well. And, of course, a special thanks to Molly for occasionally taking me down to the Madison Square dog park for a much needed break from writing and where I could bark as loudly as I wanted and wag my tail freely. Joe Tabbi was another keen and important reader, whose comments and suggestions rightfully broadened the theoretical scope of the book. I met Joe at the William Gaddis conference in Buffalo, New York, in 2005 where I presented a paper that years later proved to be the seed of chapter 5 and, truly, of the entire book. Many of the participants of that conference gave me substantive feedback, and particularly Stephen Burn and Joseph Conte, who each expressed enthusiasm for the paper and tipped me off to the existence of Richard Powers's *Gain*.

Without the English Department at Boise State University having rescued me from the melancholy life of an adjunct, I would never have had the time, stability, and resources to complete this book. A shout-out goes to Steve Olsen-Smith, whose top-notch scanner took a break from scanning Melville's marginalia to capture the wonderful Chernikhov drawing that adorns the cover of this book. Poetry, adult beverages, and nightlife were provided by Martin Corless-Smith, Janet Holmes, and Al Greenberg. Gautam Basu Thakur, Reshmi Mukherjee, and little Godot have made me feel at home in their home many times, and without too much mention of Lacan. And here's to Carrie Seymour, who loves to play possum about everything but is secretly wise as the owl. You can take me to your record store and give me a spin any time.

I would also like to thank the folks at Rutgers University Press for finding promise in the book. It is a strange thing to collaborate with someone you've never met in person, but Katie Keeran has been very helpful and patient with me. The whole editorial process has seemed deceptively easy, which is surely the mark of a great editor. Thanks also to Natalie Finkel, who is currently playing the oft-forgotten role of the all-important intern, Tim Roberts and the American Literatures Initiative, and the Arts and Humanities Institute at Boise State.

My parents have always given unquestioning support to whatever I've set my mind to and even put up with a certain cranky revisionist this last summer. So, too, did my brother, who lost some sleep over beers to make our summer nights last a little longer. And to Jeff Schroeder, for all the discussions and everything else through the years, wherever it is you're smashing pumpkins and idols these days. I mean, some of the most . . .

Last and certainly most, my heartfelt thanks to Stacey Olster, whose generosity knows no bounds and to whom I owe a debt that I couldn't repay with all the chocolate in Belgium. Instead, and in deference to her favorite color, I offer the image of a Jacaranda-lined street in a Southern California spring, flowers abloom, purple petals raining down, the soft twin paths stretching endlessly. Stacey has been an integral part of this project from its inception to its fruition and has guided me the entire way. I will refrain from mentioning the countless examples of this. More importantly, she has helped me to believe I could make some of the personal and professional leaps I've made in the past few years. In this case, Kierkegaard couldn't have done it better. She is also the only person who could ever convince me, contrary to all evidence indicating otherwise, that I am, indeed, Lena Horne.

Boise, Idaho
September 2013

FICTIONS INC.

Introduction: From Manchuria to Manchuria Inc.

It is curious to note that the 2004 remake of *The Manchurian Candidate* (1962) has little of Manchuria left in it apart from the title's resonance. To be sure, each *Manchurian Candidate* follows Captain Bennett Marco (Frank Sinatra in the original, Denzel Washington in the remake) as he inadvertently stumbles on, and ultimately foils, a plot to assassinate a prominent politician. Yet, whereas the Cold War classic simultaneously entertained American fears of both communist and McCarthyist conspiracies, its post-9/11 relative, while updating its war to the decidedly hotter topic of Iraq and Afghanistan, does not simply replace a Red scare with a shadowy terrorist network. Instead, the private equity firm and multinational corporation Manchurian Global takes the place of the communist conspiracy. This is both a notable change and a telling one. For the more recent *Manchurian Candidate* marks a shift from Cold War–era neuroses about political ideology to contemporary worries about economic power. Certainly, political ideology still resonates in the remake, as the film shows the presidential election centering on issues of terrorism, rogue states, the erosion of American liberties, and the ever-nebulous concept of "freedom." But it is not the clash of ideologies, or civilizations as Samuel Huntington might have it, that defines the central struggle in the film so much as it is the waning of democracy and the nation-state's sovereignty against the transnational power of corporations and capital. Indeed, Manchurian Global, as a friend tells Marco, is "not just a corporation ... but a goddamn geopolitical extension of policy for every president since Nixon," whose shareholders include "former presidents, deposed kings, trust fund terrorists, fallen communist dictators, ayotollahs, African warlords, and retired prime ministers." In truth, then, it is the transnational corporation that eclipses the boundaries of nations and rogue states, irrespective of their political ideologies, and whose financial ties bind American politician to terrorist insurgent. The latest *Manchurian Candidate* suggests that the enemy is no longer political ideology but economic ideology, no longer socialism in one country but the economic world-system of all.

It is further significant that the film, while condemning the power of corporations over nation-states, balks at extending this censure to the late capitalist system itself, similar to the way the original film indicts a McCarthyist paranoid politics only by reaffirming the original communist threat: McCarthyism is the "real" enemy, yet a communist conspiracy of absurd McCarthyist proportions nonetheless exists. The critique of Manchurian Global—that it engages in covert operations worldwide, employs a controversial South African researcher, and so on—reveals the corporation to be amoral at best and involved in numerous dubious global machinations. Consequently, the corporation appears too big to stop (or fail, in today's parlance). Yet the capitalist system itself requires just such an ideological belief to continue functioning. As Slavoj Žižek puts it in *The Sublime Object of Ideology*, our supposedly postideological and cynical world, while it believes itself hip to all forms of ideological manipulation, nonetheless remains in thrall to late capitalist ideology because "the fundamental level of ideology . . . is not of an illusion masking the real state of things but that of an (unconscious) fantasy structuring social reality itself" (33).

Yesteryear's communist paranoia has been ideologically unmasked and can be laughed at today for its pathological obsession, yet today's ideological unmasking of global corporate malfeasance leads only to a cynical reaffirmation of the dominance of the late capitalist system. This explains the film's fantasy ending, in which the military erases Captain Marco's image from the security camera that has captured him en route to assassinate the president and digitally replaces it with that of a former employee of Manchurian Global, later disseminating a false story to the media explaining everything. At best, this ending is a misplaced hope for financial regulation, literally coded as a government cover-up. Ultimately, the film supports Captain Marco's quest merely for the personal truth of what happened to him and his army unit (the betrayal and brainwashing), typified by his comment, "I could give a rat's ass about Manchurian Global." In the end, we learn that corporations are beyond the law and government control (except through antidemocratic tactics, like the cover-up), but also that we must accept this as a fact of life under liberal democracy. Since, as Žižek claims, "the place of [ideological] illusion is in the reality of the doing itself," the revelation about Manchurian Global becomes merely a bitter confirmation of the disavowed acceptance of the hegemonic late capitalist order, in which people "know that their idea of Freedom is masking a particular form of exploitation, but still they continue to follow this idea of Freedom" (*Sublime* 33). The latest *Manchurian Candidate* leaves us, finally, with the Gordian knot of late capitalism: capital threatens democracy, but democracy can only exist in support of capital, for to be anticapital is, by hegemonic definition, to be antidemocracy.

Nevertheless, the film is indicative both of the cultural shift in American perceptions of national threats and of the significant role that representations of corporations play in postmodern and contemporary cultural productions. In kind, the purpose of this study is to provide a detailed account of the ways in which postmodern art, literature, and popular culture have represented the corporation and, by extension, the vast and ungraspable enterprise of late capitalism. What are the forms and (dis)contents that fictional representations of corporations take on in such texts? What does it mean to make a metaphor of the corporation, to see it as a kind of monstrous beast or person, as a hero or "the Other," or even as a self-perpetuating machine or system beholden to nobody? How does an always present, yet latent, corporate presence manifest itself in a text? In what ways do individual bodies come into contact and conflict with corporate ones? How, we might ask, has the further incorporation—multi- or transnational incorporation—of America changed its understanding of itself, capitalism, and its place in the world-system?

The answers to these questions reveal several compelling conclusions. First, the corporation has increasingly become a focal point or figure—indeed, it occupies a privileged position in this case—for American financial anxieties in a global age. Second, the way in which a corporation is represented can tell us much about how these specific anxieties are related to larger economic concerns. Third, America's ambivalent relationship with corporations reveals a deep discontent with the capitalist system itself, despite capital's promise of a future market utopia and complete freedom of consumer choice, and marks a preoccupation with the loss of individual rights and freedoms as well as the possibilities of resistance to corporate capitalism.

It's the Neoliberal Economy, Stupid!

What is ultimately at stake in the texts I explore, and in this study as a whole, is the question of the ability to resist, reassess, and reimagine an economic system that, even after the ascent of the "new economy," is clearly failing. For the difficulty of being "against" capitalism, which the 2004 *Manchurian Candidate* demonstrates, ironically became the basis of the defense of the system during the 2007–2008 financial crisis. The rallying cry that certain banks were "too big too fail" established the justification of a government (read taxpayer) bailout that precluded any discussion of alternative responses to the Great Recession.[1] The fears of a return to Keynesian economic policies, best captured in the 5 February 2009 issue of the *Economist* depicting a ghoulish hand bursting forth from a grave under the title "The Return of Economic Nationalism," turned out to be pure demagoguery. Although some of the government's TARP program investments and "toxic assets" purchased as the "lender of last resort" have returned a profit (the full cost of the bailout has yet to be recouped),[2] if things had taken, or in the future do take, a slightly different financial turn, we already know precisely who will foot the bill and the drastic consequences such a debt will entail. Meanwhile there has been virtually no reform of the banks or the financial sector, showing just where the influence lies in the relationship between liberal democracies and neoliberal capital. All things told, it would appear that a neoliberalism 2.0 is on the way. This is perhaps no surprise since, as Michel Foucault writes regarding what he calls the "economic-juridical complex," or the relationship between liberal governments and the free market in the neoliberal era, "one must govern for the market, rather than because of the market" (*Birth* 121).

While economic crises are a regular feature of capitalism, neoliberalism has proven especially susceptible to them.[3] We have inherited an "economy of exception"—to alter slightly Giorgio Agamben's concept of how the sovereign's suspension of the rule of law during a time of crisis has today become the norm—in which the lender of last resort's suspension of the rule of the supposedly free market during an economic crisis has become the accepted way of doing, and pleasing, business. In Agamben's "state of exception," this means that life is essentially abandoned within the crack opened up between law and life, as "rule" becomes exception, exception the rule (*State* 85–87). In an "economy of exception," I would argue, people are abandoned to the so-called market forces of predatory lenders, banks, various forms of debt, and transnational corporations.

The "permanent state of emergency" that Agamben diagnoses in contemporary society (2–3) has become the permanent *financial and fiscal* emergencies that neoliberalism has fostered, evidenced in the widening gap between the rich and the poor despite the purported "end" of the economic crisis,[4] as well as many nations' forced adoption of "austerity measures" that even the United States has succumbed to, veiled as they are, in its fetishizing of the debt ceiling, endless federal and state budget crises, and self-imposed "sequestration."[5]

This curious contradiction of late capital, which today gladly admits to its failings and simply shrugs its shoulders in response, is symptomatic of the neoliberal era that began in the 1970s and came into its own under Ronald Reagan, the logic of which is a sort of free-market fundamentalism based on the creation and deregulation of markets and the liberalization of capital. Neoliberalism's ascent to the capitalist logic of the day was a long time in the making, as its primary adherents, Milton Friedman and Frederick Hayek, had long been proselytizing a glorious vision of a truly "free" market (Harvey, *Brief History* 19–22). Its more recent apostles have sung neoliberalism's praises under the banner of "globalization" to popular audiences in telling ways. In *The End of History and the Last Man* (1992), Frances Fukuyama famously foretold "the end of history," based on the belief that the expansion of capital to a truly global market, the failures of state-centered economies, and the fall of the Soviet Union surely meant we would all enter "the Promised Land of liberal democracy" (xv). Thomas Friedman similarly espoused a faith in globalization that minimized its discontents in *The Lexus and the Olive Tree: Understanding Globalization* (1999), in which globalization is not exactly the end of history but the beginning of a new and incontrovertible system wherein "the fundamental political question is: How do you make the best of the only hardware and operating system that works—globally integrated free-market capitalism?" (352). The summation of these and similar arguments is, paradoxically, that the global market will increase our freedoms, although there can be no choice regarding whether we accept globalization or not. In short, the temporary suspension of political freedom will consequently lead to the endless expansion of another freedom—that of consumer choice.

Essentially, it was the policies and products of neoliberalism that Occupy Wall Street and other Occupy movements were protesting when they formed in various American cities in the fall of 2011. OWS's only "unifying" slogan—"We are the 99 percent"—spoke directly to one of the hallmarks of neoliberal capitalism, which is the drastic upward redistribution of wealth in America and the world. In the United States, the top 10 percent of the population, the economic "crisis" notwithstanding, has increased its share from roughly 31 percent of overall income in 1973 to about 46 percent by 2011, and the top 1 percent of the population from roughly 7 to 17 percent (Alvaredo et al., *World Top Incomes*). The result is currently the largest gap between the rich and the poor in America since the Great Depression. This widening gap—experienced today in America as the "squeeze" on the middle class—along with cuts in social welfare programs and safety nets and a fresh crisis in capital, have left a dire fallout, not just in the United States but in the entire interconnected and globalized world of late capital.[6]

While critics complained of OWS's lack of specific demands, its curious rejection of the political system might well have been the only way to challenge the accepted orthodoxy of neoliberalism (Graeber, *Democracy* 87–99, 150–152, 233). For, as David Harvey writes in *A Brief History of Neoliberalism*, while neoliberal economic policy appears to transcend politics and is upheld by its proponents as "a *utopian* project to realize a theoretical design for the reorganization of international capitalism," in practice it is "a *political* project to re-establish the conditions for capital accumulation and to restore the power of economic elites" (19). To opt out of the accepted political process of a system that considers any questioning of its economic fundamentalism a kind of heresy is foremost a radical assertion of freedom (in distinction to global capital's "freedom") and creates what David Graeber calls "a crisis of legitimacy within the entire system by providing what a glimpse of real democracy might be like" (*Democracy* xix). Moreover, OWS, like Harvey's careful periodization of neoliberalism, serves as a reminder that we are never dealing with a monolithic Capitalism but always with capital*isms* that affect and are affected by real political decisions and policies. Thus, the neoliberal era represents the *specific mode of capitalism* of our times.

One of the most disastrous outcomes of neoliberalism has been the massive expansion of financial markets and financial services, which led directly to the 2007–2008 crisis.[7] The resulting "financialization" of the economy has invaded every aspect of American life.[8] Moreover, capital's move toward the financial-insubstantial and the corresponding decline, at least in America, of a manufacturing-based economy has since given rise to a nostalgia for the "good old days" of preglobalization industry. Dave Eggers's *A Hologram for the King* (2012), for instance, focuses on a foundering businessman, Alan Clay, who attempts to sell a state-of-the-art IT system to the king of Saudi Arabia. Clay is plagued by his own role in having accelerated America's postindustrial transformation through his outsourcing of the labor and manufacturing at the Schwinn plant he once ran, which ironically helped spur the onetime prominent bicycle company's demise. In the end, his professional and personal failures are offset by his decision not to return to America but to stay and contribute to building the king's new "economic" city. The sad state of American industry aside, Clay's final decision to create something lasting is figured as a rebirth of the salesman, global capitalist style, and is thus a curious and sincere reaffirmation of globalization. The discontent with the financial-insubstantial and attendant desire to build lasting things of value also informs the recollection of a laid-off risk-management employee in the Wall Street drama *Margin Call* (2011). At one point in the film, the employee waxes nostalgic over an important commuter bridge that a company he once worked for built. The bridge remains a public and material thing that exists in the world, the value of which lies in the tangible and metaphorical passages and connections it makes between peoples, communities, and places, whereas the financial markets amass mere intangible and individual wealth that, as the film shows, leads traders into meaningless individual competition regarding one's salary, house, and car and isolates each from the larger world where this wealth is actually created and *matters*, both literally and figuratively.

There is, then, a hidden pseudoreligious side of market fundamentalism, in which the "soul," or finance capital, seeks to escape the "body," or material conditions, of its existence. Max Weber, of course, first tied the success of American capitalism to Protestantism in *The Protestant Work Ethic and the "Spirit" of Capitalism* (1905), and in *The Great Transformation* (1944), Karl Polanyi called attention to the idealism inherent in the laissez-faire capitalism begun in Britain during the industrial revolution: "Born as a mere penchant for non-bureaucratic methods, it [economic liberalism] evolved into a veritable faith in man's secular salvation through a self-regulating market.... The liberal creed assumed its evangelical fervor only in response to the needs of a fully deployed market economy" (135). Joining capital's body/spirit dualism with neoliberal market utopianism and the Christian tendency toward eschatological thinking, it is not difficult to imagine the endgame of this desire to transcend the material world via capital. Don DeLillo does so in *Cosmopolis* (2003) through the literal and metaphysical death drive of Eric Packer, who unsuccessfully seeks to master the supposed mystical forces of the international currency market.[9] Unlike the humbled but ultimately happy Curtis Jadwin, who fails in his attempt to corner the wheat market in Frank Norris's *The Pit* (1903), Packer is cast as a kind of existential Kurtz-like hero in his apparently suicidal quest to attain the financial sublime. This is not Naturalism's defeat of man by overwhelming forces but postmodernism's coming-into-being of the posthuman in a technosociety constituted by what DeLillo, in the novel, calls "cyber-capital."

Yet neoliberalism is marked not only by an increasing financialization of the global economy but by the unparalleled growth of corporate bodies as well. Neoliberal capital may run on the logic of a total financialization of existence, but, at the end of the business day, commodities must be manufactured, distributed, marketed, and sold on a mass scale—hence the absolute necessity of the corporation to late capitalism. This was perhaps the chief lesson to be learned after the fall of Enron in 2001, which, along with the crash of Long Term Capital Management in 1999, constituted a striking rehearsal of the oncoming financial crisis.[10] Not discounting Enron's various accounting chicaneries, it was the fundamental transformation of the company into a financial trader, rather than one that actually built things, that sustained it for so long after precipitating its collapse.[11] In short, a capitalist economy requires not just the bodies and insatiable desires of consumers but corporate bodies and their productive capabilities too.[12] It could be argued, then, that a very different and more disturbing model of the posthuman than even DeLillo's Eric Packer can be found in the corporation itself. With its legal-fictional status as a "person" and corresponding constitutional rights, the corporation is treated by law as a kind of person, however unnatural a one it may be.

A Brief History of Corporate Time

The integral and dynamic role that the corporation plays in today's era of late capitalism is one that it has, in fact, long performed. In essence, the story of the corporation's evolution is one in which capital organizes itself into a sovereign body, with the help of the state, and lays claim to its share of constitutional rights.[13] Corporations were created in the fifteenth century and existed until the early nineteenth century as joint-stock companies, such as the British and Dutch East India Companies, and were usually extensions of imperial powers. As Giovanni Arrighi notes, "Joint-stock chartered companies were part-governmental, part-business organizations, which specialized *territorially*, to the exclusion of other similar organizations" (73). Thus, they were much smaller than today's corporations and were chartered and controlled by the monarchies in their countries of origin, which often dissolved them when their missions were completed.

As the corporate form developed, it benefited from the legal notions of "limited liability," which limited investors' responsibility in a company solely to their investments, and from "perpetual life," which meant the company could "outlive" its initial creators and investors. Yet, in the United States, a true glimpse of an emerging corporate sovereignty arrived in 1819, through the Supreme Court case *Dartmouth College v. Woodward*, in which the court found that New Hampshire could not revoke Dartmouth's original charter of 1769, even though King George III had granted it before American independence and New Hampshire's statehood. In short, the court found that the corporate entity's sovereignty predated and trumped state sovereignty. A corporate body had effectively eclipsed the sovereignty of a state.

However, the true milestone in the consolidation of corporate power came about through the 1886 Supreme Court decision in *Santa Clara County v. Southern Pacific Railroad* that mistakenly suggested that a corporation was, legally, a "person." Since then, courts have interpreted the decision, not without controversy (Hartmann 98–119), to mean that a corporation, as a person, is legally guaranteed full constitutional rights by dint of the Fourteenth Amendment, which was originally added to the Constitution in order to give rights to former slaves. With that ruling, however, corporations now gained the same rights and freedoms as any person. The result in the legal world is telling, as 50 percent of Fourteenth Amendment cases since then have involved the defense of a corporation and merely 1.5 percent the status of African Americans (Court 27). Further, in the years following this decision, several regulations were lifted regarding merger laws, and soon a massive corporate consolidation began, the result of which turned 1,800 corporations into 157 (Bakan 14). Apparently, the corporate body was good business.

The drastic end of the Roaring Twenties, the advent of two world wars, and the Great Depression hampered rapid corporate growth in the first half of the twentieth century (Jones 84–90), but the corporation, through its managerial and organizational skills, was nonetheless becoming increasingly integrated into a world-economy. Even FDR's New Deal, writes Harvey Wasserman, "left the power of corporations untouched—and ultimately enhanced with the coming war" (148). As capital resumed its startling growth after World War II, particularly in America due to Europe's decimated economy, a kind of *Pax Corporate Americana* was reached, wherein both labor and capital were content to strike long-term deals between them, thus ensuring the stability of the overall system. Gone were the pitched battles between capital and labor from earlier times. Collective bargaining had won good pensions and benefits for workers, the economy was booming, and corporations appeared paternalistic in their attitudes toward labor. American corporations could afford to act beneficently to their workers for the first time, and a general feeling of corporate responsibility toward America arose.

As capital reached a new crisis in the early 1970s, however, this short-lived pact was slowly eroded. The oil and energy crises, stagflation, rising unemployment, increasing international competition, and the unraveling of the Bretton Woods agreement that pegged international currency to the U.S. dollar and stabilized the world-economy led to the embrace of neoliberalism and a wave of financial liberalization supported by (supposedly) ideologically free supranational organizations such as the World Bank and the International Monetary Fund (IMF). In the United States, chiefly during the Reagan administration (though it began under Jimmy Carter's), this meant weakening the ability of certain government agencies to regulate industry and commerce, as well as ushering in a wave of deregulation, privatization, and slashing of social programs.

Corporations thrived in this environment, as the era of megamergers and megaprofits ensued. After the Reagan Revolution and Tax Revolt transformed the American economy once again, corporate profits soared, much of which was a result of financial maneuvering and tax cuts. From the 1950s to the 1980s, the percentage of all U.S. taxes that corporations paid dropped from 39 to 17 percent, while that of individuals soared from 61 to 83 percent (Korten 201). In the matter of a few decades, corporations had managed, thanks to neoliberal economic policy, to snatch record profits, even at times from the jaws of recession. With the 2010 *Citizens United* decision to grant corporations the right of "free speech" through the ability to make unlimited contributions to political parties, along with Mitt Romney's stunning response of "corporations are people" to a heckler during his unsuccessful 2012 presidential campaign, it is clear that the extent of corporate power today not only is unprecedented but is continuing to expand.

In short, the corporation has been, and remains, crucial to the history of capital. Karl Marx spoke of the dialectical relationship between technological advances and capital restructuring that allows for a greater accumulation of relative surplus value, and it would appear that no one "technological" advance has been more influential, far-reaching, or persistent than that of the corporation. The corporation has continued to mutate throughout its five-hundred-year history and remains as important, if not more important, to the system than ever before. From the joint-stock company to the corporation, along with the help of limited liability, the legal "personhood" and rights granted by the Fourteenth Amendment, and key multinational and neoliberal transformations of its powers, the corporation has proven to be a primary and dynamic motor, both affected by and affecting the multiple reconfigurations of capitalism.

Postmodernism, or the Cultural Logic of Corporate Mapping

American concerns with economic transformation are not new, of course, but they have taken on new forms in conjunction with the substantial mutations of capital over the past few decades.[14] For many initial critics of postmodernism, the post–World War II changes in the economy meant that a critique of capitalism in the postmodern era, through the arts or other means, was severely compromised, if not impossible.[15] This, of course, is largely Fredric Jameson's thesis in *Postmodernism, or, The Cultural Logic of Late Capitalism*, in which he argues that a particular market-suffused postmodern logic inspires the thrills and chills of late capitalist cultural productions, thus undercutting any potential critical-aesthetic distance that an earlier modernist art achieved (or attempted). At the same time, so dizzyingly complex has the current world economic system become that it is impossible for the individual subject to "cognitively map" his or her place within it (44).

For critics of contemporary literature whose interests shifted to the provenance of identity politics in the years of the canon wars, as John Guillory demonstrates in *Cultural Capital* (1993), Marxist criticism took a backseat to the explication of "pluralist values" that texts supposedly espouse, particularly in regard to race, class, and gender. Yet the study of class remained problematic since "while it is easy enough to conceive of a self-affirmative racial or sexual identity, it makes very little sense to posit an affirmative lower-class identity, as such an identity would have to be grounded in the experience of deprivation per se," meaning that "the *affirmation* of lower-class identity is hardly compatible with a program for the abolition of want" (13). As a result, writes Guillory, "within the discourse of liberal pluralism, . . . the category of class in the invocation race/class/gender is likely to remain merely empty" (14). By 2006, Walter Benn Michaels could lament in *The Trouble with Diversity* that "the left today obsessively interests itself in issues that have nothing to do with economic inequality" (19). Elsewhere, Michaels states that much contemporary literature has followed suit. What Michaels calls the "neoliberal novel" promotes an individualistic Thatcherite "there is no such thing as society" logic and is typified by the "substitution of cultural difference ... for class difference" that ultimately, and unknowingly, marks a wholehearted adoption of neoliberal ideology ("Going Boom").

My study, however, suggests that there is actually another tradition in postmodern and contemporary literature, perhaps a different sort of "neoliberal novel," that does not adopt the so-called logic of identity politics and that, while it does not always address or contest issues of economic inequality directly or through an analysis of class, does engage in an egalitarian critique of corporations in the neoliberal era that is inextricably bound up with larger questions about the free market, individual liberties, and economic inequality. These texts are often obsessed with economic questions in their own fashion, which is to say through the figure of the corporation. While some texts, such as *The Manchurian Candidate*, deal directly with issues of corporate power, others offer unprecedented dissections of corporate capitalism that distinguish them from even the most scathing critiques of industrialism from earlier periods, such as those of a muckraking Upton Sinclair or a socially conscious Charles Dickens. William Gaddis's *J R* (1975) and Richard Powers's *Gain* (1998), for instance, are both not only preoccupied with the effects of the corporation on American social, political, and cultural values but committed to tracing the legal-theoretical evolution of the corporation as well. These textual treatments of what Immanuel Wallerstein calls "historical capitalism"—the notion that the "modern world-system ... is and has always been a *world-economy*" and "a *capitalist* world-economy" (*World-Systems Analysis* 23)—mark a new type of engagement with questions of economic inequality and corporate capitalism.

Michaels's valid points notwithstanding, there have been recent critical reevaluations of what economic criticism was, is, and might be in the future. Many of the studies that may be loosely considered a kind of new economic criticism tend to look at the economies, symbolic and otherwise, of texts themselves or at notions of "the market."[16] What is distinct about an economic criticism that takes the figure of the corporation as its primary object of study lies in the singular position that corporations hold vis-à-vis individuals and the capitalist system itself, for the corporation is a creature born unto that system and one that arguably can exist only within it. The corporate body, with its peculiar form of sovereignty, often enjoys a mutually reinforcing relationship with capital that, in its complexity, resists a reductive "vulgar Marxist" analysis. Lending itself to Louis Althusser's notion of "overdetermination," in which there is both a "*determination in the last instance by the (economic) mode of production*" and a "*relative autonomy of the superstructures and their specific effectivity*" ("Contradiction and Overdetermination" 111), the corporation, in some sense, is both a form of the capitalist mode of production and part of the superstructure as well. Indeed, it is a key meeting point that blurs the distinction between each.

I am primarily interested in how the figure of the corporation functions at the level of textual content, both in conscious and unconscious ways, yet also in the way in which texts deal formally with trying to "solve" the economic problems that corporations represent. Thus, I look at how representations of a corporation open up into broader historical considerations of how capital has affected certain industries, from the automobile to the pharmaceutical, and vice versa. It is for this reason that I treat the metaphor of corporate personhood seriously, as do several of the texts in the study. I do not wish simply to tear back the veil and expose the "truth" of the corporation's legal-fictional existence (as if then the corporation's excesses would just disappear in a puff of smoke or be tamed by law, as the popular activist-driven books on corporate power hope) but to show the ways in which postmodern literary and cultural artifacts have provided critiques of, or windows into, late capital by following the logical extension and limit of this kind of figurative "thinking" about corporate capitalism. Corporate personhood may be a legal fiction, but the artificial person and its metaphorical body are potent nonetheless.

In functioning as a node wherein numerous economic concerns and anxieties intersect, the figure of the corporation in postmodern texts provides a means of mapping, and therefore comprehending, the vast and spectacular late capitalist system. Serving as the primary representatives of the capitalist system, figurations of corporations allow for a temporary crystallization or solidification of an economic system so dynamic that it continually dismantles social, cultural, and political structures, creating a world wherein, as Marx and Engels wrote, "all that is solid melts into air" ("Manifesto" 476). What representations of corporations do is reverse this "natural" process for a moment, condense the immaterial back into something conceivable. If nothing else, they offer ways for understanding what is responsible for the air being so smoggy, the environment so polluted. Part image construction, part material embodiment, the figure of the corporation ironically offers a kind of "face" or image of capital that suggests not just its power but a facet of its powerlessness as well.

Corporate Fictions

As I show in chapter 1, the differences in the corporate bodies figured in Frank Norris's prophetic look at the coming corporate century in *The Octopus* (1901) and Thomas Pynchon's depiction of the defaulting promises of post–World War II corporate hegemony in *The Crying of Lot 49* (1966) reveal a fundamental change in corporate presence in America throughout the twentieth century. The corporate octopus in Norris's text is monstrous but material, whereas the incorporated body of the recently deceased Pierce Inverarity in Pynchon's *Lot 49* is indistinguishable from the postmodern America for which he stands, or perhaps lies. Thus, Norris's anticipation of the decentered corporation in the metaphor of the octopus comes to fruition in Pynchon's metaphor of the real-estate developer Pierce Inverarity's "incorporation" of America itself. It would appear that corporations and capital have attained such a hold on American life that all avenues of resistance, already seen as troubled by Norris, have apparently disappeared by the time of Pynchon.

As the remake of *The Manchurian Candidate* suggests, the multinational expansion of corporate power has also challenged the sovereignty of nation-states and complicated onetime understandings of national identities. This dilemma underlies Ron Howard's comedy *Gung Ho* (1986), in which a Japanese car company reopens a failed auto plant in a small American town that, like the sputtering Detroit it stands in for, has seen the best of its economic times come and go. I contend that the film registers the fears of a fully recovered post–World War II Japanese economy that, in a sense, is returning late capitalism—with its novel and strict disciplining of old labor—to its source. The film, however, buries this more fundamental antagonism of the new transformation of capital under an array of cultural and class antagonisms between the white-collar Japanese and blue-collar American workers. Conveniently skipping over an interrogation of Detroit's own management failures, the problems of the American auto industry are instead projected onto a strict and unforgiving Japanese corporation. Thus, the film shows how a new transnational capitalism returns to its "birthplace" in the figure of an "Othered" corporation.

Worries over global economics aside, even representations of "American" corporations demonstrate that America's preoccupation with the virtues and vices of capitalism has been ongoing and, moreover, responsive to its particular historical context. Thus, in chapter 3 I trace several more popular representations of corporate power through a reading of five films—*Executive Suite* (1954), *Network* (1976), *Ghostbusters* (1984), *Tommy Boy* (1995), and *Michael Clayton* (2007)—that span five decades and give a fine example of evolving attitudes toward corporations as they affect and are affected by shifting modes of capitalist production. Not surprisingly, these films show that in times of economic boom, corporations and businesses are often seen as fairly benign, if not heroic, while in times of economic gloom, corporations become downright sinister. Oftentimes, the corporation is represented as somewhat schizophrenic—it wants to "be good," but there are people or principles governing it that are malevolent. As a result, these texts' concerns with, and critiques of, corporate power are displaced onto a particular figure (one greedy CEO) or figures (woman/television) that bear the brunt, often unfairly, of such critiques. These films, then, are unable to sustain any deeper, systemic analysis of capital. This failure results in an ever-continuing corporate morality play, marking the limits of pop culture's probing of late capitalism.

Moving from popular culture's representations of the corporation, I next consider a novel that deals with the very producers of popular productions, Don DeLillo's *White Noise* (1985), which explores the culture industry's and the media's effects on postmodern American life. The novel serves as the perfect text to examine the intersections among media, medicine, the pharmaceutical industry, and the eventual medicalization of bodies in postmodern America. Jack Gladney's comical yet overwhelming fear of death and his exposure to toxic chemicals lead him to obsess over his health, both mental and physical, as he seeks for a "solution" to the riddle of a vapid consumerist life. This he finds in Dylar, the novel's Prozac-like wonder drug, which comes to stand, I claim, for a new wave of pharmaceuticals that began to emerge during the 1980s and that have increasingly promoted the medicalizing of everyday life for profit. The uncertainty and fear generated by a spectacular media is capitalized on by corporations, specifically those of the pharmaceutical industry, as I argue, resulting in people becoming perpetual patients, life becoming beholden to a bio-economy, and the concepts of life and death being reduced to simulacral or virtual status.

The emerging example of biopower seen in the medicalization of daily life as it is captured in *White Noise* comes to the fore again in chapter 5, which deals with William Gaddis's *J R*. *J R* shows a correlation between the numerous fractured families that appear in the novel and an emerging cannibalistic capitalism that is simultaneously fracturing the world. The J R Corporation, created by the adolescent J R, comes to stand for a new kind of corporate ideal as J R employs the metaphor of a "family" of companies to promote his idea of the complete corporatization of everyday life. Working against the "play to win" capitalism the novel displays through the Typhon Corporation, Gaddis suggests, through J R's Family of Companies, that this novel and obfuscating metaphor of corporate benignity is dangerous and has potentially global consequences. In its virtual "embodiment" of capital, the J R Family of Companies embodies America and potentially the world. Biopower here becomes the eclipsing of the nation-state by multinational corporations as they attempt to expand their frontiers from corporate America to a truly corporate-governed world. This seemingly heralds Michael Hardt and Antonio Negri's argument in *Empire* that "sovereignty has taken a new form, composed of a series of national and supranational organisms united under a single logic of rule. This new global form of sovereignty is what we call Empire" (xii). Empire, a network-power spread through governmental and supragovernmental organizations, comes to dominate all facets of life, resulting in the bio-production of life itself on a world scale.

Chapter 6 returns to small-town America by looking at how Richard Powers's *Gain* (1998) juxtaposes the history and anatomy of a multinational corporation, Clare Soap and Chemical, against the history of an individual, Laura Bodey, dying of cancer. The inverse relationship between the corporate and organic body raises the issue of biopower in a less abstract and more "personal" way than in *J R* and *White Noise*. The novel suggests, through Laura's physical and psychological struggles, that what the individual human loses, the "individual" corporation gains. In treating the legal standing of the corporation as a kind of "person," Powers accepts the legal metaphor of corporate "personhood" as verbatim (instead of elaborating on it or offering a different metaphor) and investigates the ironic outcome of this "person's" life. In a sense, this exploration represents the most "self-conscious" and direct treatment of the corporation to date and suggests a certain end to corporate critiques of this type.

In the conclusion, I offer an assessment of the possibilities of corporate critique from "within" the corporation itself, as imagined in popular "white-collar" texts that register the existential boredom, pettiness, and drudgery of office jobs, as in the television show *The Office* and Joshua Ferris's *Then We Came to the End* (2007). Here I explore the ways in which a critical voice from the "inside" can be appropriated by the corporation itself, serving as a troubling model for those who argue there is no "outside" of the system and that fighting it from within is the only option. What potentialities there are for various kinds of resistance—whether a "multitude" will simultaneously emerge, as Hardt and Negri claim it must, to counter Empire's biopolitics—remains an open, if disturbing, question. Yet it would appear more imperative than ever to demand that our troubled economic system needs some kind of restructuring (if not an outright overhaul), particularly the kind that will no longer simply pander to corporate interests at the expense of individual lives. It is the corporation, the embodiment of capital, that is the driving force of capitalism in its latest formation. For all their power, influence, and pervasiveness, however, corporations also make themselves into visible, material, and substantial targets for an ever-changing system driven by unseen and immaterial capital. And while the corporate imagination is bent on finding new ways to accumulate capital and to convince consumers to purchase more and more, our own imaginations are not so easily bound so long as they remain focused on conceiving of other possible lives and other possible worlds to this one and, in the end, fostering the common commitment and the willingness to bring them about.

1 / California Dreaming: Twentieth-Century Corporate Fictions at the End of the Frontier

> *I thought IBM was born with the world,*
> *The U.S. flag would float forever,*
> *The cold opponent did pack away,*
> *The capital will have to follow,*
> *It's not eternal, imperishable,*
> *Oh yes it will go,*
> *It's not eternal, imperishable,*
> *The dinosaur law*
> —STEREOLAB, "WOW AND FLUTTER"

As the British pop group Stereolab reminds us, despite the "wow and flutter" of corporate capitalism's neon signs and glittering commodities, it is not nearly as timeless and transcendent as it projects itself to be. It is a time-and-space-bound economic system that structures the world in particular ways and compels it to particular ends. In other words, before beginning an analysis of the ways in which American fiction and popular culture have figured corporations in the era of late capital, there needs to be not only a historicizing of this peculiar institution, the corporation, but also a historicizing of its fictional representations. So we need to ask, in what ways have representations of corporations changed in American fiction throughout the twentieth century, and how do the specific realities of corporate capitalism under which such texts are produced come to bear on those representations? To answer these questions we need to select two texts that can serve as representative of their historical periods but that also display some sort of preoccupation with American capitalism. Such a choice contains a certain element of arbitrariness and pretentiousness to it, granted, but the search itself is fairly limited by its own qualifications. Nonetheless, two texts stand out as exemplary for this project.

Frank Norris's *The Octopus* comes to the fore for several reasons. First, the novel's publication date (1901) makes it one of the earliest fictional takes on a burgeoning twentieth-century corporate capitalism. Second, the novel *directly* focuses on capital's influence over social, cultural, and political life, and, even more compellingly, this focus is narrowed to a specific industry and corporation—the Railroad Trust and the Pacific and Southwestern Railroad (or P. and S.W., based on the Southern Pacific Railroad Corporation). Third, the novel is a chronicling of the 1880s amid the rough and heady days of industrialism, a key transitional time in the story of capital, and enables Norris to look forward as he looks back and to offer a fair prediction of capital's expansion during the first half of the twentieth century.

Thomas Pynchon's *The Crying of Lot 49* is a novel similarly obsessed with exploring the malaise of its present (1966) with constant reference to the past, thus making the novel the perfect companion to Norris's already "historicized" novel. *Lot 49* also depicts a corporate monster set loose in sunny California, albeit a more chameleon-like creature than the one we encounter in *The Octopus*. And, like Norris's novel, Pynchon's is perched at an important moment in the story of capital, the dawning of the era of late capitalism, which saw the corporation emerge as perhaps the most dominant institution in the world. Pynchon calls attention to corporate capitalism's increasingly deleterious effects on postmodern life: *Lot 49* not only begins to question the emerging Corporate State, it also forecasts the possibilities of resisting it in the future.

Aesthetically speaking, these two works could not be any more different, and the same could be said about much of their content. But there is a major thematic strain that runs from the one to the other, and that is the (historical) preoccupation with American capitalism and, more specifically, the corporation. The fact that the aesthetic and representational strategies of each text are wildly divergent only lends support to the claim that economic forces, here corporate capitalism, have far-ranging and far-reaching effects. In turn, aesthetic possibilities and limitations prove to have a strong influence regarding how each text represents and figures the corporation.

This, in part, explains why it is possible to read *The Octopus* and *Lot 49* as producing inverse responses to the sense of the (im)possibilities of resistance. At first reading, this much seems clear: capitalism in *The Octopus*, for all its devastation, contradictorily brings the world closer together (a nascent global capitalism) and therefore ups the chances of forming a resistant collective (The League). Even after the novel extinguishes each possible attempt to resist the system and reaches the ultimate space of despair by its end, it quickly exchanges this conclusion with a fantastic vision of triumph. Such negativity is flushed out and into the space of global capitalism, which in its immense promise can contain such anguish and doubts until they erupt at a future date.

In *Lot 49*, by contrast, an exhausted capitalist expansion has resulted in an unmappable, chaotic world, in which the subject is wholly alienated and the means and ends of political action obfuscated. The novel thus begins with the seemingly total *inconceivability* of resistance (Oedipa cannot imagine it or even care), builds to the ambiguous possibility of a resistance through the Tristero, and ends with an impending apocalyptic note of (Oedipa's) despair as the lights go out in the auction house.

Yet while *The Octopus* appears the more optimistic novel and *Lot 49* the more pessimistic one, the underlying logic suggests that the earlier novel's (re)production of despair makes it a less hopeful novel than the guardedly optimistic *Lot 49*, which (re)produces the swirling political and cultural aspirations and anxieties of the 1960s. At the very least, *Lot 49* can be argued to be *ambivalent* regarding the possibility of resistance by leaving open a space in which a "new" kind of resistance might emerge (the dispersed, more properly anarchic Tristero), whereas *The Octopus*, having foreclosed on all possibilities of resistance, retreats into questionable, if utopian, fantasies of global capital's future. An extensive and rigorous comparison of these texts, then, uncovers such complex continuities and discontinuities in both the realities and representations of corporations from the early to late twentieth century in American fiction.

In an Octopus's Garden

Frank Norris's *The Octopus* stands as one of the earliest fictional representations of a corporation in American literature. The novel dramatizes the struggle between California wheat farmers and the railroads in the San Joaquin Valley during the late nineteenth century, specifically those farmers involved in the Mussel Slough Tragedy of 1880, in which five farmers and two marshals (themselves farmers working for the railroad) were killed in a shootout over land disputes. Norris employs the infamous metaphor of the octopus to suggest the scope and influence of the Southern Pacific Railroad Corporation at the time. As the novel's poet-protagonist, Presley, imagines it, the railroad is a "vast symbol of power, huge, terrible, flinging the echo of its thunder over all the reaches of the valley, leaving blood and destruction in its path," and it is a "leviathan, with tentacles of steel clutching into the soil, soulless Force, the iron-hearted Power, the monster, the Colossus, the Octopus" (51). Norris's primary representative tentacle for the railroad arrives in the grossly adipose figure of S. Behrman, whose unctuousness enrages many of the farmers who must deal with the railroad's shady maneuverings through Behrman on a day-to-day basis. Later in the novel, after the railroad has successfully ousted the farmers from their land, Presley finds himself in a chance meeting with the president and owner of the P. and S.W., Shelgrim, a man whose power and girth easily overshadow even Behrman's impressive frame.

We have been warned about Shelgrim before, since he epitomizes "the New Finance, the reorganization of capital, the amalgamation of powers, the consolidation of enormous enterprises—no one individual was more constantly in the eye of the world; no one more hated, more dreaded" (104). When Presley, during a visit to San Francisco, stumbles onto the P. and S.W.'s headquarters, he sees the office as "the centre of all that vast ramifying system of arteries that drained the life-blood of the State; the nucleus of the web in which so many lives, so many fortunes, so many destinies had enmeshed" (569). Having witnessed firsthand the actual violent machinations of this sprawling corporation, he decides, "Why not see, face to face, the man whose power was so vast, whose will was so resistless, whose potency for evil so limitless, the man who for so long and so hopelessly they had all been fighting" (570). Following this urge, an excited Presley enters the building and, although the hour is late, finds that Shelgrim is still working and will see him shortly.

Before Presley enters Shelgrim's office, however, we might pause to consider the symbolism of this particular scene. If the railroad corporation is a kind of steel octopus, with a limitless reach, a "vast" influence, and whose tentacles suck the life-blood from the people and the land, then there arises the difficulty of ever confronting such a malevolent force, let alone challenging it. The only solution would be to find the head and chop it off, as it were. Hacking away at the mere tentacles, the novel suggests, is a futile endeavor, as hopeless as if Hercules were to slice off the Hydra's heads without searing each of its necks with a torch afterward. What Presley realizes while waiting nervously outside Shelgrim's office is that he has the chance to meet with this monster in the hideous flesh and demand accountability for the traumatic events that so recently have transpired in the San Joaquin Valley. Presley is depressed by this point in the novel, disillusioned by the real-life defeat of the vaunted farmer / common man he celebrated in his successful populist poem "The Toilers." A visit with Shelgrim, then, and a discussion with the man responsible for all the senseless violence, should be nothing short of a catharsis. It is with such a belief that Presley is ushered into Shelgrim's office and seated in front of the man's desk.

Norris makes the overarching metaphor of the novel significantly tangible at this point and transfigures Shelgrim into the octopus itself:

"Curiously enough, Shelgrim did not move his body. His arms moved, and his head, but the great bulk of the man remained immobile in its place, and as the interview proceeded, this peculiarity emphasised itself, Presley began to conceive the odd idea that Shelgrim had, as it were, placed his body in the chair to rest, while his head and brain and hands worked independently" (574). But Presley's preconceptions of Shelgrim are shattered. The man shows tolerance and charity toward a wayward alcoholic employee, and he criticizes Presley's poetry as second-rate. Presley finds that "the man was not only great, but large; many sided, of vast sympathies" (575). When Presley tries to articulate his scorn for Shelgrim, he is silenced and instead receives an admonishing lecture on the forces unleashed by capitalism. Shelgrim tells him, "Try to believe this—to begin with—*that Railroads build themselves.* Where there is demand sooner or later there will be supply. Mr. Derrick, does he grow his wheat? The Wheat grows itself. What does he count for? Does he supply the force? What do I count for? Do I build the Railroad? You are dealing with forces, young man, when you speak of Wheat and Railroads, not with men.... The Wheat is one force, the Railroad, another, and there is the law that governs them—supply and demand. Men have only little to do in the whole business" (576). Presley's reply that Shelgrim is the "head" of this business and therefore can control it elicits a similar response from the president: "I can *not* control it. It is a force born out of certain conditions, and I—no man—can stop it or control it" (576).

Shelgrim's rhetoric demonstrates a complex mix of conscious deception and unconscious revelation. Marx, for instance, would have little to disagree with in Shelgrim's assertion of the "forces" that capitalism unleashes in its transformation of nature (itself a producer) into a commodity, and money into capital. If we were to replace "the Railroad" here with "capital," then we would be left with a fair description of what capitalism does and is impelled to do, making it clear why no individual can halt such a force. As Marx puts it in *Capital*, "In so far as he [the capitalist] is capital personified, his motivating force is not the acquisition and enjoyment of use-values, but the acquisition and augmentation of exchange-values." Consequently, "Only as a personification of capital is the capitalist respectable. As such, he shares with the miser an absolute drive towards self-enrichment. But what appears in the miser as the mania of an individual is in the capitalist an effect of a social mechanism in which he is merely a cog.... Competition subordinates the individual capitalist to the immanent laws of capitalist production, as external and coercive laws. It compels him to keep extending his capital, so as to preserve it, and he can only extend it by means of progressive accumulation" (739). Shelgrim is right, at least in one sense, about his own impotence in the face of such overwhelming forces. To embrace the logic of capital means one must subscribe to it wholly, not in part.

However, Shelgrim's total denial of any responsibility for the process is also a dissemblance for two reasons. First, to swear off accountability for the initial choice that subsequently binds one to the rollercoaster of capitalism is to mystify that original decision. Certainly, Shelgrim is a cog in the capitalist machine, but he is a cog larger (literally) than most, one that assures the greasing of other wheels and cogs and institutes the most cutthroat of tactics when dealing with the farmers. Second, Shelgrim's appeal to forces such as "supply and demand" obfuscates how a supposedly "free" market actually works.[1] The forces "born out of certain conditions" and the organic metaphors of growth presume that capitalism is a "natural" force and not a force emerging from historically particular circumstances—the industrial revolution, the ideology of Manifest Destiny, free-market and monopoly capitalism, for instance. Shelgrim's naturalized view that "railroads build themselves" is meant to cut off a proper systemic analysis of capital by equating it with the uncontrollable force of nature.

Presley's reaction to this speech is significant in that it shows how persuasive Shelgrim's words are. Even though Presley came into the office with every intention of achieving some kind of justice, he is easily swayed by Shelgrim's speech. He leaves with the feeling that

> somehow he could not deny it. It rang with the clear reverberation of truth. Was no one, then, to blame for the horror at the irrigating ditch. Forces, conditions, laws of supply and demand—were these then the enemies, after all? Not enemies; they were malevolence in Nature. Colossal indifference only, a vast trend toward appointed goals. Nature was, then, a gigantic engine, a vast cyclopean power, huge, terrible, a leviathan with a heart of steel, knowing no compunction, no forgiveness, no tolerance; crushing out the human atom standing in its way, with nirvanic calm, the agony of destruction sending never a jar, never the faintest tremor through all that prodigious mechanism of wheels and cogs. (577)

Presley's tentative flirtation with the radical political movements of the day has not prepared him to combat Shelgrim's dogma and its curious translation of Marx's ideas. This is perhaps Norris's doing, whose Naturalist credo with its attendant "Social Darwinism" is itself an ideology ripe for use by the Left or the Right. If in Naturalism nature always trumps nurture, then a (mis)reading of Marx's ideas about productive forces and capital's potential to unleash ever-greater forces can easily fall in line with the doom-and-gloom notion that man is wholly determined by his biological drives, which are ultimately hard-wired by Nature itself.[2] The "law of supply and demand" becomes a holy commandment that cannot be historicized or critiqued in this view, as it is by necessity launched to the status of a transcendental signifier through which all other (natural) signs will be interpreted for their truth value.

But Norris is doing something else here as well, something as progressive as the seemingly "regressive" reading of a too-deterministic Marx refracted through Émile Zola's Naturalism. The suggestion of the physical scope and influence of corporate power, while it pessimistically "naturalizes" it, also prefigures the state of the corporation in the era of late capital, particularly when Presley confronts the "head" of this cephalopod. What Shelgrim tells him is that there is essentially no head or center to the railroad corporation, that such an idea is absurd. Presley's urge to sum up the power of the corporation, or of capital, in the figure of one man is understandable but impossible. A solution such as this would be too easy and would make it seem as if the logic of capital were subject merely to the personality quirks of its leading practitioners. The fact that capital is becoming more decentralized as it spreads is precisely what Norris is intimating here, and it is what makes capital in the era of multinational corporations so much more slippery than it was in Norris's time. In short, the despair Presley feels at the end of the nineteenth century toward an ever-disseminating capitalism is a kind of despair *avant le lettre*, not to come into its fullest expression until the new century saw capitalism develop into a more mature and properly global system.

Given the novel's suggestion of an endlessly expanding capitalism, *The Octopus* recognizes that resisting the system is no easy task. Yet as capital incessantly restructures the world, it inadvertently creates new opportunities to combat it. Nowhere is this clearer than in the wheat farmers' purchase of a "ticker" that connects the San Joaquin ranchers "by wire with San Francisco, and through that city with Minneapolis, Duluth, Chicago, New York, and at last, and most important of all, with Liverpool" (54) and that figures as the key technological innovation that will bring the global reaches of capital to light. The result is that the farmers tend to the up-to-the-minute market information as much as they do their crops and that "at such moments they no longer felt their individuality. The ranch became merely the part of an enormous whole, a unit in the vast agglomeration of wheat land the whole world round, feeling the effects of causes thousands of miles distant—a drought on the prairies of Dakota, a rain on the plains in India, a frost on the Russian steppes, a hot wind on the llanos of the Argentine" (54). What is curious about Norris's keen description of an emerging global capitalism here is that the very vastness of the world economic system with its far-reaching repercussions constitutes some kind of new totality where we would expect the individual's sense of this totality to be shattered by such a realization. Perhaps this is a result, again, of Norris's Naturalism, which sharply diverges from the soon-to-be modernist texts that embraced, in both form and content, fragmentation, rupture, and dislocation as the century's new aesthetic and zeitgeist. The new telecommunications connecting the farmers to the world economy robs them of their individuality yet replaces that loss with some wider, and not necessarily worse, sense of collective spirit. Though they are "merely a part" and a "unit," the farmers still form a "they" and "part of an enormous whole" that is linked by the imagery of nature. Norris falls short of the modernist character's existential crisis in his depiction of the farmers, for the seemingly fragmented world merely morphs from prairie to plain to steppe to llano. The earth retains a sense of wholeness throughout, which is guaranteed by an enduring Nature.

This new potential collectivity blooms when the farmers' legal fight to retain their land and purchase it at the original price "promised" by the railroad is stymied at every turn by a corrupt legal system "owned" by the Trust. In response to the railroad's increasing squeeze on their finances, the enraged farmers hold an emergency meeting and establish "The League," a collective organized to combat the Railroad Trust, to be headed by the farming community's paterfamilias, the greatly respected "Governor," Magnus Derrick. Deciding that democracy is a fraud and corruption can only be defeated by playing the game corruptly, the League quickly adopts several dirty political tactics for its arsenal, buying the votes of the Railroad Commission and electing one of Derrick's sons, Lyman, as its commissioner.

The tragedy, of course, is that the farmers have only an inkling of how this game is played. After all, this game was partly invented by the Trust. While "the League was clamorous, ubiquitous, its objects known to every urchin on the streets, . . . the Trust was silent, its ways inscrutable, the public saw only its results. It worked on in the dark, calm, disciplined, irresistible" (346). The farmers do not have the capital or the influence to defeat the enormous corruptive power of the Trust, as even the politically aspiring Lyman is bought by the railroad, leading him to turn traitor to his father, whose compromised integrity he can now ironically bring up in response to Magnus's outraged admonishments.

Not only do the farmers fail in their goals, but their reputations as respectable and honest men (particularly through the lionized figure of Magnus Derrick) are tarnished in the process. This is not entirely a surprise, as Norris refuses to romanticize the farmers' plight in the novel. Norris sums up his attitude to the farmers without pulling penned punches: "They had no love for the land. They were not attached to the soil. They worked their ranches as a quarter of a century before they had worked the mines. . . . To get all there was out of the land, to squeeze it dry, to exhaust it, seemed their policy. When, at last, the land was worn out, would refuse to yield, they would invest their money in something else; by then, they would all have made fortunes. They did not care. 'After us the deluge'" (298–299). This cynical account of the farmers as merely petty bourgeois capitalists is startlingly reminiscent of a passage in chapter 10 of *Capital*, "The Working Day," wherein Marx writes, "Capital, which has such 'good reasons' for denying the sufferings of the legions of workers surrounding it, allows its actual movement to be determined as much and as little by the sight of the coming degradation and final depopulation of the human race, as by the probable fall of the earth into the sun. In every stock-jobbing swindle everyone knows that some time or other the crash must come, but everyone hopes that it may fall on the head of his neighbour, after he himself has caught the shower of gold and placed it in secure hands. *Après moi le déluge!* is the watchword for every capitalist and of every capitalist nation" (381).

With a keen environmental eye, a pessimistic view of the ranchers' ultimate aims, and a doggedly deterministic reading of Marx, Norris ends up, if not equating the ranchers to the Trust, then judging them against the same (Marxist) measuring stick. The League, for instance, is described fairly disdainfully by Norris as "a vague engine, a machine with which to fight" (276), formed amid "the uprising of The People; the thunder of outbreak and revolt; the mob demanding to be led, aroused at last, imperious, resistless, overwhelming. It was the blind fury of insurrection, the brute, many-tongued, red-eyed, bellowing for guidance, baring its teeth, unsheathing its claws, imposing its will with abrupt, resistless pressure of the relaxed piston, inexorable, knowing no pity" (279). Remarkably, Norris's description of the League could almost double as a description of the Octopus itself, with its mixed machine and predatory animal metaphors. When Presley hears one steam engine that "whistled for road crossings, for sharp curves, for trestles; ominous notes, hoarse, bellowing, ringing with the accents of menace and defiance," he imagines the railroad as a "galloping monster, the terror of steel and steam, with its single eye, cyclopean red" (51).

The failure of the League's political machinations culminates, perhaps predictably, with recourse to violence. But even here the farmers fail to reap the rewards of collectivity, as they are once again outmaneuvered by the railroad, which moves to repossess the farmers' lands during an annual rabbit hunt and picnic (507). Without most of the six hundred members—who either balk at armed resistance, are unarmed, or realize the railroad has the proverbial jump on them—the farmers set out amid confusion and in much smaller and isolated groups than they had planned. Thus, Norris depicts the shootout at Mussel Slough (the blame of which he is careful to ascribe to neither side), which ends in the deaths of eight men, five of them League members. Violence is a waste, the narrative boldly states, and, to add a typical Naturalist insult to injury, one subplot traces how the death of the Dutch farmer, Hooven, leads inexorably to the starvation of his wife and youngest daughter and to the entry of his eldest daughter into a life of prostitution.

If Norris forecloses on the possibility of resistance through unions, essentially damning a nascent American unionism as pure militancy, he at least offers the potential of an even more radical solution: socialism or anarchism. Norris's "socialism" (Presley declares he's a "Red" at one point) is more like an attenuated anarchism, however. Nor does this anarchism entail a kind of nonhierarchical, constructive politics but merely the recapitulation of common representations of anarchists throughout history as mad bombers bent on causing chaos and destruction. The "anarchist" provocateur is the saloonkeeper, Caraher, whose wife was killed by the Trust and who espouses violence as the only way to fight the system. Merely a bitter and resentful man, and certainly no actual anarchist, Caraher inspires Dyke (the embittered train engineer turned hop farmer, who is busted by the Trust's manipulated shipping rates) to rob the Trust. But this act of guerrilla-like resistance, in which Dyke kills a man, fails as he is forced to become a fugitive and is eventually hunted down and captured, leaving his mother and daughter in tenuous economic circumstances that the once-irascible, arch-individualist Annixter (now flush with compassion due to the love for his new wife, Hilma) tries to ameliorate.

The burgeoning militancy of Presley that Caraher indirectly inspires is portrayed as equally futile. In an impassioned speech to an angry League in the Opera House after the shootout, Presley blasts the audience with revolutionary rhetoric, claiming, "Freedom is not given free to any who ask; Liberty is not born of the gods. She is a child of the People, born in the very height and heat of battle, born from death, stained with blood, grimed with powder. And she grows not to be a goddess, but a Fury, a fearful figure, slaying friend and foe alike, raging, insatiable, merciless, the Red Terror'" (552). But Presley realizes, nearly telepathically, that the crowd has not truly understood his words: its members respond only to pathos, not logic, and remain the same ignorant masses as ever, too indolent and uncomprehending to realize when their freedoms are being torn from them. Presley's rallying speech becomes simply a cri de coeur to a deaf audience. Likewise, Presley's unsuccessful attempt to kill Behrman by hurling a pipe bomb into his house is completely pointless. As Behrman remarks later on, when Presley confesses to the deed to him, "Well, that don't show no common sense.... What could you have gained by killing me?" (626). Behrman's comment underscores how he is merely one of many potential representatives of the railroad, and killing him would only lead to a comparable replacement, as the Trust's decenteredness makes it virtually an impossible target. Simply an instinctive lashing out at the closest target without consideration of the deeper consequences, Presley's act is limited to that of personal revenge and is in the end nothing but destructive nihilism.

The wheat farmers, then, pass from a completely legal challenge to the system (complaints, letter writing, legal representation) to an "illegal" strategy (collectivization, bribing, committee packing) that is employed by the Trust itself and finally to the use of violence (armed rebellion leading to the shootout). The novel, however, shows the futility of each attempt to defeat the system, and, along with casting out the solutions of a more radical politics through Presley's and Hooven's actions, *The Octopus* takes a dark look at the fight against the corporate takeover of America.

Presley's reflection on the shootout is telling in regard not only to the efficacy of any future resistance to the Trust and corporations like it but also to the collective memory of such tragedies: "Make the people believe that the faint tremor in their great engine is a menace to its function? What a folly to think it. Tell them, five years from now, the story of the fight between the League of San Joaquin and the Railroad and it will not be believed. What! a pitched battle between Farmer and Railroad, a battle that cost the lives of seven men? Impossible, it could not have happened. Your story is fiction—exaggerated" (539). Surely Presley's mildly historiographic-metafictional aside on reality and representation, as well as history and fiction, reflects some of Norris's concerns with fictionalizing what, at the time of *The Octopus*'s publication, was a twenty-one-year-old incident. Norris, in 1901, seems already at pains to convince his audience, many of whom are quite used to traveling by the comfortable and modern steam trains by then, that the transportation they have come to enjoy has come at a price dearer than they know. Norris's fears may be warranted about the amnesia of public memory here, but in the violent clashes between labor and business that continued until midway into the century, fresh scars arose to remind people of the possibilities and perils of resistance. Presley's presentiment, however, seems entirely to come to pass in *Lot 49*, where, even if memory could be stirred up (Oedipa's discovery that Beaconsfield's "charcoal filter" is made of the bones of World War II American GIs), there is still no public outlet for such painful recollections, thus further isolating those individuals seeking coherence in a baffling, broken world. In the world of *Lot 49*, as Norris feared, what should be *public memory* is interiorized or *privatized* in the individual, where, because of a lack of any "objective" truth criteria, memories remain wholly subjective, mere "fictions" with no claim to historical truth. Granted, such memory can sometimes be passed on orally, such as when the aging Mr. Thoth tells Oedipa some hazy details of what his grandfather told him about his days as a Pony Express rider. Yet Mr. Thoth reports that his memories are "all mixed in with a Porky Pig cartoon,"[3] so that reality and fiction have once again blended into something ambiguous at best (73).

Norris's ultimately pessimistic views of the efficacy of resisting the system and the pitfalls of collective memory pose a problem for the novel's ending, however. Presley's miserable realization of the hopelessness of the situation comes with a hundred pages remaining. This leaves space for Presley to meet, for the final time, the shepherd Vanamee and to reencounter the pastoral wonder of Nature that he felt at the novel's beginning. This softens his deterministic cosmology that "force only existed" by incorporating it with "the mystery of creation, the stupendous miracle of re-creation; the vast rhythm of the season, measured, alternative, the sun and stars keeping time as the eternal symphony of reproduction swung in its tremendous cadences like the colossal pendulum of an almighty machine—primordial energy flung out from the hand of the Lord God himself, immortal, calm, infinitely strong" (634). Vanamee completes Presley's intimations of immortality by assuring him that "evil is short-lived. Never judge the whole round of life by the mere segment you can see. The whole is, in the end, perfect" (636).

But the whole of the *novel*, at this point, feels far from perfect. The ending feels unearned, a result of a romanticism still running through the novel. It is the transcendent forces, those outside of Time and beyond human means, that will reestablish the good and equitable balance of the universe. Such a Whitmanian and Emersonian view is all the more suspicious when considering the novel Norris published not two years before, *McTeague* (1899), which ends with its titular protagonist handcuffed to a dead police officer in the "vast, interminable, . . . measureless leagues of Death Valley" and holding a "half-dead canary chittering feebly in its little gilt prison" (340).

In fact, it would seem that it is only the symbolism of fiction—through poetic justice, that old deus ex machina—that can "resist" the inevitability of capital. Any political struggle on the people's part is useless. Thus, when S. Behrman is buried and suffocated under his ill-gotten g(r)ains in the penultimate scene of *The Octopus*, we can rest assured that the guiding force of the *novel* has stayed true to its last line: "The larger view always and through all shams, all wickedness, discovers the Truth that will, in the end, prevail, and all things, surely inevitably, resistlessly work together for good" (652).[4] The logic of this ending makes sense when we consider Fredric Jameson's comments on narrative in *The Political Unconscious*. Jameson argues that "the aesthetic act itself is ideological, and the production of aesthetic or narrative form is to be seen as an ideological act in its own right, with the function of inventing imaginary or formal 'solutions' to unresolvable social contradictions" (79). When we recall that Norris's novel is a historical fiction, much of what Jameson details becomes clear[5] and explains why one of Norris's foremost critics, Donald Pizer, could claim substantively that "*The Octopus* is not a novel about class war or about the downtrodden, though the struggle for wealth and the realities of economic power are its subject matter. It is more a novel about man's relationship to nature than a story of man as a social being" (121). Surely it is this very "economic power" that, in being repressed to secondary status in the novel, thus returns so forcefully to shape a contradictory ending.

One of the major "unresolvable contradictions" in the novel is the *continuing* corporate dominance over American democracy and the rights of the people, who remain blissfully unaware of this fact. Yet the novel stages this "event" (indeed, constructs it as a time-bound event) twenty-one years *before* Norris publishes his novel "exposing" this event. Thus, the alarm Norris wishes to raise in his day, retroactively installed twenty-one years earlier as it is, undercuts by necessity the very pessimistic determinism that makes the retroactive "case" for corporate dominance over democracy seemingly unassailable. Essentially, Norris is arguing, in 1901, *this is happening now, so wake up!* But the novel, set in 1880, argues that *this has already happened, and there was no way to stop it!* The ending, then, as ideologically loaded as it is, still retains a utopian kernel, however degraded it may be, and is an attempt to counteract this glaring contradiction, as well as the aesthetic contradictions between an emergent Naturalism and a persistent, if attenuated, Romanticism and between a consequently deterministic reading of Marx (Norris's own) and the optimistic American outlook of the Progressive Era.

The utopian kernel, then, is essentially the recently planted seed of an emerging global market. Cedarquist, the budding financier, tells Presley at one point, "The great word of this nineteenth century has been Production. The word of the twentieth will be ... Markets" (305). Cedarquist's plan to "balance" supply and demand on a global scale—"We supply more than Europe can eat, and down go the prices. The remedy is *not* in the curtailing of our wheat areas, but in this, we *must have new markets, greater markets*" (306)—opens up the utopian hope for global capitalism. Thus Presley is converted by Cedarquist's vision of these new and vast markets and, by the novel's end, prepares to accompany a "humanitarian" shipment of wheat meant for the "hungry Hindoo" in India (648). Such a global vision, however, is fraught with contradiction and merely pushes the unresolved contradictions of capitalism into new spaces—territories (in the sense of militaristic discourse) containing peoples who will be subject to even more brutal tactics than the farmers experienced in the iron fists of capital.[6] In short, the utopian kernel—or grain, as it were—which has proven to lie not so much fallow as destructive, seems a way out in Norris's novel. Thus, the contradictions of capitalism are pushed outside the bounds of both Norris's text and ultimately America itself, at least for a brief utopian moment.

Lasting Testaments

The Crying of Lot 49 turns Norris's escapist/globalist vision back on America itself and recalls the erstwhile destructive grip of the octopus's tentacles in the penultimate scene of the novel, in which Oedipa stands on the railroad tracks trying to untie the knotty mystery of the Tristero and Pierce Inverarity: "She walked down a stretch of railroad track next to the highway. Spurs ran off here and there into factory property. Pierce may have owned these factories too. But did it matter now if he'd owned all of San Narciso? ... There was the true continuity, San

Narciso had no boundaries. No one knew yet how to draw them. She had dedicated herself, weeks ago, to making sense of what Inverarity had left behind, never suspecting that the legacy was America" (147). The tracks symbolize the end of the American frontier, as Fredrick Jackson Turner warned, and the limits of capitalist expansion, an expansion already in full imperialist swing when Norris penned *The Octopus* in 1901, at the beginning of the American Century. The sheltered suburbanite Oedipa, who earlier in the novel "believed . . . in some principle of the sea as redemption for Southern California . . . , some unvoiced idea that no matter what you did to its edges the true Pacific stayed inviolate and integrated" (41), changes her perception of America and the ever-redemptive ocean after having visited one of America's "infected" cities, where she comes face to face with the poor and disaffected. Oedipa, finding "her isolation complete, . . . tried to face toward the sea. But she'd lost her bearings" (146–147). That Inverarity's legacy, America, has been "left behind" has a double meaning here. The America he has physically left behind is a corporate and consumerist nightmare. Inverarity's real-estate empire includes Fangoso Lagoons, a housing development that boasts "canals with private landings for power boats, a floating social hall in the middle of an artificial lake, at the bottom of which lay restored galleons, imported from the Bahamas; Atlantean fragments of columns and friezes from the Canaries; real human skeletons from Italy; giant clamshells from Indonesia—all for the entertainment of Scuba enthusiasts" (20). Fangoso Lagoons has all the hokey charm of Disneyland's submarine ride, except for the irksome fact that it is a "real" housing development. And, like Disneyland, this slice of simulacra requires a pricey ticket for entry. Fangoso Lagoons is a private, "gated" community for the ridiculously rich, whose every desire has been accounted for by privately funded urban planners. Artificially constructed with the help of American capital, which has plundered at least some authentic décor from mostly third-world countries, the result is a kind of "Pirates of Fangoso Lagoons" pastiche-experience for the select few.

However, there are *other things* that must be forgotten or left behind, in a different sense. In order for such development to occur, certain things need to be destroyed, declares the proudly conservative Metzger, Pierce's lawyer assigned to assist Oedipa in executing the will: "Old cemeteries have to be ripped up. . . . Like in the path of the East San Narciso Freeway, it had no right to be *there*, so we just barrelled on through, no sweat" (46). Metzger's comment here—as subtle as the "meat cleaver" metaphor that the infamous Robert Moses employed in describing his plans to raze entire city blocks of low-income housing to clear the way for his "urban renewal" projects (the Cross Bronx Expressway in New York, for instance) from the 1930s to the 1960s—underscores the control of the definition of "rights" by private enterprise. The cemetery, which preexists the freeway, has no right to be there in the face of "progress" and development. This is John Locke on property writ wild (the same logic legitimizing the seizure of Native American lands), suggesting that any and all land not given over to capitalist development is merely land in waiting, which forfeits its "natural rights" by refusing to be developed. Land not exploited by capital thereby has no right to exist for public use, and thus Metzger's seemingly illogical statement that the old cemetery was somehow (always already) in the path of the new freeway makes a kind of twisted sense.

Oedipa's suspicion that the bones from the demolished cemetery may account for the "real skeletons" in the bottom of Lake Inverarity (an already disturbing prospect) becomes even more troubling when the remains turn out to be the bones of American GIs killed in Italy by German bombardment in World War II. Not only that, but these bones have been ground into charcoal and added as the key ingredient in a filter by Beaconsfield Cigarettes, a company owned, in part, by Inverarity. Capital here literally turns life (and death) into a commodity that can be purchased *and* consumed (as fleeting as the "smoke" it will become), as the Marxian metaphor that capital "consumes" its workers is made literal and extended by Pynchon, since the soldiers become the material grist (labor material as well as labor power) of production itself.

This is the America Inverarity has physically left behind, an America owned and controlled by the wealthy few—real-estate developers and corporate entities, who have commodified America itself. The end result is that a city like San Narciso becomes "less an identifiable city than a grouping of concepts—census tracts, special purpose bond-issue districts, shopping nuclei, all overlaid with access roads to its own highway" (24). Yet even San Narciso is merely "a name; an incident among our climatic records of dreams and what dreams became among our accumulated daylight.... There was the true continuity, San Narciso had no boundaries" (147). In short, San Narciso is a figure for all of America.

Not surprisingly, "the whitewashed bust" that sits over Inverarity's bed is that of Jay Gould (1), one of the most ruthless "robber baron" industrialists of the nineteenth century, responsible for stock-market manipulations, cornering markets, and vast corruption. Yet he is distinguishable from most other monopoly capitalists (particularly John D. Rockefeller and Andrew Carnegie) by his refusal ever to make the obligatory transition from wealthy industrialist to philanthropist. While someone such as Carnegie created various endowments and foundations to polish (whitewash), in some sense, the tarnished reputation of his name by giving something back to the public from which he took so much, Gould merely willed his estate to his heirs, scoffing at the idea of "sharing" his wealth. That the "ikon," as Oedipa calls it, that rests in Inverarity's home would be Gould speaks as much, if not more, to the notion of a "restricted" inheritance as it does to simple corruption and greed.

Yet Inverarity is ultimately less interesting as a postmodern robber baron associated with Gould than as a symbolic figure for the corporation and corporate power itself.[7] Early on in Oepida's investigation, she discovers that Inverarity's interests are multivaried and extend throughout America. He has holdings in "Arizona, Texas, New York and Florida, where Inverarity had developed real estate, and in Delaware where he'd been incorporated" (40). Surely Inverarity's vast real-estate holdings, and his incorporation in Delaware (an infamous corporate tax haven), suggest not merely that "Pierce's estate is a microcosm of America" (Schaub 48) but that Inverarity *is* America, and since Inverarity is also a corporation, so too is America. Indeed, he is described in the novel as one of the "founding fathers" of the Yoyodyne Corporation (15). Thus, Inverarity's transformation from corporeal body to corporate body is telling. In a novel playful with Greek mythology (from Oedipa to San Narciso and Echo Courts), it is perhaps Ovid's *Metamorphoses* (of course, a famous Roman bearer of said Greek myths) that best metaphorically touches on Pynchon's greatest concern in this respect. Capital, through the transformed and transformational figure of Inverarity, is corporealized in America itself. The rights of America (or its citizens) now exist solely in its private property rights and development value or, more accurately, for those who own the titles and deeds to the land.

The Mundanity of Corporate Existence

Precisely because Pierce has passed on—and *into* America itself—Pynchon gives us a world where much of the corporate underwriting remains hidden or, even more disconcerting, blasé. This is in clear contrast to the sole evil corporation in *The Octopus*, portrayed in Norris's central metaphor as a frightening beast with its tentacles sucking the life out of the entire state. One map of California, for instance, "was white, and it seemed as if all the colour which should have gone to vivify the various counties, towns, and cities marked upon it had been absorbed by that huge, sprawling organism.... It was as though the State had been sucked white and colourless, and against this pallid background the red arteries of the monster stood gorged to bursting; an excrescence, a gigantic parasite fattening upon the life-blood of an entire commonwealth" (Norris, *Octopus* 289). Moreover, this bloodsucking monster is always represented by the smarmy and obese S. Behrman as a tangible reminder of that corporate power. Despite the railroad's increasingly decentered nature, it always retains a glaring and threatening physical dimension.

In *Lot 49*, though, the giant companies that we do learn about, such as Yoyodyne, appear rather banal, represented not primarily by management and corporate hatchet men but by frustrated salaried employees in their natural cubicle-habitat. One such creature, Stanley Koteks, mistakes Oedipa for a stockholder during her visit to the company. He quickly asks her if she "can really influence policy, or make suggestions they won't just file in the garbage," and if she "can get them to drop their clause on patents" because "in signing the Yoyodyne contract, [an employee] also signed away the patent rights to any inventions he might come up with" (67). Oedipa, bemused by Koteks's complaint since she has recently been informed by the company's president about the value of teamwork, is later set straight at a bar, The Scope, where Mike Fallopian details some of the Yoyodyne employees' gripes against the company: "In school they got brainwashed, like all of us, into believing the Myth of the American Inventor—Morse and his telegraph, Bell and his telephone, Edison and his light bulb, Tom Swift and his this or that. Only one man per invention. Then when they grew up they found they had to sign over all their rights to a monster like Yoyodyne; got stuck on some 'project' or 'task force' or 'team' and started being ground into anonymity. Nobody wanted them to invent—only perform a little role in a design ritual, already set down for them in some procedures handbook" (70). Fallopian, like Koteks before him, clearly articulates the ennui of the regimented corporate grind, the dull and monotonous nine-to-five, suit-and-tie, briefcase-toting existence, outlined a decade earlier by William H. Whyte's influential *The Organization Man* (1956), which argued that a blind and unquestioning obedience to organizational structures was stifling individualism and the American character. Whyte, however, was ultimately a believer in (re)organization, contending that the individual must work with others in order to achieve particular goals. Thus, he writes, "We do need to know how to co-operate with The Organization but, more than ever, so do we need to know how to resist it" (12). Whyte, in a way, is much like the "liberal communist," in that the system is sound, so long as creativity is allowed to tinker with that system when it becomes repressive due to its inflexibility to changing circumstances.

Unlike the farmers in *The Octopus*, however, there is nothing *tangible* taken from Fallopian and others like him by the corporation. There has been no physical violence perpetrated by Yoyodyne against its workers or the community. The system that exists dispossesses people nonetheless. Because of Yoyodyne's entitlement to its workers' patents, the Yoyodyne worker, in the era of late capital, finds him- or herself in the classic position of the "free laborer" in Marx's *Capital*, who "must constantly treat his labour-power as his own property, his own commodity" (271). One can see how keenly this works in a company that thrives on technological innovation. For Yoyodyne controls the incredibly expensive and scarce resources of production that the hapless young inventor needs in order to create newer technologies, thus forcing such a worker to sell his or her labor to acquire access to the latest technologies and means of production. Instead of gaining individual freedom of expression and the means of creation, the Yoyodyne employee is like an assembly-line worker, though the products he or she works on are ideas (intellectual property), not cars or widgets. While we are no longer in the farmers' San Joaquin Valley, we find that in Yoyodyne's prototype of the 1990s Silicon Valley, many of the same basic exploitative economic principles of capital remain (even the entrepreneurial upstarts Bill Gates and Steve Jobs will eventually establish their own monolithic companies). Corporate power, having expanded well beyond the bounds of Norris's time, has made such a sacrifice of rights de rigueur for the age. Losing rights to "gain" a paycheck is something that is just part of the playing field in the era of late capitalism.

Of course, there are enormous differences between starving agricultural wage slaves and middle-class tech employees with regard to wages, health, and living standards (so much so that to "complain" about the tech employees' position seems fairly ridiculous), but in an American economy that has moved increasingly away from traditional blue-collar work to service-sector and office jobs, these are now the conditions under which capitalism is increasingly scrutinized in American culture. The beginnings of this economic shift can be traced to the immediate post–World War II years, when an expanding American economy brought unprecedented affluence and stability to American workers. At the same time, newer technologies and organizational structures utterly transformed the economy with regard to jobs and labor, as the white-collar workforce rose from roughly 30 percent in 1940 to 48 percent by 1970, while blue-collar jobs declined (Zeiger and Gall 184). It is no surprise, then, to find Fallopian and Whyte complaining about their particular kind of wage slavery. With such a massive shift in labor demographics, "white-collar" concerns with labor seem to have trumped blue-collar ones.

This economic trend has only intensified since the 1970s. Our "postindustrial age," as it is often called, means not only that there have been sweeping changes in the makeup of America's labor force (from collar switching to race and gender) but that this labor force finds its onetime secure jobs constantly in jeopardy as downsizing and outsourcing continue the sea change of an American economy that deals less and less with actual production and more and more with service-related industries. Thus, while "globalization" is praised by corporations for facilitating the flow of capital worldwide and expanding the global economy, the actual effect on American workers (and those in the rest of the world) has often been detrimental as wages have stagnated and benefits disappeared (Zeiger and Gall 242–243). Existing in a (fictional) 1960s before the decline of the aerospace industry, Fallopian is actually luckier than he thinks, considering his unfulfilling job is full-time and comes with benefits and a pension plan. As corporations in the postindustrial world continue to chip away at what people once considered "basic worker rights" in the name of staying competitive in a thriving global market, suddenly the banality of an office job might seem small computer chips next to the quiet and gradual disassembly of health care and retirement plans.

In other words, if Norris showed us the monster in the process of swallowing the State, Pynchon shows us the inside of the belly of the beast—or more precisely, its acidic digestive processes that eat slowly away at whatever remains. In *The Octopus*, the farmers either join the Trust, are killed, or are broken by its demands, but in *Lot 49*, Yoyodyne expects (to nobody's surprise) undying allegiance without any kind of physical coercion, as the songs at its stockholder meeting make clear (65). The comical, music-hall camaraderie of the Yoyodyne meeting is a far cry from the farmers' harvest celebratory barn dance in *The Octopus*. Set to the tune of Cornell's alma mater song (Pynchon's own alma mater), the Yoyodyne song is a thinly veiled oath of allegiance, not an organic folk song, and instead of being passed down by generations of friends and family, it has been passed down by corporate policy. That it is a "Hymn" is Pynchon's way of pointing to the religious underpinnings of devotion, love, worship, and submission—all of which Yoyodyne expects from its employees.

This conflation of religious and educational ideologies with business or corporate ideology is telling. One way to conceive of the corporation in this respect is through Louis Althusser's concept of the Ideological State Apparatus (ISA). As Althusser argues, "It is unimportant whether the institutions in which they [ISAs] are realized are 'public' or 'private.' What matters is how they function" ("Ideology" 18). In this regard, the institutions (corporations) of "private enterprise" clearly have ideological effects and are intricately tied to the (Repressive) State Apparatus (RSA), much in the same ways as schools and churches are. Indeed, government policy sets (or does not set) boundaries for finance, banking, and general business practices. Even in a world where the question of the transcendence of the corporation over the discipline of the nation-state remains a real issue, corporations can be said to function as ISAs.

In the era of late capital in America, this is more the case than ever. If, as Althusser writes, the RSA "functions massively and predominantly *by repression* (including physical repression), while functioning secondarily by ideology," then ISAs "function massively and predominantly *by ideology*, but they also function secondarily by repression, even if ultimately, but only ultimately, this is very attenuated and concealed, even symbolic" ("Ideology" 19). Considering the lack of *physical violence* committed by corporations in America today (unlike the pitched battles between labor and industry from industry's inception to the mid-twentieth century), Althusser's concept rings true in that corporations often function and gain their acceptance through ideology, chiefly through advertising—from slogans, spokespeople, highly researched and expensive ads, and logos. Thus, the very "attenuation" and "concealedness," the "symbolic" violence perpetrated by corporations, falls into line with the mundanity of the corporation itself. Pynchon's play with the Yoyodyne song, then, is both a humorous critique of the fraternity type of loyalty a corporation demands and a deeper dig at how such ideology calmly and silently envelops its subjects. After all, says Althusser, "That is why those who are in ideology believe themselves by definition outside ideology: one of the effects of ideology is the practical *denegation* of the ideological character of ideology by ideology" (49). The collegiate feeling of group togetherness (itself the result of an educational ISA) may mask the underlying submission to corporate authority (and later, in *Gravity's Rainbow*, to Death and the Rocket) by those who constitute the in-crowd, but Pynchon reveals to us the subtle workings of the ISA.

In *Lot 49*, corporate authority and its ideological veil are also directly tied to the military-industrial complex, as the song "Glee," which follows "Hymn," makes clear:

Bendix guides the warheads in,
Avco builds them nice.
Douglas, North American,
Grumman get their slice.
Martin launches off a pad,
Lockheed from a sub;
We can't get the R&D
On a Piper Cub.
Convair boosts the satellite
Into orbits round;
Boeing builds the Minuteman,
We stay on the ground.
Yoyodyne, Yoyodyne,
Contracts flee thee yet.
DOD has shafted thee,
Out of spite, I'll bet. (66)

It is the aerospace industry under siege here (to be joined by Dow, ITT, DuPont, and IG Farben in *Gravity's Rainbow*), and this puts Pynchon's critique of corporations very much in line with John Dos Passos's in his *U.S.A.* trilogy. The arms manufacturers and war profiteers are scorned, not so much the day-to-day functions of corporate capitalism (except by implication). Again, through the figure of the corporatized Pierce Inverarity, the land speculator and developer, Pynchon is able to carry the critique of corporations into the mundane everyday, and not just the spectacular (war)—but writing in the middle of the 1960s, he can only go so far. Pynchon is curiously in a position somewhat like that of one of his characters, Callisto, in his short story "Entropy": "He saw, for example, the younger generation responding to Madison Avenue with the same spleen his own had once reserved for wall street" (88).

Indeed, it is precisely because Pynchon reveals the fundamental way in which corporations function as ISAs as well as RSAs that his overall critique remains mired in an older paradigm of condemning corporate capitalism for funding the war machine and consequently lining the corrupt pockets of all those involved. Moreover, arms manufacturing/ dealing corporations have not garnered much public attention since Vietnam, even during the second war in Iraq, where it was Halliburton (a company engaged in "reconstruction") that garnered the most media attention due to its ties to Vice President Dick Cheney. Much of today's corporate presence manifests itself through advertising, something

Pynchon rarely touches on in *Lot 49* (with the slight exception of Beaconsfield Cigarettes). Exxon Mobil, for example, can ravage the environment, on one hand (without too much media attention), and release a commercial espousing its environmental record that depicts an eagle flying over a pristine forest, on the other. This kind of advertising puts the corporation squarely in the ISA camp, whereas the critique of arms manufacturers can more easily be traced to actual violence and destruction. Though this would still mean arms dealers can be considered ISAs too, it is important to recognize how the "secondary violence" of other kinds of corporations remains qualitatively different. Surely, Pynchon exposes the mundanity of the Corporate State in the near absence of the corporations that help produce such a world, but these days the "absence" of a corporate threat is ever more compelling since it is corporations' very unremarkable *presence* that denies or masks the fact that they are such powerful and dangerous institutions.

It is a very different practice to criticize Boeing than Pepsi Cola or Viacom, and yet the global influence of each of these corporations, as well as their commitment to profits, is essentially the same. And most people experience corporations not as malevolent forces or institutions but as the everyday companies that bring them the desired necessities of life and employ them. Such is it, then, that with the rise of a white-collar, service-sector economy come diminished expectations, a sense of being trapped in the "rat race," and a niggling frustration with the sense of one's basic nonindividuality—ironically, the same complaints blue-collar factory workers often make about their jobs. But affluence brings with it the illusion of a secure life (as the global economy becomes synonymous with temps, part-time workers, and downsizing), filled with the products and television shows that might help you forget your dismal job until Monday morning, and it certainly holds you back from rising up in arms against your employer, whom you are lucky enough to be employed by. So you "resist" instead by taking a slightly longer lunch than you should, messing around on the Internet, and IMing (or tweeting) some friends *because that's just how it goes.*

The (Im)possibilities of Resistance

Given the corporealization of capital through the figure of Inverarity in *Lot 49*, resistance in the era of late capital seems to make no sense. Resist what? Who or what is the enemy? Where is the enemy? Resistance truly is futile, in this regard. Unlike in *The Octopus*, to answer the questions regarding resistance that *Lot 49* raises asks that we rephrase or change these questions entirely because the very economic base of society that each group (the farmers in Norris and what Pynchon often calls the "preterite," after the Puritan distinction between Elect and Preterite, in his novel) would want to critique (to some degree) has been radically transformed.[8] Indeed, it is actual *physical* land the farmers are dispossessed of in *The Octopus*, whereas the preterite in *Lot 49*, having inherited this negative legacy, have also been robbed of their memories of these prior crimes (as Norris feared) and the ability to identify the cause of their ills. As Oedipa wonders, "Surely they'd forgotten by now what the Tristero was to have inherited.... What was left to inherit? The America coded in Inverarity's testament, whose was that?" (149).

The "other" America "left behind" or *left out* of the America that Inverarity bequeathed to those who hold a controlling interest in its stock is suggested by those people who come to lots not to bid on priceless antiques being auctioned, as in the book's final scene, but to haggle for life's basic necessities, as occurs in the early description of those who frequent the used-car lot in which Oedipa's husband, Mucho, once worked, "seeing people poorer than him come in,... bringing the most god-awful of trade-ins: motorized, metal extensions of themselves, of their families and what their whole lives must be like,... and when the cars were swept out you had to look at the actual residue of these lives, and there was no way of telling what things had been truly refused... and what had simply (perhaps tragically) been lost:... like a salad of despair, in a gray dressing of ash, condensed exhaust, dust, body wastes—... he could still never accept the way each owner, each shadow, filed in only to exchange a dented, malfunctioning version of himself for another, just as futureless, automotive projection of somebody else's life" (4–5). Such a pessimistic vision of a mechanized and dehumanized society is not new to American literature—even Pynchon offers such a vision of the world in *V.* (1963), the elusive titular character of which comes to be increasingly composed of material (artificial) objects. And, earlier still, Nathaniel West's *The Day of the Locust* (1939) offers a scathing critique of an America "run out of real-estate," in which the Hollywood Dream Factory is both literally and metaphorically implicated in the degradation of a once-authentic world by simulacra and grotesque fantasy. Employing a movie-screen metaphor, West divides the haves and have-nots of America (like Pynchon's "lots") into performers and viewers. The performers, of course, herald the rise of an inauthentic and capital-driven world, while the viewers compose the world of the losers, who have "come to California to die" (118) but who will be the harbingers of a societal apocalypse when their anger and resentment leads to mob violence.

But *Lot 49* is no mere rote recapitulation of the modernist theme of dehumanization. When viewed within the era of late capitalism, Pynchon's preterite appear to have no direct recourse to revolutionary change. In *The Octopus*, the shootout between the railroad's hired guns and the farmers ends dismally. Lives are lost, the farmers' cause deteriorates, and Presley can find no final justification for such violence. Yet it could be argued that the spontaneous collective organization of the farmers and their resistance serve a particular political project with specific ends. By the time we reach *The Day of the Locust* in 1939, the ressentiment of "the viewers" can only manifest itself in *spontaneous and random violence*. There is no planned political project here. The violence is sudden and destructive, and it ultimately serves in no way to elucidate a grievance to those in power. It is an even worse failure than the resistance of the farmers in Norris's novel, who at least are resisting a specific, if overwhelming, enemy. By the time we reach *Lot 49*, there appears to be no manifestation of direct resistance to the system at all.

Part of the problem of mounting a resistance in *Lot 49* is the failure of people to organize themselves collectively, which itself is partially a result of the exacerbated decenteredness of late capital. In fact, the two conditions are mutually reinforcing. Fredric Jameson claims that the ability to imagine oneself in relation to the totality (as the farmers can via Annixter's ticker) is virtually impossible in a post–World War II world because of a "mutation in space—postmodern hyperspace—[which] has finally succeeded in transcending the capacities of the individual human body to locate itself, to organize its immediate surroundings perceptually, and cognitively to map its position in a mappable external world" (*Postmodernism* 44). The farmers in *The Octopus* oddly bypass the anomie of the disconnected subject-at-sea (Oedipa) by being swept up into a larger sense of their place in a world economy. They compose a lone piece of this immense and awe-inspiring system, but they are mindful, so long as the land remains under their boots, of their place within it. There is still an idealism and possibility of collectivity for the farmers, surely the same idealism Norris must have felt in his plan to compose his "Epic of the Wheat." By contrast, Oedipa's inability to "cognitively map" herself is one of her major problems in *Lot 49*, as she is subject to a dizzying array of random events and chance encounters. As the default Maxwell's Demon in this entropic universe, Oedipa learns that the "job of sorting it all out" is hopeless.

As a result, the idealism, with regard to the vision and scope that characterizes Pynchon's works (not to mention the sheer number of pages), should be replaced by "ambitiousness," or the ambition to write a novel that attempts to totalize a worldview of what it admits, and continually draws attention to, is an untotalizable world. *Gravity's Rainbow* (1973) (and most of Pynchon's work, for that matter) is obsessed with tracing the genesis and development of various dominant and hegemonic structures of power (to put it in somewhat Foucauldian terms) at key historical moments (the end of World War II, the 1960s, etc.), when a certain set of possibilities of liberation are opened, then closed off, restructured, and reconsolidated by various economic and ruling forces (corporate entities, for instance) to suit their ends. Hence, in *Lot 49*, Oedipa imagines the Tristero's waiting, as "if not for another set of possibilities to replace those that had conditioned the land to accept any San Narciso . . . , then at least, at the very least, waiting for a symmetry of choices to break down, to go skew" (150). We might say that in *The Octopus* the individual can *act*, while in *Lot 49* the subject can only (re)act or, at best, wait.

Therefore, we pass from the (expiring) individual (with the attendant possibility of collectivity) to the isolated subject, formed in and against the structure of the system itself. This exemplifies the classic Althusserian concept of the subject who is "interpellated" or "hailed" into being. Much like the accusatory declaration of Althusser's infamous policeman, *Lot 49*'s beginning perfectly captures the feeling of such a "hailing": "One summer afternoon Mrs. Oedipa Maas came home from a Tupperware party whose hostess had put perhaps too much kirsch in the fondue to find that she, Oedipa, had been named executor, or she supposed executrix, of the estate of one Pierce Inverarity, a California real estate mogul who had once lost two million dollars in his spare time but still had assets numerous and tangled enough to make the job of sorting it all our more than honorary" (1). Pynchon's long and turbulent sentence here perfectly reproduces the feeling that Oedipa has been caught up in something beyond her power. She is hailed as an executor (a gendered term she is at least allowed to question) of a will that requires a good deal of work, and she seemingly has no choice but to accept (a choice that is no choice, which is pure ideology). The legal system literally names her here (as we learn her name for the first time as if it were a mere legal detail or aside), and Pynchon's passive construction of legal authority lends its decree the feeling of a foregone conclusion. The speed and decisiveness with which Pynchon hurls Oedipa into her quest suggests that the system precedes and constructs her subjectivity. Oedipa is literally subjected to the system's will.

The confused and isolated postmodern subject, then, formed amid the dizzying complexity of the era of late capital, cannot conceive of a more cohesive totality. This is evident when Oedipa encounters the residents of the "infected city" during her journey through San Narciso's inner city, which induces a kind of first-versus-third-world effect, all the more disquieting because we are still in America. Oedipa encounters all kinds of down-and-outs and sufferers during her wanderings through the city, which ends with her holding a lonely old man in her arms as he cries, ashamed that she cannot help him. What marks each of the people Oedipa meets (apart from their physical and emotional scars) is their apparent total isolation from one another, as well as any articulation of anger or resentment.

But if the flourishing of late capitalism destroys much of the efficacy of older collectives (the post–World War II decline of unions, for instance) in its fragmenting of a global working class, it opens up uncharted spaces that can potentially be used to forge resistance as well. For instance, Oedipa notices one thing about the residents of the city that links many of them together: "Decorating each alienation, each species of withdrawal, as cufflink, decal, aimless doodling, there was somehow always the post horn" (100). This discovery leads Oedipa to wonder if the Tristero's muted post horn serves as the secret symbol of a crypto-collective, whose members communicate with one another through the ambiguously named W.A.S.T.E. mail service. If so, then "it was not an act of treason, nor possibly even of defiance. But it was a calculated withdrawal, from the life of the Republic, from its machinery. Whatever else was being denied them out of hate, indifference to the power of their vote, loopholes, simple ignorance, this withdrawal was their own, unpublicized, private. Since they could not have withdrawn into a vacuum . . . , there had to exist the separate, silent, unsuspected world" (101). Oedipa's question as to whether the Tristero exists and whether, if it does, it is composed of these "withdrawals" is, simply put, a question as to whether there is the potential of a collective movement against the current system, and if there is, what binds it together and what is its immediate project.

The possibility of the Tristero's "silent waiting" could be read as an example of what Slavoj Žižek has termed "Bartlebian Politics" (*In Defense* 406–412; *Living* 395–401), based, of course, on the eponymous character, who "would prefer not to" in Herman Melville's short story "Bartleby the Scrivener." Žižek articulates such a politics by demanding that in a system so constraining as to "choices," which are "not choices at all," that we *not* act politically. This, says Žižek, is in order to stop knee-jerk reactionary politics that do not challenge the fundamental system itself and instead play into it. Instead, we should follow a silent, withdrawal kind of politics (that Bartleby has been argued to pursue)[9] in which we think through political problems rather than impulsively try to solve them—in a sense, think "through" the surface gripes to the deeper, fundamental antagonisms underlying them. The refusal by some people in *Lot 49* to communicate through the government's mail system can be construed as their "preferring not" to participate in a kind of government-sanctioned democratic forum, or at least it can be seen as an indirect way of stating that their actual voices have been silenced or ignored. The existence of a paramail system (instead of a paramilitary one), a mail system that, according to the history of the Tristero, various governments have clearly been at odds with since the sixteenth century, is then a way of rejecting the framing of political voices by a corporate-dominated State.

Indeed, by not communicating (at least through officially sanctioned channels), a clear message is sent—not an easy thing to do in a world where atomized individuals cannot communicate with one another (as we see with Inamorati Anonymous; 91), often due to the interference between sender and receiver that causes chronic miscommunication (Mucho calling Oedipa Maas "Edna Mosh" on the radio, believing the expected distortion will correct the mistake on air; 114). Thus, sending an indirect message or nonmessage may be the only way figuratively to send a direct message. The injunction Oedipa reads early in the novel to "Report All Obscene Mail to Your Potsmaster" is telling (33). Whether this is an intentional misspelling by the Tristero or a U.S. Postal Service typo, it serves as a reminder of how messages come to be, or not be, legitimized. The etymology of the word *obscene* can be traced to the Latin *obscenaeus*, meaning what lies *outside* of representation or what is unrepresentable. The problem here is how to send a message that is unrepresentable, which cannot be represented within the system (and perhaps Pynchon's novel itself), for by definition it represents the filth ejected outside the system's boundaries. Bartlebian politics appears to be the only way to solve the conundrum.

Oedipa, for instance, is intent on receiving messages, and her earlier avowed Young Republicanism (59) and faith in the government (she asks Genghis Cohen whether she should report her initial findings to the government; 79) are shattered by the novel's conclusion when she wonders, "How many shared Tristero's secret, as well as its exile? What would the probate judge have to say about spreading some kind of legacy among them all, all those nameless, maybe as a first installment? Oboy. He'd be on her ass in a microsecond, revoke her letters testamentary, they'd call her names, proclaim her through all Orange County as a redistributionist and pinko" (149–150). That Oedipa should even conceive of a restructuring of American society at the novel's end clearly shows that she gets the Tristero's message, no matter its corruption. Thus, the Tristero has at least the power to transform one person's worldview, whether it tangibly exists or not. As such, the Tristero is, in a sense, the abstract possibility of resistance, the residue of a utopian way out of the current state of affairs. And it is precisely through a seemingly negative Bartlebian politics that it effects a kind of change, its ultimate failure or success notwithstanding (are the letters of W.A.S.T.E. already the incinerated "Dead Letters" Bartleby dealt with?).[10]

Pynchon's pained look back at the 1960s in *Vineland* takes a fairly grim view of how the potential to resist and change the system panned out. Published in 1990, *Vineland* is set in 1984 during the Reagan years and retroactively installs the CIA and black helicopters that *Lot 49*, published in 1966, leaves out. The novel unsurprisingly seems to endorse the ominous side of the debate of some of its aging, Depression-era activists, who argue "whether the United States still lingered in a prefascist twilight, or whether darkness had fallen long stupefied years ago, and the light they thought they saw was coming only from millions of Tubes all showing the same bright colored shadows" (371). And it is a further question whether some sort of Bartlebian politics is to blame for such a state of affairs, when Jess Traverse, a onetime union organizer for loggers in the Pacific Northwest who is literally crushed (losing the use of his legs in an "accident") by industry, quotes Emerson in a supposedly hopeful tone: "Secret retributions are always restoring the level, when disturbed, of the divine justice. It is impossible to tilt the beam. All the tyrants and proprietors and monopolists of the world in vain set their shoulders to heave the bar. Settles forever more the ponderous equator to its line, the man and mote, and star and sun, must range to it, or be pulverized by the recoil" (369). Such a belief in the transcendence of justice, while it may be initially inspiring, could easily fuel a philosophy of quietism or despair. That there exists a universal justice outside the world, which can never be tampered with, is to put an enormous amount of faith into extraworldly affairs. Political action, in this philosophy, need not come from people in the world—indeed, if the tyrant cannot change the world, how could the farmer?—but from forces outside it. If the universe is inherently good, as it was for transcendentalists such as Emerson, then one can have little doubt that future justice will come to pass. But this possibly quietist philosophy is nothing like a Bartlebian one. A Bartlebian politics is founded on a sense that the material circumstances of the world are untenable and that there is an *immanent system*—whether political, economic, or social—that makes traditional resistance a near structural impossibility. If traditional resistance is ineffectual, then something extraordinary must take its place. Thus, *Lot 49*, in contrast to *Vineland*, appears the more hopeful novel—that hope hinging on the existence of a cautious, dispersed network of potential rebels.

Perhaps it is no surprise that the Pynchon immersed in the promise of the '60s could imagine an underground movement ready to burst into the mainstream, to freak out and forever change the establishment, to put it in 1960s rhetoric. But twenty years later, and buried under Reagan's neoliberal policies, such lines of resistance must have seemed ill conceived and ineffectual, as corporate dominance elevated itself to an even higher power, hitherto unimagined. But, like Norris's novel, Pynchon's earlier work is as concerned with the future as it is with the past, and *Lot 49* has proved as faithful a divining rod as *The Octopus*.

In the early 1990s, a movement against corporate power and practice arose, focusing on the branding of lifestyles and the sweatshop labor perpetrated worldwide as capitalism really kicked into global gear. Much of the military-industrial complex that Pynchon's corporate critique centered on was replaced by a scrutiny of companies such as Nike, Shell Oil, or, in keeping with one of Pynchon's prediction à la Yoyodyne, tech companies such as Microsoft. In other words, those seemingly blasé corporations were suddenly the focus of people's attention, people who resented the way in which corporations were creating "lifestyles" that increasingly commodified any form of spontaneous culture. And similar to the way Norris's novel foresaw the decentered aspect of the twentieth-century corporation, Pynchon's *Lot 49* was able to sketch a potentially new method of resistance in the Tristero—a dispersed network of individuals communicating through an "alternate" mail system, which could be argued to anticipate the ways in which activists have been able to use the Internet (though it is by no means a truly "free" space) to form local and global networks of people and, most importantly, to organize efforts to resist corporate power. It was, for instance, the Internet that facilitated the organizing of what came to be known as "The Battle for Seattle" in 1999, as numerous groups and people flocked to the streets of Seattle to protest the G6 and WTO talks scheduled there.

Both *The Octopus* and *The Crying of Lot 49*, then, offer keen predictions of America's future on the basis of the historical logic of capital.

While *The Octopus* heralds the oppressive coming of twentieth-century corporate capitalism and sees resistance to this system as obsolete, *The Crying of Lot 49* hints at the subtler changes emerging in a "peaceful" postindustrial America where corporations inspire little attention and explores a new and dynamic challenge to this system. If both novels ultimately conclude with very different visions of capitalism in America, they share a healthy skepticism of the system, as well as an understanding of its fundamental dynamism that continually restructures not just the system itself but people's ability to resist it.

These, then, are some of the major differences constituting representations of corporations in early twentieth-century and post–World War II American fiction. What we can detect in the passage from Norris's to Pynchon's novel is that corporations, having secured violent victories over people and democracy, have increasingly held sway in the social, political, and cultural arenas of life. However, this expansion of corporate capitalism into every fissure of American life after World War II has taken place quietly and unremarkably but nonetheless as ruthlessly as it did before the twentieth century. The inescapable effects of such corporate dominance are clear and visible but at the same time obfuscated, just as the shameful history of corporate capitalism has been. As a result, it is difficult to identify a cause for such a muddled state of contemporary affairs, and, even worse, a comparable single "scapegoat" kind of solution makes little sense considering the complexities of a global economic system. Thus, systemic analysis is continually thwarted by the diversity of fragmented "surface" problems and distractions, which appear to have little in common with economic matters. This makes a *pure* foundational analysis impossible and makes the work of systemic analysis often highly theoretical and abstract, although it still needs to take into consideration those immediate "surface" dilemmas. But in the absence of any easy answers, people's confusion and sense of defeat can grow, breeding a cynicism regarding the possibility that any kind of change can take place since the system is all consuming. Or worse, it can lead to the inability to imagine anything *contrary* to the system as it currently exists.

Partly as a result, American fiction and popular culture rarely explore the inequities of the capitalist system directly anymore. Pointed economical analyses of an earlier fiction (the muckraking and proletarian novels of the 1930s, for instance) are rarer and rarer, as more recent explorations of social and political problems in fiction are treated largely as if they are autonomous to such economic concerns. To be more precise, these "macroeconomic" issues are often still at play today but are relegated to the backdrop of stories and fictions, as we shall see in subsequent chapters dealing with Don DeLillo's *White Noise* and the movie *Ghostbusters*. The economic base becomes the given mise-en-scène of a fictional world, similar to the way that corporate capitalism has calmly proceeded to dominate the world today. Yet with this dominance of the corporation comes its visibility and thus a kind of temporary refinement and crystallization of the unseen "spirit" of capitalism. The corporation becomes an entry point for an analysis of capital, even if it is often conceived as an autonomous construction in and of itself, essentially free from larger economic ties. It is in the openly concealed figure of the corporation, then, that we best find both a direct and indirect critique of late capitalism, proving that while American fiction and popular culture often may not directly or consciously criticize the system, they are nonetheless unconsciously obsessed with working through the numerous contradictions of late capitalism.

2 / "Domo Arigato, Mr. Sakamoto, for the New Non-Union Contract!": (Multi)national Threats and the Decline of the American Auto Industry in Ron Howard's *Gung Ho*

In 1986, the Mitsui Real Estate Company purchased the Exxon building on Sixth Avenue in New York City for a hefty $610 million. The formidable sale gave rise to a popular story claiming that the initial asking price for the building was a mere $310 million. The Mitsui Real Estate Company had apparently overpaid by $300 million, almost double the asking price. The reason for the gross overpayment, so the story goes in Charles P. Kindleberger's venerable *Manias, Panics, and Crashes: A History of Financial Crises*, was that the company's president, awash in fresh capital, was looking for a trophy purchase, one symbolic of Japan's newfound economic might.[1] He also had apparent aims of entering into *The Guinness Book of World Records* for the largest recorded price paid for a single building. As it turned out, the story was a mere rumor, but it was not until a 15 June 1996 article on financial legends in the *Economist* that this fiction was exposed as such, something that even escaped Kindleberger's usually keen analysis. Yet, as the article put it, "if you cannot imagine anyone believing such a tall story, you don't know anything about financial markets" ("Financial Legends" 79).

What the *Economist* article makes clear is the seriousness of the perceived Japanese economic "threat" to America at the time, citing Daniel Berstein's *Yen! Japan's New Financial Empire and Its Threat to America* (1988) and Michael Crichton's *Rising Sun* (1992) as two popular examples of America's onetime preoccupation with Japan's "new empire." However, this burgeoning interest in, and wariness of, Japan was prevalent as early as the 1970s when Herman Kahn, a respected economist, wrote

The Emerging Japanese Superstate (1970), in which he explored Japan's success and asserted that "for more than one hundred years now the basic national goal of the Japanese nation has been focused on one purpose—to catch up with and surpass the West" (88). Kahn concluded his study by warning his readers that "it would be a great mistake in the case of Japan to assume that the rising sun has reached its zenith" (183). Kahn (with Thomas Pepper) amended some of his bolder predictions in 1979's *The Japanese Challenge*, yet he still emphasized Japan's eventual emergence as a world superpower. The levelheaded predictions of Japan's future made in Kahn's books (which were certainly not peddling nationalistic doggerel)[2] nonetheless resounded Paul Revere–like throughout the country, and when Americans found themselves unable to awake fully from the nightmare recession of the 1970s that continued into the 1980s, many feared not that the Japanese were coming but that they had already arrived.

Released in 1986, the same year as Mitsui's historic purchase of the Exxon Building, the Ron Howard comedy *Gung Ho* not only offers another instance of America's newfound fascination with Japan but also illustrates America's growing anxiety regarding Japanese economic might in the early 1980s by tying it directly to a suffering American economy—and specifically to a sputtering American auto industry. *Gung Ho* warrants closer study because it stands as one of the most influential instances of American pop culture's meditation on these anxieties, grossing over $36 million at the box office and leading to a short-lived television spin-off of the same name. The film rehearses numerous tensions between the two nations at the time by performing various American and Japanese stereotypes in a supposedly humorous manner, attempting to show that despite their differences, the two countries and cultures can learn from each other to the benefit of all. Yet many of the issues raised in the film are easily swept away by the lighthearted tone (Howard as a neo–Preston Sturges or Frank Capra) and Hollywood ending, which preempts the critique of corporations and late capitalism that the film initially registers. Far from remaining an attenuated comedy of cultures, then, *Gung Ho* stages a 1980s version of capitalism that, after having gone "multinational," returns from where it traveled with troubling results.

Land of the Rising Yen

Japan's emergence as a world economic power in the space of a few decades after its decimation in World War II was a remarkable feat, eventually becoming known as "The Economic Miracle." Helped, in part, by a ban on military and defense spending and an influx of Western technologies, as well as benefiting from serving as a major supplier for the UN's military needs during the Korean War, Japan began to recover from the war at a rapid pace. In addition, Japan urged along fledgling industries through its *zaibatsu* system, a kind of superconglomerate of corporations—including banks and investment firms—all working together under government direction toward the betterment of the nation. Many of these policies and practices were either recommended or instituted by the United States, which sought to establish an ally and a military base from which to fight communism after World War II. Ironically, then, America's greatest perceived economic threat of the 1980s turned out to be an economy very much a part of its making (Inkster 282).

By the 1980s, Japan had become a true player on the economic world stage, boasting the third-largest economy in the world, behind only the United States and the Soviet Union (Matray 23). But such a rapidly growing economy was eventually perceived as dangerous to the United States, whose trade deficit to Japan climbed from below $20 billion to over $50 billion between 1983 and 1986 under Reaganomics (Togo 96). Japan's surplus skyrocketed, while America's deficit ballooned, which many Americans saw as cause and effect. As a result, writes Ian Inkster, "the Japanese surplus became a symbol within America of that nation's own severe economic problems" (282).[3] Thus, the United States and Japan entered another kind of war, this time an economic one. And when an increasing deficit led the Reagan administration to devalue the dollar in 1985, the land of the Rising Sun became the land of the Rising Yen.

Much of this market battleground was fought over the importation and exportation of various commodities. Japanese imports flooded American markets with affordable and high-quality goods—mainly appliances and electronic devices—whereas Japanese markets remained fairly free from American products. The United States imposed various tariffs and struck deals to balance out its trade problems. Nowhere was this more evident than in the auto industry, where the influx of Japanese cars left the American industry in dire straits. In truth, the conditions for the decline of the Big Three automakers were already in place before the influx of the imports and the trade imbalance of the 1980s. Just as foreign car companies began to enter the U.S. market, the 1973 Arab oil embargo hit, creating widespread panic as gas prices soared and gasoline pumps dried up. Combined with the recession and the energy crisis, as well as stricter Environmental Protection Agency measures for miles per gallon and emissions, the giant, gas-guzzling cars of Detroit became outmoded steel dinosaurs. Customers began taking a closer look at the offerings of Toyota and Honda, whose cars were much more economical, more fuel efficient, and environmentally cleaner than their Detroit counterparts. Once many customers had made the switch, they discovered how dependable and durable the imports were, and henceforth Detroit's woes truly began.

While Detroit stumbled, between 1974 and 1989 Japanese production shot up from roughly seven million vehicles a year to over thirteen million (Allinson 132). American auto manufacturers, instead of evaluating their own production methods, simply lashed out at the Japanese threat. They complained about the stricter emissions standards and what they claimed were unfair advantages for Japanese auto companies. Not surprisingly, the United States sought to limit Japanese car exports. In May 1981, Japan agreed to "voluntary" restrictions on its imports to America of no more than 1.68 million vehicles a year for three years (Togo 93–94). In an ironic twist, America's hypocritical espousal of free trade by way of restrictive measures led to perhaps its biggest blunder in trying to save Detroit. Coerced into these "voluntary" restrictions and pressured by the political tactics of Detroit, the Japanese companies realized it was in their interest to build factories in the United States, thus allowing them to sidestep the voluntary tariffs and other trade barriers that were beginning to hamper them (Allinson 132). Thus, while Detroit thought it was leveling the playing field, it was in truth opening it up for the imports, which was something the imports were already planning. The imports now had direct, unimpeded access to a huge American market. American automakers found themselves facing the biggest challenge to their industry yet, and *Gung Ho* offers an early insight as to the effects of such a challenge.

Sayonara, Detroit!

Gung Ho introduces us to a small, quaint, working-class Pennsylvania town, Hadleyville (nonetheless a stand-in for Detroit), which is soon revealed to be suffering hard economic times. The auto plant that employed much of the town has recently closed, leaving most of the blue-collar inhabitants of the town unemployed and desperate for work. Businesses are closing, families are leaving, and the streets of the town are run down and desolate. Hunt Stevenson (Michael Keaton), once foreman at the defunct auto plant, has just been elected by his former employees and friends (basically the entire town) to fly to Japan and convince a Japanese auto company to reinvest in and reopen the plant, therefore saving Hadleyville and its citizenry.

Hunt appears the perfect choice to be the man who will save Hadleyville, as he possesses oodles of charm, the ability to smooth-talk anyone, and an ever-present, easy smile—qualities all perfectly portrayed by Michael Keaton. Various people wish Hunt good luck as he rides to the airport, and nobody seems worried that he could fail, although he tacitly admits to his girlfriend, Audrey (Mimi Rodgers), on the drive to the airport that failure is a real possibility. Hunt, however, hides his doubts behind his reassuring smile as he boards the plane and waves good-bye to his buddies who come to see him off, though his doubts are to return soon after landing in Japan.

Once in Tokyo, it becomes clear that Hunt is vastly underqualified for the job. His search for the corporation he is to pitch the plan to, Assan Motors, leads him astray, at one point impossibly landing him in the midst of the Japanese countryside, up to his knees in a rice paddy. Curiously, Hunt's journey to Assan Motors breaks from the familiar narratives of Westerners traveling through the East, although, as Edward Said notes, "every interpretation, every structure for the Orient . . . is a reinterpretation, a rebuilding of it" (158). Instead of serving as a mise-en-scène in which Hunt plays out his deepest desires and fantasies, Tokyo is figured as a confusing, contradictory postmodern space (from the rice-paddy feudalism to the neon streets of the postmodern city),[4] whose citizens are uninterested in the lost Westerner, who seems dwarfed by, and irrelevant in, the space. Against the shifting economic balance in the era of late capitalism, the bargaining table has been turned. Unable to brave the unfamiliar Japanese cuisine (and here the movie truly feels dated), Hunt finds refuge in the familiarity of McDonald's, where the sign's golden arches eclipse the Japanese writing covering it (since the true Esperanto of consumer capitalism is surely composed of logos and brand names) to offer a transnational postmodern Valhalla, if only momentarily. Furthermore, the only desire Hunt has is to convince Assan Motors to come to Hadleyville, and his wandering through a city hardly aware of his presence foreshadows his encounter with Assan Motors' executives. A postcolonial Matthew Perry, Hunt's only weapons are his charisma and persuasiveness, and he remains at the mercy of Assan Motors.

Hunt's slide-show pitch to Assan Motors (yet another Orientalist trope reversal here, as the Japanese executives view the carefully selected images and representations of the West that will eventually compel their "investment" in the plant) begins in a "nudge-wink" fashion. After blandly introducing the town and plant, Hunt presents a pinup-style image of a woman "working" on the production line, joking, "Whoa, how'd that get in there?" All obvious readings of the conflation of the woman's sexualized image within the space of the assembly line and mass reproduction aside, Hunt's quip is received by the stony-faced Japanese in total silence. Hunt stops the presentation, as it becomes clear it consists of the same pattern of imagery and off-color ribbing, and his exasperation leads him to plead with the board instead: "If you come over and open up that factory, these people will work *harder* for you. That's a promise." Hunt's burst of sincerity is met with the same stoicism as before, and Hunt retires from the meeting, defeated and cynical, registering his failure as he sits brooding in front of a temple, again calling attention to the irrelevance of the American worker and industrial capitalism against the surging, postmodern Japan.

Hunt returns to Hadleyville after apparently failing in his mission, but he is unable to face the town and admit his failure. Before he is forced to admit the truth, however, Assan Motors announces it is coming to Hadleyville after all. The town is elated and Hunt even more so when he is offered the job of employee liaison, a promotion for him and his first executive position. In the tide of excitement, Hunt learns that the workers are being offered a contract well below what they are accustomed to. For the plant to open, they will have to accept wage cuts and agree not to unionize. Hunt, knowing the workers will probably never go for such a deal, assures the Japanese all will be well. So begins Hunt's role as the intermediary between the management/Japan and the workers/America, as he tries to appease both sides, all the while preserving his own interests and job security too.

The State of the Union

Having sold Assan Motors on Hadleyville, Hunt must now sell Hadleyville on Assan Motors. However, the union offers an enormous obstacle to Hunt's plans, as the union representative advises the workers not to enter into a deal with Assan Motors without a contract, breaking the news to them (which Hunt has kept quiet) that they will have no contract, less pay, and fewer benefits working for Assan. The workers, frustrated and desperate for employment, distrust and shout down the union representative, calling instead for Hunt to tell them the truth of the matter. Hunt steps up to the podium and delivers his all-American smile and an all-American local legendary tale about the fourth quarter of a high-school championship basketball game when he came off the bench to lead the team to victory. Using the game as an analogy, Hunt promises the workers that all they have to do is let the Japanese have their way for a while, then turn it around to the workers' benefit. Promising such a "fourth-quarter comeback," Hunt responds to a friend's question as to whether he can "take these guys" the way he took down the opponent's star player in high school with the reply, "Yeah, I can take 'em." The crowd erupts in cheers and applause.

As liaison between Japanese managers and American workers, and as part of the managerial class with blue-collar roots and attitudes, Hunt marks the instability between the divisions of class and labor in the film, as well as the anxieties and tensions involved in class mobility in America. His peculiar position, paralleled by that of the Japanese plant manager, Oishi Kazihiro (Gedde Watanabe), allows him the space for self-reflection instead of mere self-preservation, which turns him into a kind of deliverer of knowledge to an ignorant Eden fallen on hard times. The biblical parallels are no surprise here, as Hunt is a kind of Christ figure. He "belongs" to the two worlds/classes, sacrifices his own reputation for the good of the community, and accepts the shame and frustration of the American worker as his own. His last temptation to leave the town, rather than face the consequences of his lies, is answered when he leads the walkout from the factory, and he is "crucified" onstage at the Fourth of July picnic where the mayor denounces him and the town boos him. But the all-American Jesus rises again in the fourth quarter (just as he has foretold in his union speech) and leads his believers to a last-second victory when they barely meet Assan Motors' new production quota. The question that remains for this messiah, however, is, what belief system does he espouse? On the surface, it would appear to be a reprisal of the good old Protestant work ethic. As I will show, however, there is much more to this than what is dreamed of in Hunt's philosophy.

Hunt's masterful antiunion sell to his union brothers, as well as a later scene also set in the union hall, reveals much about the film's attitudes toward labor and class in general. Set in a theater with a touch of fin de siècle décor, the union meeting resembles something out of the early twentieth century in its depiction of the energy, raucousness, and ultimate strength of labor and unions. The theater is packed to the gills, mostly by men waving fists from the balconies and floor, chanting, "Work, work, work."[5] It is fairly dark inside, and the noise, unrest, and sweat mark the space as aggressive, threatening, and overtly "masculine." Considering the economic war taking place outside the theater, this makes sense. The union hall here is a kind of training camp psyching up soldiers to go out and fight, just as the retraining course for failed Japanese executives that the film opens with resembles a boot camp in which the "dishonorable" executives must yell and confess their failure and shame while on their knees, where they are beaten with cane sticks. The animalistic and violent attitudes the union provokes in the workers, and its overdetermined staging of masculinity, mark the union as a bubbling cauldron of labor's anger and discontent. In other words, this representation is a fairly nostalgic one. Or, as Fredric Jameson argues in *Signatures of the Visible* with respect to the representation of history in Stanley Kubrik's *The Shining*, "such films do not so much express belief as they project a longing to believe and the nostalgia for an era when belief seemed possible" (131). The longed-for belief, in the case of *Gung Ho*, is a belief in the prolonged efficacy of unions.

Such a nostalgic view of the union belies the already waning power of unions in 1980s Reagan America. But since the local analysis of class and capital has been short-circuited by the impingement of the global "Japanese problem," the union is simultaneously fantasized in the film as a powerful collective with the potential to enact change *and* as a dangerous collective capable of generating a chaotic force, one which threatens the workers, the auto industry, and even America itself—hence the visual coding of an older union hall and meeting space (recalling former epic and often physical battles between unions, and specifically the UAW, and capital—Ford kept a private army for such battles—earlier in the century) that in truth is merely an empty sign for a collective liquidated of any real political power. However, the film must continue to perpetuate the illusion that the union still holds such power in order to accuse it of harming the auto industry, which, as we shall see, is the film's overall message regarding labor.

The film's refusal to explore the conditions for the state of the union means that it must omit some interesting facts about how such a state came to be and what is really at stake when unions are blamed for the American auto industry's woes. While the United Auto Workers has traditionally been one of the strongest unions in American history since its formation in response to the labor crisis of 1935, it was greatly affected by the decline of Detroit during the 1970s and 1980s. As Micheline Maynard states in *The End of Detroit*, over the years the UAW can boast of having "won some generous benefits that white-collar workers in many professions can only dream about: fully paid health care, legal advice, child care, pensions, vacation time, education benefits and job security" (300). But when the auto industry began struggling at the end of the 1970s and the onset of the early 1980s (the time period *Gung Ho* reflects and refracts), the UAW had to make cutbacks in order to help save the

Big Three, and especially Lee Iacocca's Chrysler, from bankruptcy (Rae 161). Thus, the state the UAW was in during the recession of the early 1980s appeared grim. Not able to negotiate to its advantage and stripped of the threat of a strike or walkout, the UAW's policy of making concessions severely compromised its bargaining powers. Although the UAW reestablished worker wages to their former levels years later, the scaling back of pay and benefits at the time signaled the extent of a weakened auto industry and a weakened union, a trend that continues today.

In *Gung Ho*, then, we find that the contradictory representation of the union makes a kind of twisted sense. The film must employ the figure of the union—at once powerful and impotent, dynamic yet regressive—as an outdated and harmful organization at odds with the new global economy, mired as it is in pre–World War II history and politics. The men willingly accept the nonunion contract without even attempting negotiations, which the film hints would lead to a Japanese refusal to do business with them. The unspoken message here is that American auto manufacturers, such as the former owners of the plant that closed down in Hadleyville, were saddled with weighty union contracts that made it too difficult to compete with foreign imports.[6] The new labor policies of the global economy will be union-free, and the workers had better accept this as the new order sooner than later. Hence, what is made truly threatening about the union's power is its uncontrollable, revolutionary potential (the overdetermined aggression and threat of violence), which is not *actual* political power here (the union has been stripped of that, and the union contract is refused) but the chaotic power to destroy itself, and by extension America, through a refusal to play by the new global system's rules.

The specter of that older, nostalgic union returns not just in the form of the union hall's décor, moreover, but also in the emptied content of the meeting itself. For although the workers have agreed not to unionize, they persist in calling a union meeting together (not, apparently, an official one) later in the film when they wish to voice their dissatisfaction with the new labor conditions. It is here that the contradiction of the union most evidently surfaces, for the men are nonunion members joined as a collective yet without any true power. Essentially, the lack of a union contract leaves the workers without any bargaining chips and prompts the Japanese to shut down the factory for good (at least until the ending, when everyone miraculously pulls together to save the town). In the end, the union is presented as harmful and antiquated, its power not political but physical and therefore negative and self-destructive. At the point in which the film offers a glimpse of potential rebellion put squarely in the hands of the workers, it quickly retracts that potential by casting it as self-defeating.

The reasons for the plant closing in Hadleyville in the first place are conspicuously absent from the film. They are, of course, hinted at as being similar to Detroit's problems at the time. At one point, the door handle of Hunt's car comes off in his hand, which corresponds to an earlier scene in which Japanese engineers inspecting a model of a car joke that the car is "American" when its wheel falls off. But beyond this there is nothing but a critique lodged squarely on blue-collar shoulders. The film overtly presents American blue-collar workers as lazy, incompetent, and spoiled by their union contracts. In one scene, a worker complains that his shoddy workmanship is something "the dealer can worry about," and the workers apparently clock in late and leave early, much to the management's chagrin.

The film's focus on the "blue-collar problem" effectively expunges any critique of the white-collar executives in Detroit, whose management of the Big Three put the industry in such a predicament. However, as Brock Yates claimed in 1986, in *The Decline and Fall of the American Automobile Industry*, "Nothing less than a revolution in management and labor attitude, with productivity and quality as its criteria, will save the American auto industry" (252). Detroit's hubris and its refusal to change its perception of itself and its business structures in the global economy are what have truly brought on the crisis of the auto industry. *Gung Ho*, however, is devoid of any white-collar executives who are not Japanese, as well as any closer analysis of why the factory closed in the first place. Instead, it is the blue-collar worker and the Japanese threat that appear to be the problem and solution to America's automotive-industry dilemma.

You Say, "Sashimi"; I Say, "So Sue Me": Let's Call the Whole Thing Off

Gung Ho's strange mapping of class anxieties from the local to the global is one way the film frustrates such class analysis from taking place strictly at the local level (the blue-collar workers–Hadleyville–America axis) by reconfiguring such a possible analysis against a global one (the managers–Assan Motors–Japan axis). This shift discourages a local or micro investigation by projecting all frustrations and critical inquiry outward, where it affixes to a "global threat." The result is that an antagonism is created between the two axes on the basis of perceived (stereotypical) cultural, racial, and national differences.

Yet this antagonism is merely a red, perhaps white- and blue-collared, herring. To ascribe the inability of the factory's success to cultural differences and clashing work ethics between American workers and Japanese management—sloppiness versus efficiency, individuals versus team, West versus East—is a thin ideological veil for the changes in production that a global economy mandates. And this is not to imply that there are not real cultural differences between American and Japanese workers of any collar, only that the film would like to essentialize such traits as the cause for any discontent. In an era when outsourcing will increasingly become the practice of multinational corporations, however, what seems more pertinent about the film is that it heralds such a version of late capitalism (a capitalism long ago exported to Japan via Perry, then revived and perfected during the "Economic Miracle") and signals a kind of return of the repressed, both historically and economically, of the darker side of an older capitalism in the guise of its shinier new form.

In one sense, then, the Japanese form of management, its "ruthless" brand of capitalism, is nothing more than the face of global capitalism returned to its source. With regard to this newer global power structure, the blue-collar workers of Hadleyville find themselves in a situation somewhat akin to people in the third world who are compelled to accept any form of labor that large corporations offer them (though for a pittance of what the workers in Hadleyville will make and in much more desperate living conditions). Therefore, the fears and anxieties projected onto the Japanese in the way of cultural differences can be read, in some sense, as the Otherness of that returned capital investment that was always already part and parcel of that peculiar economic institution, the multinational corporation, no matter how brightly it was wrapped in ideological and nationalistic paper when exported.

According to the film, it is the Japanese who have made capitalism and management into an inhuman, mechanical practice, and this is exacerbated in large part because American workers have lost their Protestant work ethic. Once the plant is reopened, Hunt and the workers find themselves subject to a whole host of new and rigorous production measures, from the introduction of morning exercises (which the men perform mockingly or not at all) and banishment of radios and smoking in the factory to stricter quality control and more Taylorized methods of efficiency on the assembly line, all of which greatly aggravates them. The workers soon begin grumbling to Hunt, who stalls them from action by promising them that things will relax after a while.

Yet the truth is that the conditions in American factories before and since the introduction of the transplants (foreign-owned plants operating in the United States) always have been abysmal. In *Farewell to the Factory: Auto Workers in the Late Twentieth Century*, Ruth Milkman, who views the GM-Linden plant (in New Jersey) as a fairly representative case of the decline of American auto manufacturers,[7] denies any nostalgic thinking that the older factory system was any better than today's, writing that "the combination of mindless, monotonous work, unrelenting regimentation, and inhumane supervision made the workers feel like prisoners, and they routinely employ the metaphor of the plant as a prison" (27). According to her study, relations between management and workers in the American factories were always deeply adversarial because of "the social relations of the shop floor, especially the military-style regimentation to which workers were subjected and the insensitivity of many first-line supervisors to the basic human needs of those in their charge" (27). Indeed, in *Gung Ho*, many of the tightening restrictions—the refusal to give personal days, regulation of bathroom breaks, and confiscation of reading material—that the Japanese introduce in response to early numbers showing the factory's production is well below Japanese standards were already implemented by American car manufacturers with regularity in their factories (Milkman 45–46).

Moreover, an early joint venture between Toyota and GM in 1984, the New United Motor Manufacturing Inc. (NUMMI) in Fremont, California, proved to be quite successful in instituting Toyota's methods of production. As Paul Ingrassia and Joseph B. White write in *Comeback: The Fall and Rise of the American Automobile Industry*, at NUMMI "the progress was painfully slow at first, as the workers grappled with the new system. But . . . GM's quality checkers made an astounding discovery: The hardboiled union factory hands Toyota had adopted were turning out some of the best cars GM had ever sold" (51). The NUMMI system did not work as successfully in Detroit as it did in Fremont, however, as GM's engineers and managers seemed unable to comprehend the system adequately and implement it elsewhere. But the NUMMI experiment showed the potential benefits of properly incorporating Japanese manufacturing concepts into American plants. Indeed, the NUMMI venture in Fremont could well have been a model for the auto plant in *Gung Ho*, as the workers who chafe under the "tighter" restrictions find that there is ultimately more "freedom" and benefit in playing by the new rules instead of fighting them.[8]

The point here is that while Japanese methods of production were certainly an example of increasing Taylorization of the assembly line and demanded a hardworking, disciplined worker wholly committed to the company and turning out quality products, the toll that this took on the average autoworker was often less taxing (after a period of adjustment) and more rewarding than was the older American system of auto production.[9] As Robert Sobel notes in *Car Wars*, apropos of Japanese-run plants in America, "Worker satisfaction and morale were high. Production and quality control were not only satisfactory but in some cases better than those at Japanese factories," and thus, "American management had done a poor job motivating workers" (317). While the film, in a sense, could be argued to bear out the notion that the American workers simply need time to adjust to the Japanese system, it is obvious that the more compelling critique of Detroit is lost by focusing on the Japanese, whose challenging production methods supposedly result from strict Japanese cultural norms and expectations. The film suggests that it is the cultural differences between the United States and Japan that are to blame for American workers' dissatisfaction and that such differences (individualism versus company loyalty, shoddy workmanship versus quality workmanship) are somehow so deeply ingrained in people that they are manifest in even the most trivial ways. Thus, when Hunt and Kazihiro discuss a juvenile "pissing contest," we discover that Americans shoot for distance, the Japanese for accuracy.

(Trans)national Threats

The realization that Japan was outperforming America at making cars—an original, American "apple pie" industry—inspired a reactionary patriotism and nationalistic pride in many Americans. The film reflects this nationalism and its tendency to essentialize cultural and racial differences between countries in a "friendly" softball game, where the Japanese show up in clean, new uniforms, in contrast to the ragtag, "individually" dressed Americans, prompting Hunt's friend Buster (George Wendt) to comment, ironically, "They look like the Yankees. I hate 'em already." Such national and cultural differences appear to dictate the style of play too, as the first two Japanese batters bunt for singles—a hit-and-run style, "efficient" game—until the third baseman moves up to prevent another bunt, and the Japanese begin swinging the bat just as successfully. The Americans are about to be shown up at their own national pastime when Hunt pops up in the infield for the potential last out of the game, but they win after Buster steamrolls the infielder standing in the baseline, knocking him over and preventing him from making the easy catch. No longer the result of a "friendly" game, the Americans' victory is tinged with embarrassment.

Nationalism's uglier sidekick, racism, enters here too, as the movie registers fears about the Japanese "conquering" America economically and "beating" Americans at what they do best—thus rewriting the outcome of World War II. Early Japanese imports were often disparagingly called "rice burners," and the rising Japanese challenge to Detroit was usually laughed off by complacent executives. As Maryann Keller argues in *Rude Awakening: The Rise, Fall, and Struggle for Recovery of General Motors*, "There was clearly an element of racism behind GM's initial inability to see the Japanese as viable competition. The World War II veterans who held many of the managerial positions have struggled against a deeply rooted disdain for the Japanese" (22). Keller mentions one executive's statement regarding his attempt to take Honda seriously after it opened its first plant in the United States: "The response I was met with was, 'Oh, don't worry about those little yellow Japs. They will never make a go of it in the United States'" (23). Such blatant and direct racism is absent from the film (it is, after all, a comedy), but one feels its sentiments in the depiction of American workers' attitudes toward the Japanese throughout. At one point, a worker calls the management "the Rice-a-Roni patrol," and the workers make constant fun of the Japanese, ridiculing their cuisine, their use of chopsticks, and their ritual of a prework dip in the local river. These tamed-down instances of racism and xenophobia are, in a sense, the film's calling attention to the darker underside of such behavior.

Perhaps the most glaring, yet hidden, instance of nationalism that the film evokes is in the title itself. *"Gung Ho!" The Story of Carlson's Makin Island Rangers* (1943) is the title of a World War II film about a battle in the Pacific. The film, as its title and date of release suggest, is a fairly obvious piece of jingoistic, wartime propaganda that romanticizes war and tells the "true account" of one marine battalion's training, mobilization, and successful mission after the bombing of Pearl Harbor. *Gung Ho* is, in a certain sense, the sequel to *Gung Ho!* While *Gung Ho!* champions America's retaliation against the Japanese empire, *Gung Ho* updates the earlier film by urging America to retaliate against the threat of a Japanese economic empire.

Not surprisingly, the history of World War II lies buried just below the surface of Howard's film and bubbles through on two occasions. The first is when Hunt and Kazihiro share a few beers at a bar in the local bowling alley and discuss their struggles with the workers and management, respectively. Kazihiro is similar to Hunt in that he is somewhat outside his own (business) community. He is a "failed" executive, whom

Hunt briefly encounters in Tokyo, and has been through the torturous retraining program shown at the start of the film. As he reveals to Hunt, part of his problem as an executive was that he cared too much for his employees' families and overall quality of life, which goes against the Japanese business model of total loyalty to the company. This supposedly puts Kazihiro in sympathy with the American workers. At the bowling alley, Kazihiro again tells Hunt that the American workers have no pride in their work and connects the Japanese work ethic to the resurgence of Japan during the "Economic Miracle," thus tacitly referring to World War II. Drunk by this point, he bursts into a patriotic rendition of Japan's national anthem in Japanese.

Kazihiro's narrative of the phoenix-like rise of modern Japan is nationalistic in its own right and shows a marked disregard of Japan's own imperial history leading up to the war, during which it subjugated much of Southeast Asia. The change in Kazihiro's body language suggests that the anthem is singing Kazihiro, not the other way around, and hints at Japan's inability to deal openly with its violent past, covering it instead in the ideology of national pride. Some of this Japanese nationalism can be seen as a response to the fear and bitterness that the United States and other countries felt toward Japan's "winning" an economic war after "losing" the military war. But this nationalism was fairly radical: "During 1982 a hit movie portrayed Japan as the victim, not the attacker, at Pearl Harbor. The minister of education infuriated Chinese, Koreans, and Southeast Asians when he authorized textbook revisions that stressed the benefits of Japanese colonialism, referred to Japanese aggression during World War II as 'advances,' and ignored Japan's wartime atrocities. Despite his resignation and a public apology from the Prime Minister Nakasone, few of Japan's imperialist victims accepted these acts as sincere" (Matray 23). Kazihiro's narrative of Japan's recovery and rise after the war, then, is a familiar Japanese cultural narrative of the time and shows that nationalism is not just one-sided. Moreover, it provides the deeper historical reservoir that feeds the beliefs of many of the film's characters (as well as those of American moviegoers) in the irreconcilable differences between the two nations and cultures, perhaps because this traumatic event has never been openly or forthrightly discussed by each nation. To underscore Japan's own nationalism in some sense legitimates the country as a "worthy" opponent of America, but it also dredges up (racist) American fears of an enemy so "sneaky" as to bomb Pearl Harbor and so tenacious and zealous that it once praised suicidal Zero bombers and refused to surrender until two atomic bombs had been dropped on two civilian cities. In repressing such traumatic history, the economic war that played out during the 1980s was haunted by memories of the atomic bomb and World War II.

The second time the war is mentioned, however, it is used strategically as an insult delivered by Hunt to Kazihiro. Hunt asks how Japan "lost the big one" if the Japanese are such capable managers, as compensation for his own realization that America is losing the "next one." Kazihiro tackles him, and the two wrestle for a while, until the workers finally break it up. The incident, again, shows how the trauma of history lies just under the tense relations between the countries and how it can be used as a device to shame and anger the Japanese, as much as it can be used to buttress in Americans a false sense of pride and nostalgia for America's preeminence in the world.

This kind of knee-jerk jingoism ultimately makes little sense when it comes to the status of the automobile industry, however, whether in the 1980s or today, and the nationalistic rhetoric that often surrounds much of Detroit's plea to "buy American" has to be set against the fact that companies such as Toyota and GM have long since "gone global," something *Gung Ho* unconsciously illustrates.[10] Thus, while Detroit and its advertisements harp on "buying American" and pull at patriotic heartstrings, the truth is that such multinational corporations have less allegiance to individual nations than it would seem. As Michael Hardt and Antonio Negri point out, "They tend to make nation-states merely instruments to record the flows of the commodities, monies, and populations they set in motion. The transnational corporations directly distribute labor power over various markets, functionally allocate resources, and organize hierarchically the various sectors of world production" (*Empire* 31–32). Just as transplant auto firms have affected America, so too have GM and American automakers affected various places (labor and consumer markets, as they see them) in the world. These decentralized distributors and constructors of labor and markets, then, create flows of goods, commodities, and subjectivities that overflow traditional economic and national boundaries, which the Detroit companies try and assure the customer are still intact, all the while restructuring such boundaries themselves. With regard to economics, then, the importance of nation-states rhetorically and ideologically is growing, while their actual ability to regulate commerce is being challenged and in some cases eclipsed.[11] The real transnational threat in the film (which it fails to register), then, is not the Japanese but the more and more powerful transnational corporations, newly infused with capital and freer from government regulation than ever.

Automatic Transmission

Thus, while *Gungo Ho* portrays the characters' jingoistic nationalist attitudes as harmful, it subtly reinforces a kind of nationalism, which itself is ultimately at odds with the film's heralding of the new global economy. As *Gung Ho* rigidly continues to suggest the determinism of binary differences between nations and cultures, the situation at the plant does not improve. After tensions between management and workers mount after the softball fiasco, Buster is demoted and then fired. Soon after, invited to dinner at Kazihiro's house, Hunt is also fired, only to fast-talk his way back into employment by promising Kazihiro that the workers can perform just as well as the most efficient Japanese workers and produce fifteen thousand cars in a month.

The workers, furious with the new working conditions, call another union meeting. It is only Hunt's magnificent hustling that once again quells the workers' rebellion. This time, however, Hunt outright lies to the workers. Having buttered up the crowd with jingoistic remarks about American workers' superiority to Japanese workers, he informs them that all their pay and union benefits will be restored if they can make fifteen thousand cars in a month, a Japanese record. When the workers balk at this deal and begin to doubt Hunt's earlier claim that he could deal with the Japanese, Hunt equivocates about the goal of fifteen thousand and lies, claiming that they will earn part of the raise if they make thirteen thousand cars instead. The workers leave on a high note, committing themselves to working overtime without pay and weekends, whatever measures are necessary to reach the mark and earn the raise.

The film depicts the subsequent speedup in production through a montage of devoted workers, toiling away to an unimaginative rock song, "Tough Enough." This speedup eventually leads to an accident when one of Hunt's friends gets his hand caught on the assembly line. The film portrays the accident as an outcome of the faster production methods, but it must do so in a strange fashion. *It is only when the line is jammed and work comes to a stop that the injury takes place.* Apparently, as the worker is trying to fix the problem, the assembly line jolts into action again, and he is injured. Since there is no statistical indication that there are any more accidents under Japanese auto production than American, the accident really has little bearing on the Japanese factory model, as the film would like to suggest. Indeed, the introduction of a wire in reach of the line that automatically shuts it down is a Japanese safety innovation. Again, the film would seem to belie its championing of the new capitalism by staging the accident at the point at which the new global system comes to a halt and must start up again, *not* when it is in actual motion. In doing so, *Gung Ho* undercuts the notion that the new system is more harmful to workers than the older system was.

The real danger, it seems, is in questioning, stalling, or stopping the new, fluid global economy, whether it is through unions and collective action or physically ceasing production. For, although the film suggests it is the *worker* who needs an "attitude adjustment," it is actually the new and improved assembly line—more automated with robots than ever and sped up and functioning at high efficiency under Japanese management (as representatives of the new global technologies and economy)—that *demands the workers to adjust to it*. The system only breaks down and "hurts" its workers (from the physical injury of one man to the "suffering" of all production) when its smooth functionality is undercut, stalled, or interrupted. To challenge or derail this new system (which can only ever be temporary, anyhow, for the system is ultimately unstoppable) represents the real danger here, not the system itself.

The Japanese automobile industry's innovations in assembly-line production are prime and material examples of this new global system at work. This is true especially of Toyota, which is known for revolutionizing auto manufacturing through its TQS (Total Quality Control) and its TPS (Total Production System). TPS is a system that accounts for the entire manufacturing process, down to the smallest detail, in a kind of "uber-Taylorization" of all aspects of production and emphasizing quality control ("zero defects"). Furthermore, Toyota instituted a "pull system" or "just in time" system in which products are shipped and arrive when they are needed, thus obviating warehouse stockpiling. This particular "pull system" both sped up production and lowered the cost of keeping stock and is now a regular feature of all manufacturing industries. Governing all these innovations was *kaizen*, a Japanese concept stressing "'continuous improvement,' or the process of making small changes to make a job easier, or less expensive" (Ingrassia and White 49). This concept also required a relationship between management and workers that was meant to be more open and fluid and encouraged workers to offer ideas about improving production. *Gung Ho*, however, merely represents the Japanese innovations as draconian throwbacks, entirely ignoring the more "open" relationship between managers and workers and the revolutionary "just in time" system. Moreover, Taylorizing Taylorization is merely the improvement of an *American* system of management. There is nothing essentially Japanese about it at all. As Sobel reminds us,

"As early as 1911, a translation of management philosopher Frederick Taylor's *The Secret of Saving Lost Motion* sold over 1.5 million copies in Japan" (126).

In this sense, the further Taylorization of labor in something like TPS, no matter what its benefits seem to be for the workers, is disturbing not because it is somehow "Japanese" but because it is an example of the global economic system in action. Such innovations hail the arrival of deindustrialization and the rise of the service-sector economy. Cheap labor in a global market means that old manufacturing jobs in first-world countries will decline, a "just in time" system means that warehouses are leaner and employ less people, manufacturing workers lucky enough to find work can no longer expect union contracts, and the speedup and better efficiency of production has given rise to new ways of disciplining workers, ways that the workers must accept in order for the system to perpetuate itself without any hitches. For the global system is now so all pervasive that it has convinced most people that if it is allowed to fail, it will take everyone with it. One must accept the new order, with its *requirement* of loose and fluid labor structures and financial regulations—and resulting permanent destabilization of life—and sacrifice an older assured stability for the "stability" of the system itself. As an economic structure, globalization no longer brings security and stability but insecurity and instability as well as the threat of their increase if it is allowed to fail. The ability to imagine anything outside such a Total System, to imagine the Empire's new clothes, is therefore deemed impossible.

This postindustrial dilemma is precisely what *Gung Ho* depicts when the workers walk out. Without their union contract, they are without any real voice, and Assan Motors has no qualms about pulling up stakes and letting the town deteriorate again. As we have seen, though, the film unconsciously endorses the new multinational stage of capitalism against an older industrial system bogged down by unions and pampered workers who, as a result, have lost their true-blooded, American/Protestant work ethic. Camouflaging this concern under the ruse of irreconcilable cultural differences and the traumatic history between America and Japan, the film rejects a closer analysis of America's complicity in such a global system, even after the fallout from that system returns to America's own doorstep.

A utopian moment of reconciliation and redemption is fantasized, however, in the film's ending. The wedding here between the old and new, America and Japan, is completed when management and labor work together on the line (even though the plant is officially closed), in yet another montage set to a bad rock 'n' roll song (itself another remnant of Detroit's decaying legacy). The utopian montage would appear to be the blending, then, of what has heretofore been polarized: the differences between Japanese "teamwork" and American "individualism" are transcended by the fact that management works side by side with the blue-collar workers on the line; the older system, or "American Way," works with the new system, figured as the "Japanese Way"; and the Protestant work ethic, devotion to hard work and quality control, meets the Japanese "total loyalty" to the company. Yet there is not really any merging going on at all. Nothing actually changes, except that the workers give in to what the Japanese have been demanding all along. Faced with the prospect of Assan Motors leaving, the men submit to working for no pay according to the Japanese standards of production and at the grueling pace the managers have been pushing the entire time—all to get Assan Motors to stay.

Of course, since this is the true "fourth quarter" comeback of the film, the management helps out to make the quota, and the last few cars are pushed off the line without engines and windshields. But the "victory" the workers gain when Assan's CEO, angry about the last few defective cars, relents and grants the raise is actually no victory at all. The workers and management all cheer, obviously having pulled together as a team and ironed out their differences for good, but the fact remains that the workers will have to keep up such an inordinate monthly production of cars from here on out (certainly putting in the same overtime and without management's help on the line), something it is clear they will not be able to do, even with their supposed reinvigorated work ethic. Moreover, although they now have wages equaling those they had under the union, they still lack a contract and collective voice. Essentially, the workers have been disciplined to accept the new global economy. The rules include being paid, at best, an equal wage to what they earned before (and most likely this wage will be lower than their prior salaries) and being forbidden to unionize, which thus compromises job security and bargaining power. And these rules come into effect only if there is a higher production rate than the workers are used to. In other words, employment hinges on meeting higher production goals, which will reward the workers with weakened salaries and strip them of any union benefits. However, the film's celebration of the workers' entry into multinational capitalism as they all enthusiastically perform the morning exercises they formerly snubbed in perfect unison while the credits roll to the song "Working Class Man" pushes all this outside the viewer's gaze, as the happy, Hollywood ending fantasizes this new system as a kind of utopia. In truth, Hunt's continual promise that things will "ease up" if the workers just hold on a little bit longer never comes to pass, despite the fantasy ending. It is the workers who must "ease into" the new global system, and Hunt's coaxing is late capitalism's coaxing and promise that all will be well in some future utopian market-space.

This conversion to the new system takes place at the level of blue-collar work ethic, which the film suggests has disappeared thanks to cushy union contracts. The moment of revelation, in which Hunt tells the town the "truth" about America, is telling: "You don't want the truth. You know what you want to hear? You want to hear that Americans do everything better than anybody else. [*The crowd cheers.*] They're kicking our butts, and that ain't luck, that's the truth. There's your truth. Sure, the great old do-or-die American spirit. Yeah, it's alive, but they've got it. Well, I'll tell you something. We better get it back. We better get it back damn fast. Instead, we're strutting around telling ourselves how great we are, patting each other on the back." When the workers decide to help out in the final "come-together" scene, they revive that "old do-or-die American spirit," which is apparently all they needed to do from the beginning. In truth, however, there has been little wrong with blue-collar performance in transplant factories with regard to work efficiency or quality and especially with regard to transitioning to the foreign companies' newer management and production techniques. As companies such as Toyota with its Total Production System have proved, management that establishes close ties with factory workers, and actually listens to their suggestions for improvement, tends to be successful, resulting in a happier workforce. Thus, the workers' discontent is not a reaction to the new system but precisely the opposite. Toyota even used *Gung Ho* as an example of how not to manage American workers ("Why Toyota"), though it was already sensitive to management issues before the film. In other words, in reality the Japanese system of running factories (even without union contracts) has led to not only more productivity but more contented workers. Realizing this, American manufacturers have tried to learn from the Japanese but have been unable to replicate the newer structures adequately.

What the success in productivity at the transplants and joint ventures such as NUMMI shows, then, is that the American blue-collar worker is not the root of the American auto industry's problems. There is nothing uncommonly wrong with American workers. They have not been "spoiled" by union contracts, nor have they any less work ethic than before. While *Gung Ho* suggests that Detroit's cars are defective because of careless and lazy workers, this is simply not true. It is the white-collar, corporate structure of old Detroit that is mired in the past, whose draconian factory management is more accurately reflected in the film via the "Japanese threat." Detroit's inability to initiate change at a fundamental and structural level is what has led to a further decline in the American auto industry, not a lack of American "can-do" attitude, as Hunt suggests in his revelatory speech to the town.

Hunt, even after he chooses to remain loyal to the town and holds up the mirror to its tainted image, still remains a trickster figure all the while. He is the liaison between worker and management, between Detroit and the transplants, and, most importantly, between the older, industrial capitalism and the era of the multinationals. His smooth salesmanship is ultimately the film's salesmanship to its viewer in the endorsement of a system that America need not fear if it will simply take a deep look within itself and reclaim those national and natural characteristics that it has always had—its self-reliance, toughness, pioneering spirit, and God-given work ethic. As we have seen, however, this messiah's gospel of work ethic is a ruse of sorts, pitched at the worker who will bear the brunt of this transitional state of the auto industry and global economy. If capitalism might be to blame, it is because corporations like Assan Motors, in their "foreignness," are cold, ruthless, and harbor historical resentments, but this could never be the case at home, where good, simple, and hardworking people just want to lead honest lives.

Over the (Joe) Hill and Back Again

This distinction between "home" and "over there" takes us back to the film's beginning, in which the multinational postmodern space of Tokyo offered a veritable consumerist utopia to Hunt in the form of the golden arches of McDonald's (an "American" company gone global) and not in the nostalgic space of small-town America. Coincidentally, we see no corporate fast-food restaurants in Hadleyville, nor do we get the sense there are any, as Howard must portray this America as fairly idyllic, untainted as yet by corporations and the global economy. But corporations, like McDonald's and Assan Motors, have transcended the nostalgic boundaries the film fantasizes in the name of the universal citizen—the consumer. That, for instance, is the reason foreign-owned car makers came to the United States in the first place, not for the cheap labor but to cut out tariffs and taxes and to get closer to the consumers of one of the largest car markets in the world.

Hadleyville, too, for all its sleepy, small-town nostalgia, cannot pretend its own innocence in such a world. We need only look at that ne plus ultra of consumer sites, the supermarket, to see this. Central to postmodern life, as Don DeLillo's *White Noise* registers, the supermarket encapsulates the complexity of capitalism's grip on postmodern life. Filled with the necessities of survival, food and water, it simultaneously remains a place for selling dreams, fantasies, and desires. Although the town in Howard's film is essentially dying—most of its citizens are jobless and moving away, and various businesses are closing up shop—the Hadleyville supermarket (aptly named "Food Towne") is still fairly crowded, still piping anonymous Muzak through the speakers, and still well stocked with an endless variety of goods. Hunt and Buster come to blows there, crashing into different displays until Hunt finally fells Buster, who collapses into a display of cheese curls.

That this epitome of working-class frustration, reaching a boiling point as the two old friends brawl, should take place in the supermarket seems somehow fitting. The later fight between Hunt and Kazihiro takes place in the factory, the space of production, for it is really the battle between the old and new economic systems. But the earlier fight takes place in the space of consumption, and there can be no outsourcing this rage onto a "foreign" threat. For once, the anger takes place at perhaps the true scene of the crime, though it now tears apart those who should be in solidarity, being that they suffer under the same conditions (albeit Hunt's job now effectively puts him in a white-collar position). Yet in the destruction of goods, in the smashing of displays of potato chips, paper towels, dog food, and cheese curls, there is a satisfying feeling of release, a leaking out of the truly repressed rage at the site for which all this production and misery is in service. For how can there not be a feeling of bitterness and betrayal here? In the midst of a terrible economic depression and the desolation of an entire town, even Hunt's girlfriend, Audrey, advises the stock boy to put the rows and rows of cookies on a lower shelf so that children will see them, beg their parents to buy them, and the store will move its product. The scenes in the supermarket, then, offering our only glimpse at the space of consumption in a film so critical of "Japanese" production, smash the small-town innocence of Hadleyville, revealing how much it (and America) have all along been complicit in the ever-expanding story of capital. The citizens of Hadleyville are also the citizen-consumers of the global economy and have long ago accepted its fundamental belief system.

I have attempted in this chapter to hold up a larger and wider mirror (the mirror of production) than Hunt offers Hadleyville to *Gung Ho* itself, but with the caveat that "objects in the mirror may be closer than they appear." For *Gung Ho*'s use of the Japanese and Assan Motors as a screen on which to project and distort not only the American auto industry's history and production methods but the reputation of blue-collar workers, and ultimately the ambiguous return of late capitalism with its entourage of anxieties, cannot finally contain its own *excess* (as definitions of *gung ho* suggest) in figuring the underlying historical and economic problems of capital as essentially cultural, racial, and national differences between America and Japan.

3 / Good Times, Bad Times... You Know I Had My Share(s): The Corporation in Five Popular Films

> *Even a radical film director who wished to portray culturally important social developments like the merger of two industrial concerns could only do so by showing us the dominant figures in the office, at the conference table or in their mansions. Even if they were thereby revealed as monstrous characters, their monstrousness would still be sanctioned as a quality of individual human beings in a way that would tend to obscure the monstrousness of the system whose servile functionaries they are.*
> —T. W. ADORNO, "THE SCHEMA OF MASS CULTURE"

Representations of corporations or depictions of corporate power have become familiar tropes in and throughout the image repertoire of popular culture. In movies and television shows, corporations are often cast as the bad guys, coldly calculating in their pursuit of profits, unsympathetic to the human cost of their business (trans)actions. The castigation of a heartless capitalism has become fairly commonplace in such media, so commonplace, in fact, that it might be useful to take a closer look at these fairly one-dimensional representations of corporations to discover the cost of such "flattening" depictions. We might argue that corporations in popular culture have become stereotyped, in a sense, and that such stereotyped tropes signify all too easily a certain emotional complex in the viewer, which can block, in its immediate stimulus, any attempt to think through such tropes. What we end up with is a kind of Manichean view of corporations wherein a temporary aberration in capitalism is ultimately good for the system, instead of a dialectical approach that offers a base from which to examine the rise of such a contradictory view, and what seems to be a change in content remains merely one of (n)ever-changing form.

The satirical cartoon *South Park*, for instance, exemplifies this sort of binary trapping of thought, particularly in an episode dealing with corporate power and influence. This episode, "Something Wall-Mart This Way Comes," depicts the opening of a Wall-Mart (instead of Wal-Mart) in the little town of South Park, Colorado. The opening of the Wall-Mart leads to the closing of various mom-and-pop stores, due in part to South

Park's population being literally hypnotized by the store after initially having embraced its bulk-priced bargains. The store turns out to be a kind of monster, seeking to swallow the town, and the episode clearly lampoons not only Wal-Mart but rampant consumer capitalism as well. Shoppers are like zombies, it implies, and corporations mystify, through hypnosis/ideology, the true state of things: that it is you who are being consumed, not you who are consuming.

Finally becoming aware of this threat, the town attempts to stop Wall-Mart by burning it down, only to have another Wall-Mart immediately take its place. In frustration, the children (the protagonists: Stan, Kyle, Kenny, and Cartman) travel to Wall-Mart's headquarters in Bentonville, Arkansas, to find out how to destroy the store. In yet another fictional-fantasy meeting with a CEO, the children meet Harvey Brown, who fears nothing can stop the Wall-Mart because it is running itself (the same line that Shelgrim gives Presley in *The Octopus*). However, armed with Brown's advice to "find and destroy" the store's heart, the children return to South Park, where they track down their target behind a plasma-screen television in the electronics department. The "heart" of Wall-Mart turns out to be a mirror, wherein after the children witness their reflections, they are told that the true heart of Wall-Mart is themselves (the customers), but even more specifically their "desire." They smash the mirror, and the Wall-Mart self-destructs. The town's subsequent choice to shop only at mom-and-pop stores to counter the corporate menace implodes after a montage shows the rapid growth of a local shop to multinational proportions, after which the town burns it down—and the cycle continues.

While the show's solution to the dilemma of corporate capitalism is wanting, it at least represents a fairly self-conscious view of the role of corporations in American daily life. Such an episode stands at the end of a long line of corporate representations that similarly attempt to grapple with capitalism's troubling contradictions. This chapter looks at five such films that also deal with corporations in a fairly straightforward manner, with one exception. The films have been selected, in part, for this reason, but also because it is helpful to read the logic of each of the films as fairly descriptive of the changes in corporate capitalism over the past fifty years. The stories these films tell of corporate capitalism in postwar America might also be seen as a microcosm of America's popular (un)consciousness and understanding of the thrills and chills, the mania and panic of late capitalist life. *Executive Suite* (1954), for instance, speaks to the relative security felt during post–World War II American affluence. The individual and the family find themselves challenged by corporate capitalism, which is well meaning enough in its goals to be reined in before its destructive capabilities are fully realized. Much of this postwar stability and security is questioned in the 1960s, and by the time *Network* (1976) is released, the welfare state is not faring so well after all. Corporations are clearly no longer the paternal organizations they were in the 1950s and 1960s. They have gone multinational, and a lingering, media-compromised 1960s radicalism tries in vain to call them to account. When *Ghostbusters* (1984) hits the screen, the neoliberal agenda feared in *Network* is in full swing. With the economy surging, there is a sense of reprieve from the 1970s recession and a lighthearted embrace of the free market and all its benefits. The hurdy-gurdy economic times that followed—the market crash in 1987 and the recession in the early 1990s—gave way to some mild concerns with the struggles of smaller businesses as mergers and corporate takeovers seemed the order of the decade. *Tommy Boy* (1995), riding on the tail of this recession, can begin to see the economic upswing of the Clinton years as news enough to have a nostalgic vision of the renewed roots of American capitalism, somewhat akin to the vision of *Executive Suite*. Yet *Michael Clayton* (2007), released during the "War on Terror," seems to look at the effects of the global economy as politically, morally, and culturally bankrupt. This colorless world seems in a kind of limbo, with no sensible prehistory to explain its conditions and no possibility of changing them.

Furthermore, in the interest of discovering telling continuities and discontinuities among these films' representations of corporations, the five films discussed span a variety of genres, from drama (*Executive Suite*) to comedy (*Tommy Boy* and *Ghostbusters*) to thriller (*Michael Clayton*) to cultural and political satire (*Network*). These films are telling in that, like the Wal-Mart episode of *South Park*, however critical or uncritical their analyses of corporate capitalism might be, none of them is able to uncover fully the systemic and structural problems in the economic system itself. As a result, the films tend to end either positively, by pushing the concerns raised outside their frames, or pessimistically, by reaffirming the unstoppable and malevolent forces of capitalism. We end up locked, once again, in the binary of either/or and good/evil, which merely reiterates the same views of corporations and capitalism and offers little hope for change.[1]

The Essential Goodness of Capitalism

An early film that serves as a kind of model for the pervasive view of the corporation as evil is Robert Wise's *Executive Suite* (1954). In the film, the death of Avery Bullard, president of the Tredway Corporation, leaves a power vacuum that the remaining six board members seek to fill. After some mild backroom wheeling and dealing (none of it too underhanded early on), Loren Shaw (Fredric March) emerges as the most likely candidate to succeed as president. But Shaw, the most fiscally rigorous and cutthroat of all the board members, is not well liked by the others. They blanch at his single-minded pursuit of profit, which never tallies the human cost of business in the final reckoning. While we are given glimpses of the other board members' troubled lives (for they are "as human as you and I," the narrator promises us at the beginning of the film), Shaw is always in the office, making it clear that he lives only for and through the Tredway Corporation. Shaw is the true "company man."

Shaw's cool-headed business strategy and extreme dedication are ultimately depicted as dangerous in the film. Shaw, however, is curiously dispassionate for a "villain." In an early scene, he defends his numbers, charts, and ruthless pursuit of profit as simply following the law that dictates corporations must return dividends to their stockholders. He is genuinely confused by any argument to the contrary, remaining as stoic as Spock when listening to any argument that does not adhere to the logic of capital. In the end, Shaw is less a character than the representative of the kind of corporation emerging at this time, as corporate financial restructuring and stratification led to more efficient and streamlined business models, more committed than ever to a profit-first mentality (Baskin and Miranti, 226). Shaw himself is an accountant, beholden to numbers and unarguable mathematical conclusions, and his scholarliness is apparent in his love of such data. He thus encompasses the more and more professionalized managerial class (despite his being middle-aged) with its ever-more-standardized accounting practices and its subsequent attention to its growing number of and more-educated-than-ever stockholders.

Shaw's foil is Don Walling (William Holden), whom we first encounter working in a furniture-manufacturing shop on a special project, unlike the number-crunching Shaw perched high in his office. While Shaw is devoid of passion, Walling is bursting with it. Although he is a board member, Walling works with his hands on the factory floor among blue-collar workers. He has a love of physical labor and creation that Shaw can never know. But Walling is dissatisfied with the furniture that the company is currently turning out. Tredway's products used to be of superior quality, but the pursuit of profit and mass-production techniques have reduced them to cheap and shoddy commodities. One of

Walling's foremen laments this at one point, complaining, like Walling, that there is no joy or satisfaction in making such commodities.

The film's logic here, in simple Marxist terms, is that Walling understands that labor itself is individually fulfilling, as well as productive. There is an immediate gratification for the laborer in creating something that is unique from other commodities because of the attention and craftsmanship that went into its manufacture. Once such a commodity is sold—the commodity's transformation from pure exchange-value (the seller) to pure use-value (the purchaser)—it will have a lasting effect on the world, surely greater than that of a commodity of inferior quality. In other words, the film suggests that labor engaged in the production of high-quality commodities, complemented by equally high business ideals, affords a strong bond between worker and commodity—under such conditions, the film argues, labor is *not* alienated. Since there is care and craftsmanship evident in the production of such commodities, their creation (even in a factory setting) shares more in common with feudal artisanship than mass production. It is only when efficiency and profits rule the space of production that the worker becomes entirely alienated from his or her labor and is reduced to an object as worthless and disposable as the commodities he or she makes. You are what you make, the film suggests.

The real tension the film reveals, then, is the one between a newer, streamlined, dispassionate corporation bent on obtaining profits (people and products be damned) and an "older," idealistic and paternalistic corporation that equates the quality of its product with the quality of American life and the good of the country in general. The former is, by law, the goal of every corporation; the latter is a belief, an ideal to which a company may or may not subscribe. As such, this dialectic remains at the core of the corporation and is subsequently manifested routinely in popular culture by proxy of the "bad" executive versus the "good" one. We see this when Walling eventually opposes Shaw's candidacy for company president. By this time, however, Shaw has blackmailed enough board members to ensure his victory.

In a moralistic, Capra-esque ending, Walling chastises the board for the current state of the company and launches into a speech emphasizing the Tredway Corporation's, and Avery Bullard's, original laudatory ideals. He reminds the members of the kind of high-end merchandise they used to make and punctuates his point by smashing a cheap piece of office furniture to pieces. The speech, of course, wins the board members over, so impressed are they by Walling's youthful passion and formidable vision. Thus, the son steps into the father's re-*soled* shoes and re-treads Tredway's recently misguided path. The capitalist system has been righted once again by a reinvigoration of the system's founding principles.

Consequently, the film sets up a formula that became standard for many such films dealing with a business or corporate restructuring: there is a "good" capitalism that treats its workers with care and respect and a "bad" capitalism that is inhuman in its sole pursuit of sales and profit. This contest always takes place between two people or camps—whether executives, board members, or owners—and is usually refined (as it is in *Executive Suite*) into two main characters at odds with each other. In general, the character espousing "bad" capitalism is portrayed as corrupt, immoral, and evil. To remove the offending agent is to save the day, as is the case in *Executive Suite* when Shaw is defeated.

In this sense, the film deserves mention in that its "villain," though he gets wrapped up in the play for power, is truly no villain at all. Shaw, it might be argued, is corrupted by the system itself, which explains the "it's nothing personal" attitude he exemplifies in his quest for the presidency and his desire to fulfill the corporate mission. Shaw is so imbued with the legal corporate directive that his attitude is no pose; it is the pure embodiment of this principle of the profit motive, more amoral than immoral. Even when he is defeated in his bid for the presidency, he immediately and respectfully congratulates Walling. And while most offending agents are ejected from the company in such films, Shaw merely retreats back to his charts and graphs. Shaw is cold, certainly, but without an ounce of malice.

We might even go so far as to accuse the film's ideology itself, as embodied by Walling's character, as being the real "villain." Could it be that Walling is the true villain after all? There is something refreshingly honest about Shaw's subscription to pure capitalism and to the corporate directive. He attempts to hide nothing and breaks no business rules. Outside of his blackmailing some executives to gain the presidency, which is truly a moral dilemma for him, he merely follows the system's rules to their logical fruition. Shaw is so transparent in his aims, so absent of duplicity in his business philosophy, that he retains an odd kind of innocence, or at least naiveté, regarding his and the company's actions.

Can the same be said for Walling, however? Might it not be argued that Walling is even the more committed capitalist than Shaw is, that in his redemption of the system by injecting it with noble ideals and a sense of purpose once again, Walling does more good for the corporation than Shaw does? After all, Walling tells the board members that they can make the same kinds of profits while still retaining the sense that their mission goes well beyond such mere material aims. He even cures Julia Tredway of her anger at her father by twisting Tredway's remiss parenting into a great sacrifice, that of the few for the many. Now Julia must also sacrifice her resentment (and thus her painful childhood) to purify the corporation once again. Tredway's psychological damaging of his daughter for the company's benefit (ominous scenes suggest the same could happen to Walling regarding his son) is apparently acceptable as long as the ideals of which it is in service are lofty enough. Shaw, though he harms nobody in this way, is somehow more monstrous. His lack of interest in principles that supposedly transcend the cash nexus exposes a raw truth about the corporation that the other executives would like to forget.

In the end, will the only difference remaining between a supposedly "bad" and "good" capitalism hinge on the quality of the product and the unexamined assumption, à la Adam Smith, that the wealth and health of the nation rely on a simple commitment by capital's main proponents to some kind of humanist ideal? Is not this redemption of capital by such honorable intentions and ideals *ideology in its purest form*? Who, then, is more duplicitous, the transparently principled Shaw or the visionary Walling, who would have us believe that we can have our capital and share it too?

All this is to say that when considering the corporate structure itself, *it is vital to remember that it shapes the individuals within it*. The ideals of even the well intentioned, such as Don Walling, are routinely twisted into their opposites by the structure of the corporation itself. Good intentions or not, the corporation will not allow such a "good" model to last indefinitely. Surely, in the 1950s, this darker side of capitalism could be suppressed rather easily. Yet this early indicator of the shift from a commitment to more stable, long-term growth of industry and capital to the myopic chasing after short-term gains and focus on up-to-the-minute market fluctuations is a harbinger of the crises in late capitalism to come.

Nonetheless, without consciously seeking to do so, *Executive Suite*, through its depiction of one corporation's internal power struggle, exposes the structure lying beneath the boardroom drama. Avery Bullard's vacated presidency, his empty chair, reveals an opening through which one can glimpse the internal contradictions inherent in the structure itself. Bullard's absence is the symptom of a deeper lack of structural integrity. In the end (or the beginning), there can be no Wallings without Shaws, and vice versa. Shaw and his agenda may be repressed, he may be forced back into his office to tabulate numbers, but he is the unconscious foundation of the entire edifice, which the others would like to forget. Once a crack in the structure appears, however, the repressed returns with a vengeance, until the imaginary order is once again restored. Just as Marx said that the crises of capital are not merely singular events but instead reveal the fundamental internal contradictions in the system itself, so, too, do the crises of corporations uncover the latent inconsistencies in their own construction.

Corporate Seductions and Pandora's New Box

The vast changes in American society and culture during the 1960s and 1970s saw the rise of a new generation skeptical of political and economic power. No more was capital's crisis a mild one, easily assuaged as it was in *Executive Suite*. In the sputtering economy of the 1970s, such an optimistic outlook was virtually impossible, as evidenced in another film dealing with corporate power, Sidney Lumet's prescient and darkly comic *Network* (1976), written by Paddy Cheyefsky. The film follows the sea-channel change in network television's programming during the 1970s, as the ruthless pursuit of ratings and profits began to dictate what shows the networks produced and aired. UBS, a failing fictional television network, has recently been purchased by CCA, Communications Company of America. Motivated purely by profit, CCA guts the ailing news division, starting with the firing of longtime anchor Howard Beale (Peter Finch), in order to streamline its operations and raise ratings.

The representative of the corporate drive (he is probably UBS's CFO) is the aptly named Frank Hackett (Robert Duvall). Hackett cares little for the integrity of the news division and its onetime cachet unless it brings in market shares. He is the true "company man" with ambitions of securing a seat on the board of directors at CCA. With the CCA merger, Hackett realizes that corporate restructuring can pay both personal and shareholder dividends, and he sets forth a plan to reorganize the structure of financial accountability at UBS. Aware that the members of the old guard are unwilling to embrace the new protocol, Hackett manipulates them until they all but ask for their own dismissals.

The old guard, led by the president of the news division, Max Shumacher (William Holden, now playing a man embittered by the system, instead of one rejuvenating it), soon finds itself either without jobs or succumbing to the new order. Amid the shake-up, the firings and rehirings, Shumacher and Beale reminisce about what Beale calls "the great early days of television" and the "grand old men of news." The two recall their days with Edward R. Murrow, Harry Reasoner, Walter Cronkite, and the whole CBS gang. Here we find the distinction between the old and new guard. Shumacher's idea of journalism and news in America comes from a time in the 1950s when media had to struggle against a highly conservative and reactionary Eisenhower era and its attendant guard dog, Joseph McCarthy. Producing an objective analysis of the country at the time was a seemingly noble and heroic pursuit, with people like Murrow standing up to the bullying and conspiracy-mongering tactics of McCarthy. Coming from such a background, Shumacher sees himself and his work as ethically upstanding and crucial to sustaining a healthy democracy.

The new guard, however, is little concerned with the ethics of television broadcasting. For those who compose it, television is all about ratings and profits. Although it seems as if Hackett leads the new guard in his role as corporate hatchet man, that position is reserved for Diana Christensen (Faye Dunaway). At first, Christensen's reality-based programs have nothing to do with the news, until she seizes on an idea for a show, *The Mao Zse-Dong Hour*, using real-life footage of a bank robbery and kidnapping sent in by the Ecumenical Liberation Army (based on the Symbionese Liberation Army / Patty Hearst affair). After UBS's CEO, Edward Ruddy, is hospitalized by a heart attack (he eventually dies), Hackett is put in charge of the company. He promptly fires Shumacher and puts Christensen in charge of the news. With the news compromised by programming, Christensen builds a tawdry news hour around Beale's rants (Beale is rehired after his last on-air tirade proves a hit), including segments with "Sybil the Soothsayer," "Vox Populi," and "Skeletons in the Closet." The show is a massive hit, and UBS's ratings and profits continue to soar.

The film then follows the rising fortunes of UBS and CCA under the sway of Hackett and Christensen. Christensen moves forward with production on *The Mao Zse-Dong Hour* with the help of a communist organization eager to cash in on the profits. She also renews an affair with Shumacher (the two once slept together), who is now out of work and suffering a midlife crisis. Smitten with Christensen, Shumacher leaves his wife of twenty-five years and moves in with her. But the relationship hardly lasts six months before it falls apart, which is apparently how all Christensen's romantic relationships end. This is partly, Christensen says, because she is too "masculine." She is a terrible lover, she claims, too uncaring, too unwomanly, and men have told her "what a lousy lay I am." This is due to what she calls her "masculine temperament" of quickly climaxing and dropping off to sleep soon after. Indeed, we see her making love to one man while watching the television, completely uninterested in her lover. In a humorous weekend-getaway montage with Shumacher, she talks of nothing but her work as the two take a romantic walk on the beach, have a candlelit dinner, and end the evening by making love. Shumacher is silent in every scene, dreamily listening. Christensen continues the chatter during sex (she is, of course, on top), reaching a rapid climax as she announces her latest successes. Silenced and sexually "used" as Shumacher is, conventional gender roles are put off-kilter here. Later, when Shumacher moves into her apartment, his depression and midlife crisis are referred to by Christensen as "menopausal decay." This "masculine" woman has clearly upset the gender roles Shumacher is habituated to, though it will take him some time to realize this.

The woman who enters the masculine world of the corporate structure, then, must at once be masculine enough to get her heel in the door yet is damned for doing so. She must empty herself of her "natural" femininity for masculine traits, a kind of gender bending that leaves her contorted and not quite human. Women's "natural" duplicity and inconstancy, combined with an aggressive masculine drive, can only end in trouble, the film suggests. It is better to remain in the domestic sphere, like Shumacher's wife, where such instability can be contained by patriarchy, and the man can have his little affairs (as Shumacher has had with his secretaries over the years), thus reaffirming his "manhood." Loosed from such domestic "bonds," the sexually and economically liberated woman is a force that is viewed by the film as uncontrollable.

It is fairly easy to see *Network* as registering male fears of women during the second-wave feminism of the 1970s as white, middle- to upper-class, educated women began to make inroads in formerly male occupations. After all, Beale and Shumacher lament the passing of the "grand old men" of news and the hard-drinking, joke-telling, back-slapping "masculine" world that goes with it. But such male anxiety of the influence of feminism's second wave and the ramifications of decisions such as *Roe v. Wade* remains only a partial explanation of Christensen's character. There is much more to it than that, particularly with regard to what "woman" in the film is associated with. For instance, although the film registers dismay at how corporate power reduces the news to newstainment, its critique hits hardest at the specific programming that enacts this reduction, which is Christensen's forte. But this is to emphasize the symptom over the disease. Frank Hackett is also presented as one of the villains in the film, but as the angry and ruthless force of capital, he is fully understood by the characters as well as the viewer. Hackett is straightforward about his devotion to ratings and profits, and in this sense, he remains heartless but predictable. Furthermore, the news division has always been accountable to corporate oversight, though with the understanding that running it would always entail a manageable loss of profits. Where Hackett really stands out in his evildoing is in tinkering with the corporate structure that tears down the boundary between news and profits, and though this constitutes half of the "problem" that the film investigates, it receives less of the blame. Indeed, it is this restructuring that initially worries Shumacher and the old guard. Once it has been completed, they no longer consider it a relevant issue. Shumacher is upset that his control over the news may be weakened, but never is he concerned with larger economic forces at work.

Christensen, moreover, is clearly figured as the alluring and deceptive femme fatale. Like Hackett, she too is driven by ratings, but her creation of various shows that ultimately confuse the distinction between informative, meaningful news and cheap entertainment masked as meaningful news receives the brunt of the film's scorn. Christensen blurs boundaries (gender roles, news versus entertainment), and to the older generation, of which Shumacher is a part, she embodies the channel-surfing postmodern generation, content to remain giddily and schizophrenically skimming the televised waves of simulacra, wiping out responsibility and meaning.

That this most villainous of villains should be figured as a woman here is no surprise. As Suzanne Leonard argues, in an examination of representations of "career women" and adultery in popular culture, "public anxiety about female work is frequently filtered through the adultery narrative such that the narrative offers a means not only of regulating and controlling that anxiety but also of displacing it onto an easily identifiable target. Patriarchal culture's need to keep the working woman 'under surveillance' lest she get too heady with power (or lust) is also an obvious animating factor in some popular representations" (111). In *Network*, Christensen's boundary blurring is deceptive, seductive, and ultimately a kind of *adultery* since it respects no established bounds, rules, or loyalties—and who better to represent such trickery than a woman? After all, the "masculine" Hackett takes apart an older corporate structure and "erects" another that allows him to promote his objectives, while the masculine-acting-but-still-feminine-in-destructive-potential Christensen blurs and obfuscates conventional boundaries and structures. When Shumacher faces Hackett in a showdown, voices are raised, desks are pounded by clenched fists, and each man knows where he stands. Indeed, men are "men" and remain masculine and aggressive in such confrontations. But with Christensen, Shumacher is seduced by the feminine (sex), and his masculinity is consequently challenged by shifting and "adulterated" gender roles.

Herein lies the hypocritical contradiction at the core of Shumacher's character and the film's overall message. As much a proponent for the older paradigm of news programming (with its emphasis on moral responsibility and accountability) as he is, Shumacher renounces the secure and substantive domestic life that is attendant to that paradigm and expresses the same values: "respect and allegiance," his wife says (we might imagine here a kind of 1950s domesticity to match the vaunted 1950s journalism). Shumacher's inability to maintain his ideals at the public and the private level—for they both stem from the same (phallic) root—discloses his own complicity with the changing paradigm. Thus, he makes up for his impotence to halt change at the executive level by a show of potency via the sexual act at the personal level in his affair with Christensen. This act is therefore an admission of powerlessness (with the illusion of agency by sexual "conquest") and a tacit acceptance of the new state of affairs. For it is Christensen who openly (as she tells him) scripts the seduction of Shumacher, and as the ideological gap between them widens and the affair ends, Shumacher realizes that he has been "duped" just like the viewing public for which he apparently stands. He remains impotent in both spheres of influence and has even risked his twenty-five-year marriage. Although he eventually denounces Christensen and all she stands for, he has clearly "sold out" for a quick bang. We might say that Shumacher, since he ends up choosing to compromise his personal life (adultery, the bang) rather than compromise his professional/public reputation (endorsing newstainment, the buck), receives more bang for his buck, opting to invest in a libidinal rather than monetary economy. However, since these economical spheres, like the spheres of public and private, have blurred into each other and long since lost their autonomy, Shumacher is as guilty and compromised as the programmers and public he despises.

Shumacher and the film, therefore, unleash most of their frustration and rage, which have been building throughout the movie, onto Christensen, not Hackett. Shumacher takes the moral high ground after his relationship with Christensen fails, telling her, "Everything you and the institution of television touch is destroyed" and "[You are] television incarnate: indifferent to suffering, insensitive to joy. All of life is reduced to the common rubble of banality. You're madness." Christensen is the perfect figure for "television incarnate" since she is deceptive, seductive, and surface oriented. She can be only a mere shell or repository for her career. She is "filled" with ideas for shows, at the price of having any inner substance or depth, and her character gives credence to Laura Mulvey's argument in "The Myth of Pandora" that "myths and images have frequently, in the history of patriarchal culture, materialized into a polarization between a visible and seductive surface and a secret and dangerous essence. This topography privileges the visible surface of beauty, while projecting onto it the instability of masquerade" (3). Typically, then, a woman's "appearance dissembles her essence. The topography is one of binary opposition, a split between an inside and an outside, between seductive surface and dangerous depth" (5). That the film remains obsessed with form and its capacity to mask content, or the lack thereof, is thus a kind of displacement, in part responsible for its inability to wage a more effective critique of capital, to which it makes mere overtures instead.

Thus it is that the new television programming represents the dangerous form on which the film fixates. With its shallow inconstant images, prostituting of the cheapest shows, and seduction and pacification of the viewer, television remains the greatest threat to American democracy, perhaps greater than the capitalist system that ultimately dictates its (empty) content. But, of course, the film conflates television with Christensen, who is deemed "television incarnate," and thus we see that the film genders television as "female." And since Christensen, our femme fatale-cum-Pandora, fits into what Mulvey points out is a "series of images of femininity as artifice" (6), it should be no surprise that this postmodern Pandora carries with her a new, postmodern box: the television. As Mulvey argues, "The box repeats the topography of Pandora herself: her exterior mask of beauty concealing an interior of combined mystery and danger. The box, then, can be interpreted as a displacement of Pandora's seductive danger onto an emblem of female sexuality described in the myth, as the source of all the evils of the world" (8). The new television, the film argues, is feminine, a neo–Pandora's box, and is the true culprit behind America's ills. It will render the public passive, empty people of "simple human decency," and eventually create a world of "dehumanized" cogs, as Beale later puts it. The seduced and pacified spectator loses the ability to act and fight back, supposedly masculine traits. Capitalism, though (as embodied by Hackett), remains corrupt but masculine in its brutal honesty and unfeeling nature. The film's true jeremiad, then, is reserved for a female-gendered television at the expense of a masculine arena of capital. Christensen/television/woman stands as the ultimate seductress and pacifier of the public.

In this case, it is no surprise that Shumacher's conflation of Christensen and television comes just after she challenges his sexual prowess in one of their last arguments before breaking up. Feeling conciliatory, Christensen tells him that she lied about him being a "bad lay," but Shumacher laughs it off, wondering aloud why women always try to hurt a man most by trying to "impugn his cocksmanship," something about which he has long ceased to care. But the hypocrisy is tangible here, as clearly Shumacher's affairs have long attested to his belief in "cocksmanship" as a marker of masculinity. That his attack on Christensen conflates her "true" deceptive feminine nature with the dangerous illusion of a gendered television merely reinforces the gender struggle going on unconsciously. Ironically, in Christensen's inability to see Shumacher as an individual with feelings (as he rightly complains), she objectifies him by reducing him solely to his "cocksmanship." At a deeper level, then, Shumacher's terror is that his masculinity has been reduced to his biological sex—the penis—which is a tacit acknowledgment that it is Christensen who has the phallus. His last-ditch effort to foreswear the cult of the cock here only reveals, once again, that he has been rendered impotent in both his personal and professional life. His moral sermonizing and his fusing of television with woman allow him the illusion that the 1950s gender roles that have clearly been eclipsed have somehow returned through the back door via his noble ethical vision of television news, which allows him to condemn Christensen as representative of an attenuated, feminized, tele-generation.

The closest the film comes to examining the economic conditions under which such newstainment arises is through the figure of the "insane" character, the unhinged news anchor Howard Beale. What begins as a bad depression for Beale after being forced to retire soon morphs into complete mental imbalance. Beale, apparently in a manic episode, begins to believe in his own status as a "latter-day prophet" and tells Shumacher he feels a kind of "oneness" with the universe, which he describes as if it were some kind of Whitmanesque tele-vision he will broadcast to America. Under this neo-Whit*mania*, he is soon hearing voices as well. As a kind of holy maniac uttering God's truths, dubbed "the mad prophet of the airwaves," Beale appeals to the public as a divinely inspired prophet of doom. Despite Shumacher's plea to Christensen to take him off the air, and a similar one to Beale himself to seek help, Christensen soon builds a new show around him to showcase his "talents." As we might expect, the show's set contains religious iconography—a large stained-glass window, a pulpit-like area from which Beale can preach—and Beale is let loose each night to a cheering audience, to which he delivers a sermon and then collapses in a kind of epileptic fit.

Moreover, Beale's rants eventually prove to be more than the average spiel, revealing themselves to be veritable jeremiads, as Christensen points out. The American jeremiad is a familiar trope in American literature and culture, as Sacvan Bercovitch details in *The American Jeremiad*. The jeremiad functioned as "a ritual designed to join social criticism to spiritual renewal, public to private identity, the shifting 'signs of the times' to certain traditional metaphors, themes, and symbols" (xi). In the jeremiad, the speaker berates society for moral turpitude and corruption, adding a rhetorical flourish with apocalyptic overtones. After such a verbal scouring, the speaker often exhorts listeners to change their way of life in order to counteract the destruction and desolation that their present path is leading toward. In actuality, Beale's ongoing jeremiad is more of what Bercovitch calls the "anti-jeremiad" since "both the jeremiad and the anti-jeremiad foreclosed alternatives: the one by absorbing the hopes of mankind into the meaning of America, the other by reading into America the futility and fraud of hope itself" (191). Beale's finest moment in this tradition of the jeremiad arrives with his infamous line, in which he exhorts his audience members to yell out of their windows, "I'm mad as hell, and I'm not going to take this anymore!" Through this jeremiad, Beale expresses not just his own personal anger and frustration with the world but the public's as well. His command is followed, and we see numerous people opening their windows and screaming Beale's words into the night. The chaotic chorus builds, and a sudden rolling thunder sounds ominously at the scene's end.

Notably, it is the "irrational" character, Beale, who is allowed to utter certain truths that the rational characters cannot or will not address. There are, of course, other characters who challenge the powers that be— Shumacher and the old guard. But the challenge the old guard offers is strictly focused on the dynamics of newscasting and is waged within the network itself. One wonders what their reply would be to Hackett and Christensen, who, in response to the critique of their new programming as being of the "lowest common denominator," would argue that they give the public what it wants, in true "democratic" fashion. We might expect a somewhat "elitist" response from Shumacher and company, arguing that the public has been made vapid by the very vacuity of the programs it has been forced to consume. But here we would end in a chicken-and-egg dilemma in which both sides have an equal claim to certain truths.

It is also important to consider that the old guard has already fallen below its own high newscasting standards by airing as much soft as hard news. As Christensen tells Shumacher when she tries convincing him to build the news hour around Beale, UBS's news has already been cheapened (she gives him a compelling segment-by-segment breakdown of the last news hour to prove her point), so "if you're going to hustle, at least do it right." It is Christensen who understands the public discontent with Vietnam, Watergate, inflation, and OPEC's oil embargo and calls for "angry shows," thus seeing the potential in Beale's jeremiads. It is unclear how much responsibility someone like Shumacher takes for this decline in viewership. The film suggests that the angry mob that follows Beale's, hence television's, every word is somehow to blame in its mindless stupidity. The film shows a disdain for mass viewership that Shumacher (due to his disgust with Christensen and her "television" generation) would probably agree with, despite his claims to believe in "simple human decency." This is apparently what is lacking in the new generation that has been raised on television, though it is unclear how a generation of people raised on television could be held entirely responsible for the tube's deleterious effects on it.

Thus, the nobility of the old guard is somewhat tarnished, and the look back to the good old days of Edward R. Murrow and CBS, when the unequivocal stance against fascism and Nazi Germany gave one a clear sense of moral probity, proves to be more than a little nostalgic for a world untouched by the heady years of the 1960s and beyond. It is not merely a desire for a time when news mattered but also a desire for a time when a moral society felt that news mattered. In a strange way, such a desire for a unified and uniform society relies on the oppressive conformity that existed in the Manichean Cold War, pre-civil-rights world. Honor and integrity appear more distinct when an enemy, whether abroad (the USSR, Hitler's Germany) or at home (McCarthyism), can be clearly delineated. When boundaries become blurred, so too do the distinctions between good and evil, as the film's excessive condemnation of Christensen attests. But, again, if anyone is "to blame," it would seem shortsighted to pin all the blame on television and a generation raised on it, however convenient doing so is for the preservation of the noble ideals of an earlier generation.

Beale, in contrast, engages with the public directly and tries to empower his audience by revealing the manipulations and lies that are hidden from it, especially regarding the medium of television itself. His critique is external, not internal. This is what makes him ultimately the unstable and dangerous "irrational" element that threatens to remain uncontainable. Indeed, Beale is eventually perceived to be a great threat by the network itself when he dedicates one show to critiquing something nobody else (not even Shumacher) in the film ever does: multinational corporate capitalism. After learning of some of the behind-the-scenes corporate machinations at the network, Beale spends an entire show informing the public about the power and pervasiveness of global capitalism and America's dependence on foreign oil and Middle East investment. He exposes an impending deal between CCA and something called the Western World Funding Corporation, a global consortium of banks. WWC is about to acquire CCA without any disclosure as to the owners of WWC, who Beale reports xenophobically are "Arab" (they turn out to be a Saudi Arabian consortium). He warns that these "Arabs" now own much of America and the world. Beale finishes his jeremiad by urging that the audience send telegrams to the White House demanding the government stop the deal. The public is inspired, the White House is flooded with telegrams, and the deal is halted.

This is too much for the network and CCA. Beale needs to be reined in for his comments, and he is called to a meeting with CCA's president and chairman of the board, Arthur Jensen (Ned Beatty). With a charismatic "personal touch," Jensen embraces Beale and tells him that he is himself a former salesman: "They say I can sell anything. I'd like to try and sell something to you." In a spectacular scene set in a darkened corporate boardroom ("Valhalla," Jensen calls it), Beale sits down as Jensen paces around and talks. Playing on Beale's belief that he is a prophet, Jensen poses as God. In a booming voice, he delivers to Beale the gospel of consumer capitalism, which is worth quoting at length:

> You have meddled with the primal forces of nature, Mr. Beale, and I won't have it. Is that clear? You think you merely stopped a business deal—that is not the case! The Arabs have taken billions of dollars out of this country, and now they must put it back. It is ebb and flow, tidal gravity. It is ecological balance! You are an old man who thinks in term of nations and peoples. There are no nations! There are no peoples! There are no Russians! There are no Arabs! There are no third worlds! There is no West! There is only one

holistic system of systems, one vast and immane, interwoven, interacting, multivariate, multi-national dominion of dollars. . . . It is the international system of currency that determines the totality of life on this planet! That is the natural order of things today! That is the atomic, subatomic, and galactic structure of things today! And you have meddled with the primal forces of nature, and you will atone. . . .

There is no America. There is no democracy. There is only IBM and ITT and AT&T and DuPont, Dow, Union Carbide, and Exxon. Those are the nations of the world today. . . . We no longer live in a world of nations and ideologies, Mr. Beale. The world is a college of corporations, inexorably determined by the immutable by-laws of business. The world is a business, Mr. Beale! It has been since man crawled out of the slime, and our children will live, Mr. Beale, to see that perfect world in which there is no war and famine, oppression and brutality—one vast and ecumenical holding company, for whom all men will work to serve a common profit, in which all men will hold a share of stock, all necessities provided, all anxieties tranquilized, all boredom amused. And I have chosen you, Mr. Beale, to preach this evangel.

Such a description of the utopian end of late capitalism, in a veritable orgy of products and satisfied customers, would make Frances Fukuyama proud. Moreover, the emphasis on "forces of nature" adopts a Marxian notion of the dynamism of capitalism ("All that's solid melts into air," as the *Communist Manifesto* informs us) but combines it with an Adam Smith-like "Invisible Hand" that guides these forces to a fulfillment in a consumers' paradise. Capitalism is here naturalized—it is a "primal force of nature" and an "ecology"—and described much in the same way as it is in Shelgrim's speech to Presley in Norris's *The Octopus*. Whereas Marx would say capitalism unleashes such forces of nature, Jensen has it that capitalism is itself the force and rule of nature.

Moreover, there is a curious "democratization" that occurs as capital continues to transform the world. The suggestion here is of a utopian world without national boundaries and wars. Thus, at one level, Beale's "Arab" fears are no longer tenable. Capital as a transcendent force apparently makes everyone an equal stakeholder, a "citizen of the world," unless, of course, you cannot pay the cost of admission, the price tag of which the CEO fails to mention. And since the film registers an angry public, as well as several active terrorist groups, it is clear that not everyone can afford the cost of joining this world-company. Even if such national and racial boundaries were to be theoretically transcended successfully by capitalism, there would still remain the very real issue of class. But Jensen delivers his gospel with equal parts exhortation and majesty. He truly believes in his own triumphant teleology of capital. Beale is awestruck and left believing he has "seen the face of God." Thus, the CEO sells this bill of goods to Beale in its entirety, and the ideologically satisfied customer indeed changes his tune on the next show. The prophet of the future is now the *profit* of the future.

The irrational factor in the film, then, is eventually contained when Beale is channeled and controlled by the system. This is really no surprise, since Beale has been manipulated step by step in his recent rise. In a world where everything can potentially be co-opted by the system, particularly through the commodification of the image, the seemingly humanistic cri de coeur of Howard Beale, "I'm mad as hell, and I'm not going to take this anymore," ends up becoming not the rallying and revolutionary command that it could have been but a mere slogan that the studio audience yells during the opening credits of his show. Yet Beale, as the irrational rationalized by the system, is the only character to show a larger understanding of the forces at play in such a world.

There are brief sparks of revolutionary potential to change the system, such as Beale's populist letter-writing campaign that gets him into trouble with Jensen. The film, however, forecloses quickly on this possibility as soon as Jensen speaks to Beale about it. The same goes for any radical politics or what Christensen calls "mutilated Marxism" at one point in the film. The satirical depiction of a pseudo–Black Panther revolutionary group that agrees to have its operations recorded and aired, so long as the compensation is adequate, suggests the revolution will be televised and hence commodified. Overall, the film is as pessimistic about political change as it is about the endurance of the human spirit, ending with Beale's assassination by the network executives and offering a dark punch line to the entire movie: "Harold Beale, the first man to be killed because of low ratings."

Thus, *Network*, through the rage and despair of Shumacher and Beale, depicts a radical and fundamental change in the economic structure of American capitalism. With the utopian potential of the 1960s thoroughly exhausted, however, it appears that the utopian vision of global capital has taken its place, even if this vision, delivered near the film's end by its newest adherent, Howard Beale, means dismal ratings and dissatisfaction. The public's distrust of such a vision, however, will prove to be fickle when economic fortunes become brighter. All will soon be forgiven and forgotten and faith in the system restored, and *Network* itself will prove to be a last-gasp cri de coeur against the rise of global capitalism.

Neoliberal Phantoms and Fantasies

At the end of the 1970s, the troubled Carter administration, unable to enact an economic turnaround by the 1980 presidential election, found itself ousted by the upstart Republican nominee, Ronald Reagan. The former California governor had some novel ideas about economic stimulation, and although the early years of his first term saw a continued economic downslide, by the time *Ghostbusters* (1984, written by Harold Ramis and directed by Ivan Reitman) was released, America was undergoing an economic upswing. Thus, while at first glance this supernatural comedy seems to have little to do with Reaganomics, *Ghostbusters*, as we shall see, is a telling fable of corporate capitalism's relatively quiet, "glorious" revolution. Set in the midst of the neoliberal Reagan era of wild privatization and deregulation—the decade when pure capitalism was unleashed in all its fury—*Ghostbusters* captures the social and cultural dilemmas that capital promised to solve if only it were set free to do its work.

The key to understanding the economic backdrop in *Ghostbusters* is to focus on its setting: New York City in the early 1980s. At this time, New York was beginning to recover from the dismal end of the 1970s, when the city faced its worst fiscal crisis to date, crime ran rampant, and President Gerald Ford and the federal government turned their backs on Mayor Abraham Beame's pleas for financial assistance—as the now-famous *New York Daily News* headline read on 30 October 1975, "Ford to City: Drop Dead." Much of the modern gritty lore of New York emerged during these years in films such as *Taxi Driver* (1976), *The Warriors* (1979), and *Escape from New York* (1981). The city was often depicted as a crime-infested, postapocalyptic wasteland, and not without good reason. Even Woody Allen's nostalgic, Gershwin-scored love letter to the Big Apple, *Manhattan* (1980), though it portrays a safe and secure Upper East Side existence (moral decline notwithstanding), admits to the gestalt of the city, when the narrator complains, "I don't care what anyone says, I love this city." Such a line in the fully gentrified, post-Giuliani New York City makes absolutely no sense today—unless it is used, ironically, to *defend* the corporate and wealthy takeover of much of the city.

Ghostbusters has been rightly identified as a film championing "urban renewal,"[2] the more positive-sounding phrase used for the darker aspects of gentrification. Max Page, for example, argues in *The City's End: Two Centuries of Fantasies, Fears, and Premonitions of New York's Destruction*, that the film "is a camp takeoff on a disaster movie, playing on the tropes of urban crisis and New Yorkers' emotional need for heroes" due to the fact that "the city had survived the worst and was about to enter two decades of robust economic development and resurgent wealth" (169). But to see the film as merely embedded in the logic of urban renewal is to miss the impact of the larger economic forces at work in the redevelopment of New York City and America during the 1980s. As William K. Tabb makes clear in *The Long Default: New York City and the Urban Fiscal Crisis*, the eventual assistance from the federal government came with the caveat that New York City adopt strict financial "austerity measures." These resembled "the sort of budget the International Monetary Fund imposes on third world countries as a condition for renewed borrowing," which meant that "New York City lost control of its affairs and was forced to accept a debt-restructuring program that left it, by 1980—after its 'rescue'—using 20 percent of locally raised revenues to service its debt" (21). The city also bowed to a probusiness agenda that was reflective of nationwide economic and political policies and trends. In *Remaking New York*, William Sites writes, "After the late Carter administration began to cut direct assistance to cities and to refocus federal urban policy on stimulating private investment, Reagan policies went considerably further. Enacting sweeping tax cuts, deregulation measures, and decreases in federal aid to cities, national policy makers helped create an economic environment that reinforced the need for cities to cater to investors, developers, and mobile corporations" (42). With this larger economic picture of neoliberal, free-market capitalism as a backdrop, we can enter into the political intricacies lurking behind such apparently laudatory projects of "urban renewal" as they play out in *Ghostbusters*.

At the film's beginning, we meet Dr. Peter Venckman (Bill Murray) and Dr. Ray Stantz (Dan Aykroyd), who are Columbia University–employed "parapsychologists." As their official titles suggest, their research area is dubious at best, and Venckman spends his time falsifying experiments in order to try and sleep with certain attractive female subjects. A sudden university budget crisis gives the university's president the final leverage he needs to close down the program, and Venckman and Stantz find themselves jobless and without research facilities. Down and out, the two muse over what to do, and Stantz pitches Venckman an idea to start a company, a company that will deal with paranormal problems and disturbances: the Ghostbusters. Stantz uses a second mortgage on a house he inherited from his parents as leverage to secure a large loan, and the Ghostbusters are in business.

What the Ghostbusters actually are, of course, is a corporation. They are a private company that is highly paid to deal with certain "disturbances." At first, this seems a relatively benign service, as the Ghostbusters are merely another small business struggling to cover operating costs. A cheesy television advertisement shows them rather stiffly announcing the services they provide, while a phone number flashes at the bottom of the screen. It is a low-budget affair and casts them as exterminators of a sort. They may as well be spraying for roaches as for ghosts, since their job is essentially pest control. Business is excruciatingly slow at first, though the film would seem to champion small businesses and their savvy entrepreneurs as a way to stimulate economic growth.

However, as the number of ghosts begins to increase, the Ghostbusters' service becomes essential to the city and its citizens. There is simply nobody else to turn to. The Ghostbusters subsequently become heroes and celebrities. We see them on the cover of newspapers and magazines and appearing on talk shows. Business becomes hectic, and they are forced to "expand" and hire another member. Since they form a kind of monopoly, the Ghostbusters are increasingly called on to take care of the city's problems. As Stantz predicted earlier, "ghostbusting" has become a lucrative business and opened up an entirely new industry, in a sense.

Although we see a montage of the Ghostbusters' jobs (including, for humorous effect, a restaurant in Chinatown that rewards them with several ducks), most of the Ghostbusters' clients appear to be fairly affluent. The crew's first job is to capture a ghost terrorizing an upscale hotel. Though they cause a large amount of damage that the hotel's manager complains about in a bid to deny payment, the Ghostbusters' threat to set the ghost free quickly earns them their fee. So too is a later client, Dana Barrett (Sigourney Weaver), comfortably well-off, ensconced as she is in a large apartment building in Central Park West. In any event, if the Ghostbusters' rates are the same from job to job, it would appear that this increasingly necessary service is one that only certain people can afford.[3]

As the threat of Gozer (a Sumerian god bent on destroying the earth) and the apocalypse grows, the city finds itself unable to cope with the problem. Gradually, the Ghostbusters become more and more integral to "solving" it. In other words, as fear and confusion reign, the city turns to a private company to "save" it from disaster. This is precisely the place in which New York City found itself in the 1970s and 1980s, when redevelopment resulted in ceding large amounts of real estate to corporations and businesses, along with the attendant subsidies and tax breaks, in order to stimulate "urban renewal." This meant selling off large chunks of Manhattan to (often international) corporations for next to nothing, as the city tried coaxing businesses into putting money into redevelopment. As one study points out, "With the new federalism, New York City government depended increasingly on private developers and public/private partnerships for the provision of new and rehabilitated housing" (Harloe, Marcuse, and Smith 194). The result was that people in the lower economic stratum, often minorities, found themselves uprooted and cleared out of an increasingly corporatized city.

The Faustian bargain that New York (and other American cities) made with capital, then, is much the same as the one the mayor and the city make with the Ghostbusters in the film. Before the crucial meeting with the mayor, we have already seen the police delivering the possessed Louis Tully (Rick Moranis) to the Ghostbusters instead of taking him to jail, admitting that they have no idea how to handle his curious ramblings and that the Ghostbusters would probably know best what to do with him. Likewise, in the face of impending disaster, the mayor gives total power and authority to the Ghostbusters to do whatever they must to save the city. What each of these scenes portrays is the failure of local, city government and municipal services to deal with a crisis. Whether it is the police or the local officials, the city is helpless to solve its own problems and must look to a private company to bail it out. Hence, the Ghostbusters, a private corporation, essentially trumps the capabilities of New York City itself.

Consider the main "problem" of the film, for instance, which ostensibly is the ghosts. What are these ghosts supposed to represent? They do little actual damage throughout the film—they scare people, crash cars, steal food, read books, and fly aimlessly around. *Ghostbusters*, when one considers it, is not much of a traditional ghost story, wherein a specific haunting takes place that is metaphorically charged (the return of the past/history, whether public or private). It is essentially a comedy, and the ghosts are not really meant to be frightening, as Page has written(171). It is tempting to write them off as mere phantoms of the problems—crime, poverty, decaying infrastructure and city services—of that older, more troublesome New York. The Ghostbusters, in a pre-Giuliani New York, are heroically cleaning up the city, getting rid of those despicable beings that infest its streets. But it is important at this point to pause and recall precisely what such "cleaning up the streets" and urban renewal meant to various minorities and lower-income people living in New York City at the time.

The revitalization of Times Square and Forty-Second Street can serve as one example.[4] The area had been the symbolic center of the deterioration of New York City for a while. Throughout its history, it had been associated with vice and shadiness, and in the 1970s, such a notion reached its zenith. The scene in Martin Scorcese's *Taxi Driver* in which Travis Bickel drives through Times Square and sermonizes about the scum of the earth captures this feeling perfectly.[5] After the end of New York's fiscal crisis, Times Square and Forty-Second Street became the nexus of a huge redevelopment program (led by the Forty-Second Street Development Corporation) that furthered the city's probusiness agenda by playing on such images of a desolated city.

Like many development projects in New York that, as Sites notes, "served to subsidize businesses and developers and to exclude the wider public" ("Public Action" 197), the Times Square and Forty-Second Street transformation benefited a certain class at the expense of others. The proponents in the city government and media were happy to play off the historically media-fed, (white) public's view of the area as a veritable war zone. In *Reconstructing Times Square: Politics and Culture in Urban Development*, Alexander J. Reichl writes, "Public reports emphasized concerns about crime, drugs, violence, and pornography in the area; but the language of urban decline derives much of its potency from racial anxieties, and lurking beneath the surface of redevelopment proposals was the persistent theme that West Forty-second Street had become the domain of a menacing population of young African-Americans and Latinos" (2). Yet, "contrary to widely held perception, especially among suburbanites, that Forty-second Street had become a 'ghetto street,' studies found that whites constituted a 'numerically dominant group' of persons on the street at almost all times of day" (62).

Thus, much of the rhetoric of redevelopment, as it often does, adopted carefully coded racial messages, as well as military metaphors, to make its case. Territory needs to be reclaimed; a certain "element" needs to be removed or contained for the safety of "everyone." Most of the homeless in the area, for instance, were "ship[ped] to the South Bronx" (Davis 391). Yet, as Reichl writes, "there are certainly important misconceptions at work when racial integration is perceived as a minority takeover, but these anxieties are deeply rooted in a society that continues to be characterized by racial segregation and inequality" (62). Added to this, writes Sites, was a tendency to blame New York's fiscal troubles mostly on "the unworthy and dependent poor, the misguided generosity of social reformers, the unreasonable demands of racial minorities, [and] the irresponsibility of free-spending politicians," instead of on "developers who had overbuilt, [and the] financial institutions that encouraged and profited from irresponsible municipal borrowing . . . , let alone the corporate decisions and federal policies that long favored suburbanization at the expense of urban centers" (*Remaking* 39).[6] Such scapegoating thus tapped into long-held American beliefs in self-reliance and a strong (Protestant) work ethic, as well as traditional (white) fears of a racial or ethnic "other," who is simultaneously a burden and a threat to American prosperity.

As the film transfigures it, the "problem" of minorities and the poor, who must be swept out of the way for the good of all, becomes the ghosts themselves. Although they used to be human, they no longer are seen as such. They are vaporous, easily blown away by the winds of economic change. Yet they also remain and resist, haunting their former streets and neighborhoods in protest. "Uprooted" from their "rest," much as many people were uprooted from their homes, the persistence of such phantoms attests to the fact that this "problem" can never be fully solved by the thoughtless and callous machinations behind gentrification (perhaps, in part, the reason for *Ghostbusters II* and the soon-to-be-released *III*). As H. V. Savitch writes in *Post-Industrial Cities*, "The CBD [Central Business District] boom, gentrification, and the displacement of working-class households have worsened existing imbalances. The CBD is saturated with investment, the remainder of the urban core is overcrowded" and "falls deeper into poverty" (48–49). In short, writes Sites, "displacement was an inevitable consequence of private reinvestment" ("Public Action" 199). These displaced people do not simply disappear, however (as the ghosts do in the urban-renewal championing of the film, where they are "contained" in a storage unit—yet burst free again), but are merely pushed into less desirable neighborhoods or "contained" in ghettos. Much like the scene in which Louis Tully collapses against the window of a luxurious restaurant in Central Park, whose elegant diners pay him hardly a second of interest, such people may as well exist in another world—and in a sense, like the ghosts, *they do*.

Reichl sums it up nicely, writing, "In the transition from the Great White Way to the Dangerous Deuce, whites saw the decline of their civilization and its subordination to an alien culture that threatened to displace them from the central areas of the city" (117). This puts a "neighborhood watch" twist on the Ray Parker Jr. hit theme song, which rhetorically asks who one should call if there is any strangeness, weirdness, or trouble in the neighborhood. If the people who are likely to call the Ghostbusters are, as we have seen, the wealthy and an ailing city eager to stimulate private enterprise whatever the cost, then it becomes clear who probably constitutes the "weird" and "strange" disturbances.

In the end, the "problem" of Times Square and Forty-Second Street was solved without too much difficulty. Through several economic downturns, the Forty-Second Street Development Corporation eventually did its job. As Reichl writes, "It took two decades to transform Forty-Second Street and Times Square from a symbol of urban decline into a thriving Disneyspace" (17). Likewise, the ghosts themselves are shown to be easily "containable" in the Ghostbusters' Containment Unit, and even their leader, Gozer, who is intent on destroying the earth, is eventually defeated.

So what, then, is the film's deeper problem, if the ghosts pose little actual threat? Tellingly, it is not until the ghosts are released that the real trouble begins. And this is where we find our true villain. It is, of course, Walter Peck (William Atherton) of the Environmental Protection Agency, which turns out to be the main culprit behind Gozer's success. From his first appearance, when he clashes with Venckman and demands to inspect the Ghostbusters' Containment Unit, Peck is shown to be the most troublesome element in the film. But why is he so suspicious and untrusting of the Ghostbusters? A sympathetic voice might say it is because the Ghostbusters' Containment Unit is run by nuclear power, as are the weapons they regularly use to capture ghosts, meaning the Ghostbusters operate a modest nuclear device/reactor in their basement that nobody but themselves knows how to work, smack dab in the middle of New York City. And all of this is completely unregulated. Most people would find this alarming, particularly in the 1980s, when fears of nuclear accidents (think *The China Syndrome* [1979], Three Mile Island, and the soon-to-be Chernobyl) were understandably high. But oddly enough, we cannot but hate Peck and the EPA for their intrusive and meddling ways. In a wonderful ideological sleight of hand, the film's test audiences found themselves cheering when the mayor has Peck arrested and puts his faith in the Ghostbusters to save the city.[7]

There is no clearer parable of the 1980s love affair with privatization and deregulation than this scene in which the mayor must choose between the EPA and the Ghostbusters. The Ghostbusters now hold a sole monopoly on a service we would expect the city or federal government to provide, since it is now necessary to the safety and well-being of America. And the only real threat to the Ghostbusters providing such a service is regulation and government red tape. The accursed EPA with its regulations and restrictions not only is limiting the potential of capital to grow exponentially but is also undercutting the very fabric of American society, putting us all in danger by tying up our only possible savior. The incredible power the Ghostbusters hold at this moment, a power that eclipses that of local and state government, is the obvious analogue to the preeminence of the corporation in the 1980s, as Reagan's economic policies increased capital's control over essential public services (for which Reagan had slashed funding) and limited government's role in the well-being of its citizens. "These federal policies," writes Sites, "provided a new set of carrots and sticks for cities seeking to right themselves. Reinforcing vulnerability to market forces, such measures reduced most national urban commitments and actively spurred the mobility of foot-loose corporations" (*Remaking* 43). That the Ghostbusters headquarters is housed in a renovated firehouse in a neighborhood that one of the crew describes as resembling "a demilitarized zone" underscores this point, as does the fact that their vehicle is an outdated ambulance. As basic, underfunded public services meet their demise, it is the private sector that rushes in to take their place.

So who eventually foots the (Ghostbusters') bill? What is the outcome of such economic policies? What are the dreams and desires of such policies? The central desire is, of course, for that same consumerist utopia that *Network*'s Arthur Jensen espouses. After all, the Ghostbusters defeat Gozer and her minions, thus saving the city. The parable of private enterprise to the rescue seems complete as the film ends with a citywide parade of gratitude for its saviors. If we carry the film's logic from New York City to the rest of America, we might be filled with a vision of a national Ghostbusters franchise, with the Ghostbuster as well known as the Orkin man. Yet there is one intentionally humorous crack in this laudatory façade, which occurs in the final battle between the Ghostbusters and Gozer atop a skyscraper. When the Ghostbusters fail to harm Gozer with their nuclear-powered lasers, a playful Gozer announces that she will allow the group to choose its own form of death. In defense, the Ghostbusters form a huddle and agree to keep their minds clear of any thoughts to frustrate Gozer's plan. But after only a few seconds, Gozer claims the choice has been made, and, punctuated by the sound of earth-rumbling footsteps, Stantz admits he could not help thinking of something. This something appears soon after as the infamous Stay Puft Marshmallow Man.

Should we be surprised here? Is not this mild satirical swipe at the monstrousness of consumer culture also an instance of the return of the repressed—the film's unabashed embrace of the new free-market economic policy and its consumerist utopian ends? Is it not telling that with the "freedom to choose" Stantz is unable to resist thinking of not merely marshmallows, one of the most trivial of commodities (sugar, water, and gelatin), but of the brand-name version's mascot? The foreshadowing of the marsh-monster in the glimpse of the bag of marshmallows on Barrett's counter early on in the film, then, is also the revelation of this (unconsciously) supposed consumer paradise.[8] Is it any wonder, too, that Gozer's portal into the world exists in Barrett's refrigerator, the space in which many such commodities will come to rest? In this sense, the real battle occurs between the Ghostbusters as private-industry/entrepreneurial heroes and the Stay Puft Marshmallow Man, representative of the commodity-driven culture that such private enterprise gleefully creates. This final showdown realizes the core contradiction in the film's unconscious embrace of Reagan's free market and its conscious and light lampooning of rampant consumerism. Here emerges the true dark underside of the world that *Ghostbusters* unconsciously glorifies. The logic of late capital would like to project such economic policy and consumer imperative as complementary, as achieving the perfect balance between lucrative supply and fulfilling demand, but the apocalyptic fears actually stem from the original repressed contradiction, which erupts in full force regardless, like the marshmallow that bursts all over the crowd when Stay Puft is defeated. For the actual effect of such neoliberal, free-market economic policy, even in the late 1980s, was a forced dependence on corporate America that resulted in an increased income inequality between rich and poor, particularly for racial and ethnic minorities. Such income disparity continues to grow today in New York, as well as in America as a whole. As the current fiscal crisis continues to plague America and the world, one might be tempted to ask, once again, "Who you gonna call?"

The subsequent transformation of public space results in a world not so different from the Hollywood set on which the Ghostbusters blast Stay Puft to pieces—it is a simulated and surreal one, simultaneously creating and attempting to satisfy consumer desire. This remains a disconcerting prospect for other areas targeted for such "renewal," which seems no more than privatized public space, complete with signs, logos, and fabricated shopping "experiences." In this sense, *Ghostbusters* figures as one of the most subtle and disturbing films depicting corporations and their discontents. For while it champions the renaissance of New York City, it disregards the larger price paid for this rebirth, as well as the macroeconomic forces that all but necessitated these costly and specific methods of renewal at the local level.

Rebirth of a Salesman

Even as innocuous a film as the late *Saturday Night Live* alumnus Chris Farley's comedy *Tommy Boy* (1995) represents corporations in light of the economic climate of its own production. *Tommy Boy* follows a bumbling son, Tommy (Chris Farley), as he attempts to save the family business, Callahan Auto Parts, from financial ruin. Tommy, a recent college graduate (surprisingly, for he is a shade darker than dim), has just come home to blue-collar Sandusky, Ohio, to work for Callahan when his father dies. With "Big Tom" no longer at the helm, the company and its employees see grim days ahead. To make matters worse, Big Tom's widow, Beverly (Bo Derek), whom he had recently wed, only married him for monetary gain. She and her "son," Paul (who is not Beverly's son but her husband, played by Rob Lowe), conspire against Tommy the entire film to advance their plan of selling the factory to a competitor since Beverly was left with Callahan preferred stock instead of cash when the estate was settled.

Moreover, since, as Big Tom puts it, "in auto parts, you're either growing or you're dying," Callahan had been in the process of manufacturing a new line of brake pads with hopes of revolutionizing the industry. With Big Tom having sunk all of Callahan's capital into the project, the company is cash poor. Before his death, Big Tom was in the middle of negotiating a large bank loan to help open a plant devoted solely to fabricating the new brake pads, but without Big Tom in the mix, the bank refuses the risky loan, which hinged on Tom's convincing his clients to sell the new brake-pad line. Callahan's board of directors decides that, without this loan, selling the company while its stock is still high is the only option to avoid bankruptcy, although it will mean shutting down the plant, laying off three hundred workers, and essentially destroying the entire town. This potential industrial wasteland, exemplary of the Rust Belt, has already been glimpsed when Tommy is driven home from the airport, and he notices that several auto-parts businesses have long since closed up shop. The remaining industry in the town is in jeopardy of shutting down and Sandusky with it.

But Tommy, distraught by his father's death and desperate to prove he deserves to run the family business (thus fulfilling Big Tom's wish that "this always has been, and always will be, a family firm"), offers his entire inheritance as security for the denied bank loan. With this equity, the bank grants the loan, and Tommy attempts a last-ditch, on-the-road sales trip with his childhood friend and Big Tom's trusted executive Richard (David Spade) to sell the new line of brake pads. A party animal and confidence-lacking ne'er-do-well, Tommy turns an ill-fated trip into a successful one (with Richard's help) by learning the "personal" side of business—he gets the customers to like him (just like good ol' dad did) by stressing the quality of his products and the special bond of trust any company is sure to form with his family-run operation. As Richard counsels him, "People are buying you, not the brake pads." In other words, Tommy sells his awkward, but homely, personality, as well as the image of a Main Street, USA, mom-and-pop store rather than the image of the small (but growing) factory-owning company that Callahan actually is.

Tommy is able to do this, in part, because Zalinsky's Industries, the rival company, is a larger and more media-savvy company than Callahan is. We see several of Zalinsky's commercials and billboard advertisements throughout the film, and Zalinsky's is clearly growing and moving into the territory Callahan is losing. Moreover, Tommy must continually deal with the fact that Zalinsky's is profitable enough to offer a guarantee on each of its products, a guarantee that Callahan claims it provides but does not display on its products' packaging. Zalinsky's canny advertising campaign, as well as its carefully constructed image and packaging, have propelled it to the forefront of auto-parts manufacturing.

But once Tommy figures out the "personal" side of business—that sales can be achieved through a smile, dogged persistence, and earnest straightforwardness—he is able to use the nostalgic Main Street, USA, image to his advantage. When he hears a potential client complain that his customers like to see a guarantee on the box, Tommy taps into the sales wisdom that his father espoused earlier in the film: "A guarantee is only as good as the man who writes it." Tommy's screwball sales pitch, delivered in a "confidential" tone, echoes his father's homespun wisdom. Tommy argues that a guarantee on the box may make the buyer feel secure but that this feeling has little to do with the merchandise itself, since it is possible that "all they sold you is a guaranteed piece of shit. That's all it is, isn't it?" However, as everyone knows, Callahan means quality, so a guarantee on the box is wholly unnecessary. Much like Don Walling's vaunted well-crafted commodity in *Executive Suite*, Tommy can play on his customers' similar desire to idealize the commodities they purchase. That a guarantee should be more a cause for suspicion than reassurance is a stroke of sales genius that Tommy adapts from the repertoire of his father, whose salesmanship is legendary, much like Arthur Jensen's in *Network*. As Richard tells Tommy, Big Tom "could sell a ketchup popsicle to a woman wearing white gloves." Indeed, Big Tom's most famous line that he uses to convince on-the-fence clients to buy from him without further scrutiny is, "I could get a helluva good look at a T-bone steak by sticking my head up a bull's ass, but I'll take the butcher's word for it." Such a folksy "anecdote," with its small-town vision of butchers and farmers, provides a sense of an open precapitalist marketplace (an actual physical market) where exchanges are made person to person by trusted "experts" in their fields. Because individual consumers are also honest producers, they each respect the autonomy and status of those with whom they bargain. The anecdote of the bull simultaneously claims that there "is no bull here" and is a fine example of ideological mystification in its purest form.

Tommy turns the guarantee around by evoking small-town suspicion of the "guarantee," which is surely nothing but some big-city lawyers' and ad men's huckstering words. In place of this suspect legal-speak, Tommy reaffirms his father's tradition of meeting face to face with clients, armed with a firm handshake and an honest smile. There is no double dealing here, such a sales pitch suggests, just trustworthy products from a real-life trustworthy guy. Thus, the film evokes a nostalgic vision of an era of sales that took place before corporations had put together niche-marketing teams that strategized by the numbers, a bygone time before twentieth-century media brought the most powerful sales pitch yet into every living room in America via television. *Tommy Boy* suggests a kind of sentimental rebirth of the salesman. Gone is the rage and suffering of Willy Loman, gone is the desperation and the "fuck or be fucked" hypermasculine morality of David Mamet's *Glengarry, Glen Ross*. Callahan is a "family firm" run by people, not capital. Instead, we are back with Willy's esteemed salesman, who "put on his green velvet slippers . . . and pick[ed] up his phone and call[ed] the buyers, and without leaving his room" (*Death* 81), a Horatio Alger type, whose "luck, pluck, and virtue" will always carry the day's sales.

In distinction to Callahan, Zalinsky's empire has apparently grown too large for such one-on-one salesmanship. Zalinsky's Industries is a major corporation, one well known to the public, and its level of business includes buying out companies like Callahan in order to use each company's name and reputation to increase its own sales. Zalinsky himself is everywhere via his commercials, but as spokesman in his ads, he has become as much of an image as he is owner of the company. While he establishes a familiarity and fame for the company, it comes at the sacrifice of the person-to-person business model that Tommy and the smaller Callahan can exploit. Everybody knows Zalinsky's, but nobody *knows* Zalinsky. What they do "know" of him comes from his reassuring ads, in which he claims, "I make car parts for the American working man because that's what I am, and that's who I care about."

As different as Callahan and Zalinsky's are in their size and business philosophy, they are not exactly set at odds in the film. Zalinsky serves as a foil to Callahan throughout, but the real danger to Callahan comes from within—from Beverly and Paul, the scheming widow and her husband, who would gain from the company's sale. Paul's efforts to destroy Tommy's sales success eventually work, and Callahan will have to go forward with its plans to sell the factory to Zalinsky. But on seeing another Zalinsky's commercial, Tommy decides to confront Zalinsky (Dan Aykroyd) in person about the impending sale of Callahan. The naive Tommy, unable to separate signifier (Zalinsky's image) from the signified (Zalinsky's Industries), believes in the ideology of Zalinsky's commercials and banks on the fact that Zalinsky knew his father and will understand and help out Callahan. The destination of this trip is, of course, Detroit, with its literal and symbolic ties to the American auto industry and blue-collar workers (whom Tommy, beloved by the Callahan workers, is trying to save).

Not surprisingly, Zalinsky turns out to be the antithesis of what his ads project him to be. Zalinsky scoffs at Tommy's attempt to beg for financial mercy, claiming, "That's life. America's in a state of renewal," and that capitalism is based on the bigger fish swallowing the littler fish, which is nothing but a necessary duty of large companies like Zalinsky's, whose job it is to "thin the corporate herd. . . . The weaker animals always go." Zalinsky's social Darwinist (and Naturalist) vision of capitalism turns the tables on the extortion and violence of corporations like his own and sees them as saviors of the system itself. Such free-market ideology must have worn a little thin considering the S&L crisis of the late 1980s that cost the government—that is, the taxpayers—billions of dollars, which were used to bail out large banks and investment companies on the verge of bankruptcy, a practice in direct violation of a free market, laissez-faire ideology. But Zalinsky pitches such callous business tactics as simply going along with the nature of how things work in America. When Tommy asks about the promise to the American worker in his ads, Zalinsky replies, "What the American public doesn't know is what makes it the American public." Here private capital and media propaganda help to create a mass public ripe for manipulation.

Tommy, now enlightened to the power of images, (re)presentation, and salesmanship, realizes that if the medium is the message, it must also constitute the means of challenging that message. Strapping some flares to his chest to resemble dynamite, Tommy forces his way into the boardroom where Zalinsky is about to purchase Callahan. Armed with the recent knowledge of Paul and Beverly's bigamous relationship and a local news camera crew, Tommy puts Zalinsky on the spot on a live "breaking news" broadcast by informing him of the consequences to Callahan and Sandusky if Zalinsky buys the company. Tendering an order for enough brake pads to save Callahan, Tommy urges Zalinsky to purchase the products, thus saving the company and the town. With the cameras rolling, Zalinsky must perform his carefully constructed media role and signs the order, believing that his impending purchase of the company will soon make the order moot anyway. But after Tommy next exposes Paul and Beverly's bigamous relationship, it becomes clear to all involved that Beverly's inheritance (the preferred stock that gave her a controlling stake in the company) will become Tommy's. Thus, Tommy becomes Callahan's principal stockholder, and Zalinsky's debt-saving order is legally binding. Callahan is saved.

The film's underlying message regarding corporations is thus relatively conservative and not a little idealistic. Where we might expect to see a protracted struggle between a failing company and a rapidly growing company concerned only with increasing profits by squelching its competitors, instead we witness a wedding of the two. Zalinsky congratulates Tommy on his clever maneuvers and wishes him luck. After all, Zalinsky was once the "little guy," too. As the sole owner and individual face of the corporation, he can remember his own embodiment of rags-to-riches capitalism and thus respect his old rival Callahan. After all, is it not the free market and competition that only makes us stronger? And are not both Callahan and Zalinsky pure products of the immigrant's American dream, as their Irish and possibly Polish (or eastern European) surnames suggest?

Poised at the point of exposing the rapaciousness of capital, in which the shark gobbles up the little fish, the film (to some degree) rehumanizes Zalinsky's Industries through the figure of its founder. Zalinsky, for all his camera time and glossy ads, is still a fair player in the arena of capital, who enjoys a tough adversary. It is the purging of Beverly and Paul that truly saves Callahan. Beverly and Paul, then, become the real reason (after Tommy's initial incompetence in sales is overcome) that Callahan is foundering. The internal struggle is what held the company back, not the state of the market or the ravenous competition (though the industrial wasteland depicted in the film's beginning lingers). Competition, in the end, is good for Callahan and Tommy, who will now use such success to help Callahan grow. Tommy, as the good CEO, will ensure that Callahan also acts as a trustworthy and benevolent company. With such sound business principles subscribed to successfully, there is no reason, the film suggests, that a company should not flourish.

Yet this seeming binary between the small-town, "honest" Callahan and the corporate, image-driven Zalinsky's Industries, is no binary at all as much as it is two positions on the "ladder" of capital. Callahan may be several rungs lower than Zalinsky's, but as the natural metaphor of either "growing or dying" endorsed by Big Tom suggests, Callahan will be moving up this ladder. In other words, if Callahan continues to grow, it will be subject to the same business and advertising strategies as Zalinsky's. Tommy may be the beneficent owner and CEO at the moment, but there is nothing to suggest that an expanding Callahan would be able to maintain such "small-town" business sense and practices as it grows.

Corporate Agenda / Corporate Gender

The continued ignorance of the basic structure of the corporation means that the morality play of good and bad capitalism will continue indefinitely, as it does most recently in *Michael Clayton* (2007), though with some interesting twists. In the film, Michael Clayton (George Clooney) is a "fixer," a lawyer who cleans up after corporate messes. Clayton appears to be existentially flat-lining through middle age. His job is ethically questionable, he is a single father with no love life, and he has a large amount of outstanding debt due to a failed restaurant venture with his junkie brother, who ripped him off and disappeared. Moreover, since his creditor is a shady, underground source who demands payment on his debt immediately, Clayton has a renewed gambling problem.

However, Clayton's request for a loan from his firm is granted when he agrees to see through another mop-up job for a corporation. Clayton's good friend and mentor, Arthur Edens (Tom Wilkinson), a corporate defense lawyer, has recently suffered a manic episode in Minnesota during the deposition of a case he has been working on for eight years involving a multimillion-dollar lawsuit alleging that U/North, a chemical company, knowingly dumped harmful contaminants into a populated area. Edens's breakdown threatens to lose the case for U/North, and Clayton is called in to settle down the worried U/North and establish whether Edens is well enough to continue the case.

Clayton has helped Edens, who is a classic manic-depressive, through such an episode years before. But when he encounters Edens in the hospital, he finds the man still at the zenith of a manic episode. Edens excitedly tells Clayton about the case, particularly about some information he has—a paper signed by U/North's CEO that recognizes the danger of certain chemicals—that proves U/North is guilty. Clayton does not want to get involved in the case since his firm is in the midst of a megamerger and his loan hinges on getting Edens back to normal, and he tries to convince Edens to forget his recent crusader rhetoric. But the savvy older lawyer has apparently gained a conscience during his breakdown, and he questions the ethics of what he and Clayton have been doing for years by defending the interests of powerful corporate clients. After escaping from Clayton's stewardship, Edens returns to his apartment in New York's meatpacking district to build his case against U/North, all the while maintaining an insane love affair via telephone with one of the plaintiffs, whom he eventually convinces to visit him.

Although the film attributes Edens's new outlook on life to a mental disorder, his breakdown, like Howard Beale's in *Network*, figures as more than one individual's psychological imbalance. Edens's "insanity," however, one-ups that of the one-dimensional Beale, who functions as one tine in a two-pronged attack on television and capital that is eventually recouped. Edens, through his manic episodes, is released as the voice of honesty and passionate concern in *Michal Clayton*, and like a Shakespearean Fool, he can speak truth to power, especially in legalese. Set against the Prufrockian pallor of Clayton (whose name suggests a heavy, dull, moldable lump, while Edens's suggests his quixotic and utopian temper) and the gloomy dispassionate tone of the film itself, Edens functions as the sole figure embodying the repressed conscience of those who are complicit with a corrupt system, and his crusading drive to expose the truth functions as a kind of (literally) suicidal death drive, in which either he or the system must be destroyed. In a sort of paradox, Edens's mania makes him the only passionate character in the film. U/North's public-relations person and designated evildoer, Karen Crowder (Tilda Swinton), shows an intense drive to establish a good image for U/North and to climb the corporate ladder, but she is more driven *by* a goal than *she* is driving *toward* one. The "insane" Edens can transcend the ethical quandary of the film (the inability to find an "outside" from which to resist the system effectively) and devote himself to the goal of changing it, but the "rational" Crowder, immersed within the logic of capital and the system, can only be driven by the concerns of the system itself.

Clearly, the film suggests that to support the system actively—whether as corporate lawyer, "fixer," or executive—one must become hollow, empty of any moral and ethical considerations, and devoid of any drive or passion not in service of the system itself. For not only is Clayton existentially wiped out and compromised (he is a former prosecuting district attorney, who gave up the pursuit of justice and ended up using his connections to become a successful "fixer"), but so is his nemesis, Crowder, whom we witness early in the film (unbeknown to us) as a reflection in the mirror in which she rehearses a public-relations speech for U/North, signifying the liquidation of her own "self" by the corporate speak and corporate face she has adopted, a mask that we later learn has long since ceased to be a mask.

The depths of Crowder's commitment to U/North and its CEO are exposed after Edens goes missing. Clayton, under pressure from U/North and his firm to find and neutralize the now legally dangerous Edens, is unable to bring his friend back into the corporate fold(er). Crowder, who is aware that the information Edens holds can crush U/North, has Edens killed to look like suicide. Clayton is suspicious of his friend's suicide and begins to look into the U/North case, which leads the assassins and Crowder to believe that Clayton has been helping Edens and has the documents for which they have been searching. Eventually discovering a box of reports damning U/North that Edens was holding at a local Kinko's, Clayton decides to finish the case his friend began. This leads to an assassination attempt on his own life—a car bomb that detonates after Clayton has vacated his car, causing his would-be killers to believe he has died in the explosion. With such a cover, he is able to set up a successful sting operation, luring Crowder into admitting her guilt, all with the help of his brothers and old police buddies, marking a kind of resurrection of Clayton's character—his ethics, personal integrity, old friends, and family are restored in serving justice. U/North will lose the case, and Edens has been avenged.

Michael Clayton follows the model set by other films that blame corporate malfeasance on particular executives (here the CEO and Karen Crowder), but it does so in a curious fashion. The damning evidence of U/North's responsibility for its misdeeds is the paper signed by the CEO, Don Jeffries himself. Thus, in terms of the highest level of accountability, we would expect Jeffries to be the main villain of the film, since he has knowingly initiated an illegal and dangerous business practice that has directly harmed a number of people. But the majority of the blame and condemnation for this act is deflected from Jeffries and U/North and redirected onto Karen Crowder.

That the film's true villain turns out to be a woman at first seems odd, considering the gender imbalance at the executive level of corporate America. Yet Crowder is the one who orders the two murders (one of which is successful) and who schemes, unbeknown to Jeffries, to save U/North's image and case by hunting down the compromising documents. Several times we see Crowder in the position of shielding Jeffries from knowledge of her illegal activities, all to maintain the image, even to him, that U/North is having no difficulties with the lawsuit. Yet it is clear from the beginning (and from the signed document) that Jeffries is aware of his illegal activities and thus somewhat unclear as to why Crowder continually covers for him. She apparently enjoys her power and reputation to such a degree that she will murder in order to secure it, but, again, Jeffries is the party guilty of the "original sin." That Crowder somehow comes to bear the brunt of all the illegal activity in the film by committing a murder is strange. Yet she is clearly the main villain in the film, even though it is Jeffries and other executives who have caused the sickness and potential deaths of many more people, as well as the destruction of the environment. But the "vulgar" murder and selfish scheming of Crowder is somehow supposed to put the more massive crimes of the corporation and its CEO out of our minds.

Certainly Clayton sees it this way. Like the typical film-noir antihero (the film has noir-like elements in tone and style, as well as in Clayton's character), he is drawn against his better judgment into something larger than he imagined. His sympathies are at odds with his desire to remain true to his own ethical code, a tough, ultimately selfish attitude (combined with his particular moral exhaustion) that is only breached when his friend is killed (à la Sam Spade in *The Maltese Falcon* [1930] or Philip Marlowe in *The Long Goodbye* [1953]). Moreover, Clayton's mission is never anything more than a personal one. He does not pretend to care about the U/North case or its victims much. That he will ultimately help the victims win their case becomes just a byproduct of his true aim. Instead, he wants solely to avenge Edens's death and the attempt on his own life. The last scene of the film is telling in this regard. Clayton does not wish to speak to the CEO about the company's transgressions but to Crowder concerning hers. Granted, he is wired and must get her verbal confession, but it is telling in that Crowder tries convincing the confused

Jeffries to go back to the board meeting, safe from the lurking danger of Clayton, and receives the full force of Clayton's vitriol.

Clayton and Crowder have, of course, met once before, when Clayton tries to reassure her in Minnesota that Edens will do no more damage to the case. The meeting takes place at a bar and ends quickly and disastrously with a furious Crowder berating Clayton about his failure to contain Edens, who represents the irrational, the libidinal. That a client should rage at him is common in Clayton's job (as the film's opening scene shows us), but here it takes on an edge, since it eventually leads to Crowder's despair and decision to kill Edens. Had Clayton succeeded in his mission, Crowder probably would have had no need to silence Edens. Hence, Clayton's emasculation in this scene must leave a particular sting.

This failed meeting feels like a blind date gone horribly wrong. That the two should meet under potentially romantic circumstances, which the film rapidly forecloses on, cannot liquidate its own libidinal investment so easily. Mixing the handsome Hollywood darling, George Clooney, into a spy-thriller/noir genre in which viewers expect to find a femme fatale but instead find desexed and empty characters forces the film to find some kind of outlet for such raging libidinal seas. Or perhaps Clayton's miserably failed "pseudodate" is yet another reason why his pent-up anger and frustration must be vented on a female character? In any event, it is Crowder who must fill this vacant position.

As a kind of femme fatale, Crowder becomes the repository for all of the corporation's deception. For if the corporate image pretends to be a kind of soul when it is really nothing but exterior image—a sort of mask—then the femme fatale, with her alluring deceitfulness and beauty that "masks" an inner corruption, serves as the perfect figure to dramatize this threat, especially in a noir-ish film that lacks any female love interest. Again, we first see Crowder as an image in the mirror, fixing her makeup, putting on her "corporate face" that will represent the image of U/North. As she inspects her body in the mirror, the seduction to follow will not be a physical one, as was Christensen's in *Network*, but a seduction by the corporate image and rhetoric.

For there can be no traditional femme fatale character who literally seduces the hero in *Michael Clayton*. None of the film's main characters appears to have any kind of respectable love life. Clayton is divorced, Crowder is married to her job, and Edens has recently left his wife of over thirty years, though he professes a "love" for one plaintiff, which the film presents as a product of his insanity (thus, true love in the film is also irrational). So we are introduced to an unconventional femme fatale in Crowder instead, one who fuses together the corrupt corporation with the familiar trope of the two-faced woman. This conflation successfully channels the libidinal currents of the film that otherwise would remain frustrated. The "climax" of the film, then, occurs when Clayton "exposes" Crowder and verbally excoriates her, not in wrapping up the U/North case. It is one of the rare moments of emotional expression we receive from the stoic Clayton, and the moment is a catharsis for him, as well as for the viewer.

This is to say that Clayton and the film's rage at the corporation is not aimed at the logic of capital and the corporation but at the false image it maintains, as evidenced in the squeaky-clean U/North commercial that Edens, during a scene set in his apartment, maddeningly plays over and over at maximum volume. Thus, if the corporation is a fairly masculine space where men in boardrooms puff on cigars and exemplify a kind of rapacious and aggressive pursuit of capital, then there is nothing much wrong with this. Such a (war) game can be understood by all the participants equally, and if the playing field is never exactly level, that is simply because part of the game is to manipulate the field itself. But in the case of the corporate image and public relations, the game is complete deception, and this is, as the single Clayton knows, surely a woman's game. Competition that is acknowledged as competition is fine, but competition that masks itself as something other than it is, that requires not brute strength or force to defeat it but the ability to dissemble, shape shift, and carefully read the nuances of others, is unfair. Such competition is anathema. As a result, even Clayton must engage in these "weak" tactics to defeat such an enemy, arming himself with a hidden wire and goading Crowder into a confession.

Clayton's real enemy is never the U/North guilty of the destruction of the environment and human lives—the logic of the corporation—but the deceptive image of U/North embodied by Crowder. Clayton and the film, like the prisoners in Plato's cave, remain fixed on the shadows playing on the wall. Or, to be more precise, the freed prisoner, Clayton, is not interested in escaping from the cave so much as he is with confronting his captors, the puppeteers. Why the cave should be as it is, and what could possibly be outside it, are of no concern to him. Thus, in *Michael Clayton*, the dominance of corporations in the era of late capitalism is so pervasive and unquestioned that even attempting to imagine something outside such a system is irrelevant or results in madness.

As we have seen, to embrace irrationality is apparently the only way to act freely within such a system. Since the rational, which the system has converted into its opposite, is now the irrational, the real irrationality lies in the "rational" system itself. But this can only be signified in the excess of madness, either by the freedom of Edens's mental instability or through Crowder as the overly ambitious executive who resorts to assassinating her rivals in cold blood rather than in frigid legalese or cold, hard, cash settlements. Such a fantastic, international-spy-thriller motif is fairly ridiculous in the world of *Michael Clayton*. It is more a throwback to the days when capital and labor exploded into actual violent struggle (such as the California farmers' riots against the railroads in the nineteenth century as depicted in Frank Norris's *The Octopus*) or at least is closer to what occurs today in many third-world countries where corporations, often working closely with authoritarian governments, hold sway.[9]

But we are no longer in a time when such bloody confrontations occur over corporate misdeeds in America. Having won such battles, corporations in the era of late capitalism have settled down to a seemingly mundane existence. The contradictions of capital and labor have been "resolved" at the surface level, although not fundamentally. This, in part, explains the pervasive cynicism of the film that change can never truly be effective. More so, it proves that the *excess* of violence (of irrationality)—the exploding cars, the stealthy assassins—is the only way to represent *the actual everydayness and dullness of corporate violence*. This kind of violence is what Slavoj Žižek calls "'systemic violence,' or the often catastrophic consequences of the smooth functioning of our economic and political systems" (*Violence* 2). Such systemic violence "must be taken into account if one is to make sense of what otherwise seem to be 'irrational' explosions of subjective violence" (2). The slow poisoning of the water in the Midwest by U/North, for instance, cannot be represented directly (or visually) in the film. There is nothing shocking and spectacular about the act of pollution; it is essentially boring. Such violence is invisible and quiet, *but it is violence nonetheless*; and this banal form of violence must be converted into the unbelievable and impossible to function as a credible threat to viewers.

In having to resort to such a representation of the unrepresentable, *Michael Clayton* simultaneously downplays the threat of corporate power (its everydayness or naturalization in our world) and exaggerates it. In the end, it is the corporation, not the shady loan shark of the underworld, which participates in brutal and spectacular violence. Who would not denounce such corporate misdeeds, on the right or the left? Such an attenuated view of corporate violence becomes less a critique of corporate power than an inverted denunciation of a potential revolution against the system. After all, if legal maneuverings will never fundamentally change the system, and if violence (as in its industrial capitalist forms) is represented in the film as an irrational and dangerous method used by malevolent forces (here the corporation but perhaps revolutionaries one day), then there is nothing effective that can be done to alter such an untenable state of affairs. *Michael Clayton* offers a bleak vision of late capitalism in which real resistance to corporate power is futile or, worse, unimaginable. Even as the seemingly rehabilitated Clayton leaves the U/North building victoriously, his last act of getting into a cab and telling the driver to give him fifty dollars' worth of driving signifies the continuing aimlessness of his, and everyone's, life in such a world.

Corporations have long since won a quiet and secret conquest of the earth in *Michael Clayton*, and there is no possibility of changing the system as it is. *Network*, appearing twenty years earlier, can at least register rage at this burgeoning situation. By the time we reach *Michael Clayton*, the exhausted rallying cry "I'm mad as hell, and I'm not going to take this anymore" becomes "I know I'm going to have to take this, so just leave me be." These bleak visions of the world offer little compensation in the way of hope or a glimpse of a more utopian future radically different from the one proposed by the likes of Arthur Jensen.

While corporations remain prevalent in a variety of American films and television shows, they often function only as a rudimentary way of commenting on the underlying economic system. There is always a tension, whether heightened or relaxed, when a corporation is figured in popular culture because, whether consciously or not, some kind of comment is being made about capitalism itself. In times of economic prosperity, when enough of the corporation's profits trickle down the economic ladder, popular culture tends to view the corporation with suspicion but ultimately finds that the capitalist system can be redeemed with a sensible nudge in the right direction—usually through the possibilities inherent in small-business owners and their cutting-edge ideas that will reinvigorate the system. In times of crisis, however, when the economy is bleak, representations of corporations are much more likely to begin to uncover the political machinations behind corporate power. There is an attempt to grasp more fundamental and systemic issues regarding capitalism, yet these analyses always seem to be coated in an apocalyptic pallor and an inability to see any brighter future. Nevertheless, the corporation retains its grip as a perennial "bad guy" in popular culture, now somewhat benign, now hell-bent on profits, but always to be viewed with both awe and suspicion.

4 / A Capital Death: Medicine, Technology, and the Care of the Self in Don DeLillo's *White Noise*

Don DeLillo's *White Noise* has long stood as a perfect primer on postmodern American life in its humorous depiction of one postnuclear family's mundane day-to-day in a media-saturated world where the strange is rendered familiar and the familiar strange. The unspectacular "hero" of the novel is angst-ridden Jack Gladney, who frets daily over the myriad possibilities of death threatening his safe suburban existence and gropes for answers to the meaning of life in the spiritual dark. His fear of death is so great that it appears to have partially influenced his latest marriage and his career choice as chair of "Hitler Studies." What makes Gladney's obsession with death especially interesting, however, is not his overwhelming fear and anxiety (which would merely signal neurosis) but the terms under which he comes to see himself suffering. Gladney discovers a new kind of death, what we might call a "postmodern death," and he struggles to comprehend it throughout the novel.

Equipped with an existential view of life and death, Gladney is unprepared to deal with death's newest guises. In a discussion of the human understanding of death with Gladney, his colleague Murray Jay Siskind alludes to Tolstoy's *The Death of Ivan Ilyich*, noting that "Ivan Ilyich screamed for three days. That's about as intelligent as we get" (282). Things are not so "easy" for Gladney, however. Even the possibility of an Ivan Ilyich–like horror-stricken scream (which echoed far into the modernist's existential void) has been subsumed by the white noise of postmodern life, "a dull and unlocatable roar, as of some form of swarming life just outside the range of human apprehension" (36). For, as Gladney states, the ways and means of death are constantly changing: "Man's guilt in history and in the tides of his own blood has been complicated by technology, the daily seeping falsehearted death" (22). Gladney's comment here is shrewd because it underscores the workings behind the event of what we normally think of as "death." As science and technology evolve, so too does "death," which in turn changes the way people come to understand mortality itself.

White Noise reveals this complex interplay among science, technology, and death as Gladney searches for a style of dying he can come to terms with, a kind of "death-style" to match the unobtrusive lifestyle he has chosen. Through his quest, the novel evinces the shortcomings of medical science in an age of simulation and uncertainty and points to its failures in dealing with death by suggesting that some of its preventative methods may be as harmful as they are helpful, especially in their effects on people's comprehension of health, illness, and mortality. Yet this critique of science, technology, and medicine is not limited in its scope and truly takes on weight when it is set within the context of the novel's greater concern with exposing the problems and paradoxes of a simulated postmodern world, a place of confusion and contradiction where the arbiters of truth are those authorities bearing the latest information and who gain and hold power by generating, purchasing, storing, retrieving, and disseminating such information. In short, it is a world in which corporations help create and "solve" such seeming chaos. *White Noise*, then, situates the discourse of death in relation to other social discourses to show that, far from being a universal condition, "postmodern death" is a highly particularized cultural construct, ultimately subject to corporations, the market, and capital.

Choosing a Death That's Right for You

Gladney's attempts to quell his fears of death uncover a host of assumptions he holds about death and indicate some of the greater narratives that have informed his views.[1] Tellingly, none of these narratives is explicitly tied to the narrative of late capitalism and its most powerful representatives, corporations. As we shall see, many of Gladney's narratives offer transcendent or "natural" views of death that are somehow outside the realm of what the novel shows is an increasing "corporatizing" of life under late capitalism.

Gladney's first imagining of death occurs early in the novel. After awaking suddenly one night from a "muscular contraction known as the myoclonic jerk," Gladney wonders, "Is this what it's like, abrupt, peremptory? Shouldn't death, I thought, be a swan dive, graceful, white-winged and smooth, leaving the surface undisturbed?" (18). This Romantic image of death recalls Rilke's poem "The Swan," in which an "awkward walking" swan enters a pond:

> And death, where we no longer comprehend
> the very ground on which we daily stand,
> is like the anxious letting-himself-go
> into the water, soft against his breast,
> which now how easily together flows
> . . . .
> while he, infinitely silent, self-possessed,
> and ever more mature, is pleased to move
> serenely on his majestic way. (ll. 4–12)

Here, life merges into death harmoniously, and the swan figures as a beautiful and heroic emblem of this meeting, which is nothing short of the culmination of a natural process. Gladney's image of death as a swan dive evokes the same effortlessness of passage, the same nobility in bearing. The aestheticizing of death turns death into an artistic technique (perhaps a "death d[r]ive") that can be practiced and mastered, not merely by Rilke but by Gladney as well. The diver's art is one of precision, the dive itself a triumph of form over materiality. The diver slips under the water's surface as smoothly as possible, and the act becomes one of beauty. The myoclonic spasm, however, is a profound belly flop: "I seemed to fall through myself, a shallow heart-stopping plunge" (*White Noise* 18).

Death as a sudden fall that cannot be rehearsed, where one plummets through the self as through a void, is a fine example of a modern, existential notion of death. Gladney's fanciful wish for a kinder, gentler death is antiquated and absurd in the face of the randomness of postmodern death. He even goes so far as to idealize Attila the Hun's death, which, as John Frow points out, allows him to valorize "a heroic lack of self-consciousness, [and] a naive immediacy to life and death" (42). Gladney's attempts to romanticize and aestheticize death are hopeless and inevitably sink into the existential abyss. If that were not enough, the metaphor of passing into death via calm waters is effectively smashed when Dimitri Cotsakis, another colleague, drowns in a surfing accident (*White Noise* 168).

The modern, existential vision of death is Gladney's most trusted narrative. As Leonard Wilcox argues, Gladney "is a modernist displaced in a postmodern world. He exhibits a Kierkegaardian 'fear and trembling' regarding death and attempts to preserve earlier notions of authentic and coherent identity" (99). Frank Lentricchia similarly claims that Gladney's plot to kill Gray near the novel's end "embodies his dream of existential self-determination" (94). Gladney's comfort with existential discourse is evident during his and Babette's ongoing conversation over which of them should die first: "She claims my death would leave a bigger hole in her life than her death would leave in mine. This is the level of our discourse. The relative size of holes, abysses and gaps. We have serious arguments on this level. She says if her death is capable of leaving a large hole in my life, my death would leave an abyss in hers, a great yawning gulf. I counter with a profound depth or void" (*White Noise* 101). This despairing one-upmanship uncovers the influence of existentialist discourse on death from Martin Heidegger to Albert Camus.[2] Death here can only (not) be imagined as nothingness, and the more massive, the more gaping the void, the more anxiety of death one has. Thus, the sober existentialist taking stock of the meaninglessness of existence— the heroic Nietzschean gaze into the abyss—becomes *de*void of any metaphorical power. The exhausted language of existentialism in part restricts the articulation of a "postmodern death" and results in simply a humorous contest about whose void is bigger.

Gladney's desperate search for a suitable death is thus complicated as this existentialist discourse overlaps with other discourses, as each narrative strains, unsuccessfully, to articulate the new form of "postmodern death." The result is a smorgasbord of "death-style" choices, as if seeking an understanding of life and death were the same as shopping for a new shirt at the mall. Murray hawks Tibetan Buddhism early in the novel, and Babette, a devotee of supermarket tabloids, reads Gladney a story titled "Life After Death Guaranteed" that, after detailing several incredible stories of persons remembering their "former lives," becomes a sales pitch: "The no-risk bonus coupon below gives you guaranteed access to dozens of documented cases of life after death, everlasting life, previous-life experiences" (143–144). In this hodge-podge of postmodern "faiths," various narratives compete, intersect, and replace one another—particularly as all have been reduced to commodities and carefully marketed by corporations in the age of late capitalism.

At one point, Gladney even slips into a medieval conceptualization of death when he awakes early one morning to find a white-haired man in his backyard. Gladney approaches the man, certain that "he would be Death, or Death's errand runner, a hollow-eyed technician from the plague era, from the era of inquisitions, endless wars, of bedlams and leprosariums.... He would be the aphorist of last things, giving me the barest glance—civilized, ironic—as he spoke his deft and stylish line about my journey out" (243). Gladney's personification of death, with all its "allegorical force" (243), is a combination of various media- and artistically fed fables about man "playing against" Death for a longer life, a trope perhaps best employed by Ingmar Bergman in *The Seventh Seal* (1957). In such cases, Death is figured as a doggedly determined gamesman, linked to a higher cosmic and spiritual order, who willingly gives his opponent a (seemingly) sporting chance to defeat him. Defying death becomes a game or competition in this way of thinking (and one that can never be won, thus the heroic potentiality).

This notion is undercut when the white-haired man turns out to be Gladney's father-in-law. But the gamesmanship, the attempt to "cheat" death, is never far from Gladney's thoughts. In fact, this trope of gaming with a "civilized Death" moves from the medieval rhetorical tendency toward personification and allegory into the postmodern preference for synecdoche and metonymy, most noticeably in the figure of the doctor, who stands in for science and technology. The doctor, like Death personified, is also a "technician" but a technician of the postmodern world who has mastery over the latest science and technology, someone who can understand the latest computers, machines, and data, someone who "knows the symbols" (281). It is precisely Gladney's loss of a symbolically ordered Death in a postmodern world, in which symbols are merely signs to be interpreted, that puts him at the mercy not of the religio-spiritual order but of a techno-scientific one instead.

This, then, is what a "postmodern death" entails, living (dying) amid the strangeness of new technologies. Gladney tells Murray near the novel's end, "There's something artificial about my death. It's shallow, unfulfilling. I don't belong to the earth or sky. They ought to carve an aerosol can on my tombstone" (283). To be sure, it is computer data that confirms this elusive "death" for Gladney: "It is when death is ... televised so to speak, that you sense an eerie separation between your condition and yourself.... It makes you feel a stranger to your own dying" (141–142). The televised, computer-screen death is a simulated one that lacks the authentic intimacy and immediacy of "real" death. Thus, for Gladney, an unmediated death is a natural one, and it is a death always imaginatively staged in the past, when death apparently held true to the natural order of things.

Murray later tells Gladney that "modern death,... has a life independent of us" and "adapts, like a viral agent" (150). This argument of a kind of living-evolving death may appear to renaturalize death under the sign of evolution, but it signals an acceptance that as the world changes, so does our understanding of death. This questioning lays the groundwork for seeing the ways in which death is culturally and historically negotiated. If Gladney's search for a "death-style" reveals the social and cultural discourses surrounding death, then Murray's refusal to romanticize death creates a space from which to interrogate the concept of "natural death," the sort of death for which Gladney yearns.

Because We Cannot Stop for Death

Critics have long employed Jean Baudrillard's concept of the simulacra in their readings of *White Noise* to emphasize the role of the media in a spectacular society, but Baudrillard's thought is helpful in interrogating the notion of *death* as well. In *Symbolic Exchange and Death*, for instance, Baudrillard maps the relationship between political economy and death. For Baudrillard, political economy in late capitalism has been reduced to the political economy of the sign, as he puts forth in *For a Critique of the Political Economy of the Sign*. In short, this entails a reduction and liquidation of any possibility of a (former) symbolic order or value, as exchange value effectively trumps use value, collapsing older Marxist critiques of capital and heralding the new "political economy of the sign": "*This semiological reduction of the symbolic properly constitutes the ideological process*" (98).

In other words, for Baudrillard, the ideological triumph of the sign, the image, the simulacrum, or exchange value gives rise to a late capitalist system in which free-floating signifiers empty out the possibility of depth or symbolic meaning (and of an older Marxist critique of ideology as well) by creating a strict binary code governing all meaning. DeLillo plays with this triumph of the sign in *White Noise* when Gladney listens to Steffie talking in her sleep and expects her to mutter a revelation, which turns out to be "Toyota Celica." In frustration, Gladney complains that Steffie "was only repeating some TV voice. Toyota Corolla, Toyota Celica, Toyota Cressida. Supranational names, computer-generated, more or less universally pronounced" (155). Indeed, each car's name signifies something that has nothing to do with driving (Corolla, flower petals; Celica from the Latin *coelica* for "heavenly" or "celestial"; and Cressida, a satellite of Uranus or Trojan lover of Troilus in medieval romances). Thus, DeLillo humorously strips Gladney of yet another symbolic dimension of meaning by replacing it with a pure sign or code, the cultural code that he recognizes as not merely ad-speak but the true transnational postmodern Esperanto (as when Hunt clings to a McDonald's in Japan in *Gung Ho*)—the corporate logo.

Expanding on this concept of the "semiological reduction of the symbolic" in a reading of political economy and death in *Symbolic Exchange and Death*, Baudrillard writes that in postmodern times, "little by little, *the dead cease to exist*. They are thrown out of the group's symbolic circulation. They are no longer beings with a full role to play, worthy partners in exchange" (126). This "out of mind" phenomenon is mirrored by an "out of sight" one too, since, in contrast to former times when cemeteries "remain[ed] in the heart of the village or town," now they "prefigur[e] every future ghetto" and are "thrown further and further from the centre towards the periphery" (126). *White Noise* offers a scene somewhat akin to Baudrillard's comments on cemeteries and the dead. When Gladney stops to visit "the old burying ground" of Blacksmith Village, he finds the "headstones were small, tilted, pockmarked, spotted with fungus or moss, the names and dates barely legible.... Embedded in the dirt before one of the markers was a narrow vase containing three small American flags, the only sign that someone had preceded me to this place in this century" (97). Like the dead that Baudrillard suggests are symbolically silenced, so too are the dead in this graveyard essentially silent and forgotten. Gladney somberly reflects that "the power of the dead is that we think they see us all the time. The dead have a presence. Is there a level of energy composed solely of the dead?" (98), but it is hard to see how much presence and power the dead have in such a rarely visited, dilapidated graveyard. Gladney sees the fact that he is "beyond the traffic noise, the intermittent stir of factories" (97) as indicating how well placed the graveyard is with respect to mourning, yet this location obviously functions to keep the all-but-forgotten dead well away from the living as well, both literally and figuratively. Ye olde village burial ground, now accessible via the expressway (ominously so, when we recall the cemetery razed by Inverarity in *The Crying of Lot 49*), also signals the change from the small-town atmosphere and life Gladney so desires from Blacksmith, whose original and historical burial ground is now nearly entirely forgotten.

With the dead silenced and removed, so to speak, the ability of the dead, and death itself, to function symbolically is lost. Stripped of such social and symbolic significance, death consequently becomes the individual's solipsistic obsession, as it is with Gladney, who is the perfect example of the customer in such a political economy of death because he cannot accept the terms and conditions that apply to his situation, the very terms and conditions that have underwritten his condition (life) as something that will one day be reckoned and expire, and so he pays and pays and pays.

The Pre-scribed Life

The symbolically bereft binary construct of life/death lends itself to a linear (capitalist) time scheme, so that people like Gladney often feel they are "running out of time" or that an early death "shortchanges" them. Life, extended out like a credit line, eventually expires. Under such linear time constraints, people come to expect a "natural death" the way they might expect a service to be fulfilled, and barring any accidents, this death should be deferred as much as possible by medicine, science, and technology. Yet the idea of "natural death," as Baudrillard writes, "signifies not the acceptance of death within 'the order of things,' but a systematic denegation of death. Natural death is subject to science, and death's call is to be exterminated by science. . . . The only good death is a death that has been defeated and subject to the law: this is the ideal of natural death" (*Symbolic* 162).

Gladney's belief that his death will be "artificial," "alien," or unnatural may be a consequence of the technology he is unable to put his faith in, but his longing for a "natural" death reinscribes the very conditions of death that science sets out to eradicate. Hence, Gladney's desire for a "natural death" is no longer possible because postmodernism's simulated death implodes the distinction between "artificial" and "natural" death. Artificial death is now natural death in the sense that it is the postmodern mode of death, and thus it is a natural death that would truly be unnatural in this world. At one point, Gladney comments, "I recalled with a shock that I was technically dead" (158). His comment is more astute than he realizes, for although Gladney speaks figuratively here, he literally (and inadvertently) refers to his death as simulated by the SIMUVAC worker on a computer screen. We are far from the refined, artistic "technique" of Romantic death here and have entered the screen of the simulated, scientific "technical" postmodern one.

Thus, the only possible way to cheat death is to cheat the system itself. Gaming with Death is replaced by being disingenuous with one's doctor. The doctor as postmodern technician holds the key to life or death in his wealth of superior knowledge. He, like Death, metes out life or death sentences according to a higher authority (science instead of God). The authority of the doctor causes patients to adopt a simultaneously fawning and duplicitous manner, as revealed when Gladney and Babette take Wilder to the doctor for his incessant crying. The two "anticipated questions the doctor would ask and rehearsed [their] answers carefully" because "doctors lose interest in people who contradict each other" (75). Since, for Gladney, "this fear has long informed my relationship with doctors, that they would lose interest in me, . . . take my dying for granted" (76), each visit to the doctor becomes a worrisome, rehearsed performance and one that reveals the importance placed on the authority of the doctor, who is there not so much to cure the ill as to tend to the (living) dead or dying. Such a view of doctors and medicine is alarming because life itself becomes little more, as Baudrillard suggests, than the attempt to fit the model or contract of a life that society perceives is owed or granted to us. As Dr. Chakravarty explains to Gladney during a visit, "People tend to forget they are patients. Once they leave the doctor's office or the hospital, they simply put it out of their minds. But you are all permanent patients, like it or not. I am the doctor, you the patient. Doctor doesn't cease being doctor at close of day. Neither should patient. People expect the doctor to go about things with the utmost seriousness, skill and experience. But what about patient? How professional is he?" (260). This, in part, helps explain why Gladney is so terrified of doctors' offices. The distinctions between doctor and patient are rigidly enforced here, and the doctors are happy to keep it that way. Indeed, remarks Mark Conroy in an essay that maps the transmission of cultural narratives and figures of authority in *White Noise*, "authority, at least in the world of this text, is above and before all positional" (158). If the doctor plays the role of the doctor/authority, then the patient is subsequently forced into a role of patient/subject.

In Foucauldian terms, Gladney's body has been made "docile" or "normalized" in these interactions with the SIMUVAC technician and Dr. Chakravarty. As Foucault writes in *Discipline and Punish*, "the body is . . . directly involved in a political field; power relations have an immediate hold upon it; they invest it, mark it, train it, torture it, force it to carry out tasks, to perform ceremonies, emit signs" (25). Gladney's array of tests, benign as they seemingly are, nonetheless subjects him to the ceremonies and signs of postmodern medicine. Medical techniques and practices also encapsulate perfectly Foucault's notion of "biopower," a sort of mutation of power that, Foucault argues in volume one of *The History of Sexuality*, arose during the shift from classical to modern society, so that "the old power of death that symbolized sovereign power was now carefully supplanted by the administration of bodies and the calculated management of life" (*History* 139–140). Thus, "it was the taking charge of life, more than the threat of death, that gave power its access even to the body" (*History* 143). The extension of this notion of biopower to postmodern times leads to the "professionalization" of the patient (like the encouragement of victimhood that Jack's daughter, Steffie, signals in her desire to play a victim in a disaster simulation; *White Noise* 206–207), which takes medicine from the realm of merely treating the sick and ailing to administering life itself.

Consequently, when Gladney lies to his doctors about his medical history, it constitutes his way of disrupting the medical system and its mediation of life and death. By imparting false facts about his history, Gladney hopes to receive a clean bill of health in return, an extended warranty on his life. However, his lie to Dr. Chakravarty about not being exposed to chemicals is ineffectual since medical science has itself become a simulation. In feeding "false" signs into the system, Gladney thinks he is separating the signifier (his exposure / symptoms) from the signified (the effects / his death). His question about whether "the numbers show some sign of possible exposure" is countered by Dr. Chakravarty: "If you haven't been exposed, then they couldn't very well show a sign, could they?" (261). Gladney's response, "Then we agree," is formed as a statement (not a question), to which Dr. Chakravarty does not respond. Nothing is agreed on, and whatever the signs on Dr. Chakravarty's chart indicate, they are clearly already circulating free of their "real" referents.

A nearly identical scene occurs when Gladney visits a specialist on Dr. Chakravarty's referral (276–281). Gladney lies three times during his tests and matches his answers to the doctor's questions with what the doctor tells him most people's responses are:

> "What about appetite?" he said.
> "I could go either way on that."
> "That's more or less how I could go, based on the printout."
> "In other words you're saying sometimes I have appetitive reinforcement, sometimes I don't?"
> "Are you telling me or asking me?"
> "It depends on what the numbers say."
> "Then we agree." (278)

Again, nothing is agreed on here but the tacit acknowledgment that Gladney's answers should coincide with the data displayed on the printout. The simulated symptoms take precedent over the (lack of) "real" ones. Moreover, it is not because Gladney tries to lie about his exposure to Nyodene D that the system founders. When Gladney slips up and is forced to admit his lie, the results of the diagnosis do not change. The doctor tells him, "We have some conflicting data that says exposure to this substance can definitely lead to a mass" (280). The oxymoronic "can definitely" attests to the inability of medical science to draw conclusions about the chemical's effects. Gladney learns nothing here that the SIMUVAC technician did not already tell him at the evacuation center (140–141). The "diagnosis" is *virtually* meaningless: "This doesn't mean anything is going to happen to you as such, at least not today or tomorrow. It just means you are the sum total of your data. No man escapes that" (141). Here, DeLillo gives Sartre's contention that "man is . . . nothing else than the ensemble of his acts" (47) an ironic postmodern twist. Life as data, death as data. Life, death, and medicine—all are emptied of their power to signify under the weight of technology and simulation. The final absurdity is that it may take approximately fifteen to thirty years to discover if Gladney is indeed in danger from the exposure, at which time Gladney will be anywhere from sixty-seven to eighty-two years old.

DeLillo also calls attention to the limitations of modern science in a postmodern world during the evacuation prompted by the Airborne Toxic Event. When Steffie psychosomatically (re)produces the symptoms of exposure she hears on the radio broadcasts, Gladney wonders, "What if she was developing real symptoms by natural means? . . . Which was worse, the real condition or the self-created one, and did it matter? . . . Is a symptom a sign or a thing? What is a thing and how do we know it's not another thing?" (126). If suggestion and simulacra are able to create the "real," then Gladney's frantic questions unveil a disturbing problem inherent in modern medicine. As Baudrillard describes it in *Simulacra and Simulations*, "if any symptom can be 'produced,' and can no longer be taken as a fact of nature, then every illness can be considered as simulatable and simulated, and medicine loses its meaning since it only knows how to treat 'real' illness according to objective causes" (3). "Real" medicine in *White Noise* is reduced in the end to a lone question—How do you feel? (which is the question all three of Gladney's doctors ask him)—while the seemingly "unreal" spread of déjà vu warrants a "toll-free hotline" with "counselors on duty around the clock" (176). In *White Noise*, medicine falters in the face of simulation, which separates the symptom from its referent. Diagnosis is endlessly deferred, and therefore we are always already patients.

This is not to say, in a kind of instigative Baudrillardian way, that modern medicine and health care *are in reality ineffective*. DeLillo's aim is not a ridiculous dismissal of medicine-as-simulation (similar to

Baudrillard's purposely provocative insistence that the first Gulf War did not "take place" in *The Gulf War Did Not Take Place* [1995]) but to expose, through Gladney's exposure to Nyodene D, how the "creeping daily false-hearted Death" has its partner in a speculative and preventative idea of medicine, a kind of mundane view of medicine as a regulated, daily, truthful life guarantor.

Dr. Chakravarty sees his and Gladney's developing relationship framed by such an idea of medicine: "Together, as doctor and patient, we can do things neither of us could do separately. There is not enough emphasis on prevention. An ounce of prevention, goes the saying" (261). Indeed, the old adage "an apple a day," which through its employment of a "natural" symbol of wholeness and health (banished today yet reinvented in various health-food and organic-food crazes) attempts to offer the key to health and happiness, ultimately fails to give assurance in the postmodern world as compared with aspirin—an aspirin a day, not an apple, keeps the heart attack away. Here we perhaps find an odd postmodernized parable in which the knowledge resulting from tasting the aspirin leads to the fall from the garden with its old apple of common, folk knowledge, and banishment to a world of authoritative, scientific knowledge with its daily administering of life. For the result appears to be an ironic one: life is not exactly lived so much as it is administered and pre-scribed (that is, prewritten, modeled, and simulated, as well as "ordered" for one's health) by modern medicine in daily doses. Slavoj Žižek lists some of the features of a world where virtuality reigns supreme in *Welcome to the Desert of the Real*: "On today's market, we find a whole series of products deprived of their malignant properties: coffee without caffeine, cream without fat, beer without alcohol, . . . virtual sex as sex, . . . warfare without warfare, [and] the contemporary redefinition of politics as the art of expert administration, that is politics without politics" (10–11). Medical science is no exception to this trend. It must banish death from the scene, as Baudrillard states, and thus it must banish "life" as well. We are always already patients, always already preventing a death that will (not) come, by pre-scribing a life that will (not) be lived.

The Ever-Patient Customer

More than just a humorous depiction of the collapse of certainty in a simulated world governed by signs, *White Noise* asks the question, what, given such dilemmas of the postmodern world, is the ultimate goal or end to science and medicine, particularly in light of the practice of preventative medicine, and what are the effects of the pursuit of such an end? Steven Best and Douglas Kellner argue that to understand science in postmodern times, it is important "to reflect on the science/society nexus; the coevolution of science, technology, and capital; and the ways that social relations, discourses, and metaphors shape scientific understanding" (114). The answers to the preceding question, therefore, will not be grounded in a simple cause-and-effect analysis, since it is apparent that cultural and social beliefs inform science and technology, which in turn inform cultural and social beliefs, and the total sum of such beliefs affect and are affected by late capitalist economics and the influence of corporations—more specifically the pharmaceutical industry in the case of health care and medicine.

Not surprisingly, the climate of confusion and fear governs the world of *White Noise* and compels the characters to cling with a religious fervor to anything that will give them assurance or allay their anxieties. To live one's life in the novel is to be on the lookout for one's possible death, thus turning people who would otherwise be considered healthy into patients of sorts. The professional and perpetual patient's job is always to be preoccupied with disease and death and to take every precaution necessary to protect him- or herself from infection. Indeed, numerous characters in the novel constantly attend to the health of their bodies. Denise reads the *Physicians' Desk Reference* (36, 132), Babette tries a health-food diet of "yogurt and wheat germ" (7), Steffie and Denise perennially police Babette's eating habits (43), and Alfonse Stompanato expounds on the necessity of having a "good internist" when living in New York (217). It is no wonder, then, that a drug like Dylar (purported to extinguish the fear of death) is developed. Science and technology design the strategies for dealing with the very problems they have helped create. Ambivalent as Gladney is about technology and postmodern life, he too succumbs to the allure of Dylar and its promise to expunge the anxiety of death when he searches madly through the trash for the bottle of pills (259).

With the emergence of a self-conscious, ever-patient customer, which Gladney embodies to a tee, there is thus born a vast, new market. Such a market was quickly tapped into during the 1980s by the pharmaceutical industry, which was suffering a crisis of sorts in the early years of the decade and was searching for new inroads to consumers. Winnie, a neurochemist and colleague of Gladney's, exposes the corporate underpinnings of the Dylar project to Gladney after she reads an article in *American Psychobiologist*: "Such a group [studying the fear of death and developing Dylar] definitely existed. Supported by a multinational giant. Operating in the deepest secrecy in an unmarked building just outside

Iron City" (299). That the Dylar project was shrouded in secrecy—"To prevent espionage by competitive giants" (299)—also implies that there is indeed a fertile market to be harvested here and one of which other companies are surely aware. The multinational aspect of the corporation is important here too, as it gestures to the exploitation of third-world countries' natural resources. Earlier, Denise's listing of third-world nations' in relation to their minerals and exports clearly shows the United States' regard for these countries: "Peru has the llama. . . . Bolivia has tin. Chile has copper and iron" (81). Moreover, the global reaches of the multinational company's research and development branch is apparent in the "rogue scientist" and Dylar creator, Willie Mink, who is an immigrant of indeterminate ethnic origin (at least to Gladney) and a "westernized" patchwork of American culture in appearance and speech (307).

Clearly, *White Noise* is prescient in its treatment of the pharmaceutical industry and prescription-drug use during the 1980s (and especially the 1990s), which soared to unprecedented heights under the Reagan administration's deregulatory economic policies and with the passage of the Bayh-Dole Act (1980) and Hatch-Waxman Act (1984).[3] As Linda Marsa puts it in *Prescription for Profits*, "the Reagan White House encouraged government researchers to forge ties with industry, which transformed the once pristine laboratory into a hotbed of commerce" (7). In 1988, two years after the publication of the novel, and perhaps fittingly amid the Iran-Contra scandal, Prozac was approved by the FDA for use against depression. This heralded a new age in the pharmaceutical industry in regard to the treatment of depression, obsessive-compulsive disorder, and anxiety.

Moreover, Dylar is very much a forerunner of Prozac and, like Prozac, is distinctively different from the kinds of barbiturates (Seconal, Nembutal, and Valium) that may well have inspired DeLillo's fictional drug (Valium was the number-one prescription drug from 1969 to 1982, its sales spiking in 1978; Sample 29). At the time, the popularity of barbiturates, which had helped fuel industry profits in prior decades, was waning due to the drugs' often deleterious effects on users. In *The Cult of Pharmacology*, Richard DeGrandpre writes that sales of such drugs peaked in "1973, when over eighty million prescriptions were filled. By 1986, this number had fallen to sixty-one million. As the number continued to decline, a hole in the domestic drug market began to widen" (52). Essentially, this "hole" was filled by SSRI drugs (selective serotonin reuptake inhibitors), led by the neural-trailblazing Prozac—a new drug for a new age.

Dylar qualifies as such a technologically innovative drug in search of a fresh market. Earlier in the novel, Winnie describes Dylar as "not a tablet in the old sense" but "a drug delivery system. It doesn't dissolve right away" (187). She identifies it as "some kind of psychopharmaceutical. It's probably designed to interact with a distant part of the cortex" (189), and she calls it "a wonderful little system" (188). Dylar, then, is a state-of-the-art designer drug and, as such, can be seen as representing the new kinds of SSRI drugs that began to flood the market after Prozac led the way (the most successful being Paxil [1997], Zoloft [1999], and Celexa [1998]),[4] at a time when "drug discovery became based on an understanding of processes at the molecular level. Molecular and computer-driven models of chemical structure drove 'rational drug design' and 'combinatory chemistry'" (Kaplan 45). The complex chemical makeup of these newer drugs ironically made them more dangerous than their discredited barbiturate brethren were and exemplified the enormous effects that modern chemicals could have on the brain. Considering *White Noise*'s entertainment of Heinrich's deterministic brain theories that so upset Gladney, it comes as no surprise that Dylar is not merely a mind-numbing drug like Valium but *a drug meant to interact and chemically alter one's state of mind*. Even Winnie is impressed by the *technological prowess* of the drug. Though Gladney fears the possibility that "we're the sum of our chemical impulses," the fact is that Dylar's success as a neurochemical drug relies on such a hypothesis. Gladney's hope that the drug might work is thus pinned to a theory of human behavior that he is unwilling to accept.

The fetishization of Dylar is the perfect symbol for science and technology's quest to destroy death or the next best thing—the fear that death instills in people. In a world in which the media spectacularizes death to the degree that "every disaster made us wish for more, for something bigger, grander, more sweeping" (*White Noise* 64), technology and television function to promote fear and to channel it. Fear is thus the underwriter of every program and commercial, which advertisers can then tap into, as Babette realizes: "It is all a corporate tie-in.... The sunscreen, the marketing, the fear, the disease. You can't have one without the other" (264). Dylar, under these conditions, is hardly a drug created for the betterment of human life. It is the ultimate product, the commodity ne plus ultra. In Dylar, the already intersecting lines of media and consumerism are fused. The drug's effects on Willie Mink (he cannot separate words/suggestion from reality) make clear the conflation of media suggestion and belief (which the novel interrogates throughout its course) with a purchased, anaesthetized consciousness. Yet "consciousness" is a misnomer, for the state Mink is in resembles in part the "mediated deaths" of the television-watching zombies, the Thanatoids, in Pynchon's *Vineland*.

Such media saturation/suggestion can help "produce" symptoms (as in Steffie's reproduction of the symptoms of exposure to Nyodene D that she hears on the radio) and thus helps in producing the kinds of conditions it hopes to treat. Later in the novel, Denise also begins to experience déjà vu, despite her religious reading of the authoritative *Physicians' Desk Reference*. Denise's susceptibility to media suggestion, however, is quite different from Steffie's reproduction of symptoms and illustrates the pharmaceutical industry's direct blurring of "education" and marketing that helps spur on the neurosis of the ever-patient customer. Denise's views of disease and disorder are filtered not only through the mainstream media but through a seemingly "official" medical book, the *Physicians' Desk Reference* (PDR), which is commonly consulted by physicians. Yet, as Leonard J. Weber point out in *Profits before People?*, "[the] information in the PDR is written by drug companies and the companies that support financially the distribution of free copies to 500,000 physicians, hospitals, and libraries." Thus, "the information in the PDR does not come from independent sources," and its "free distribution every year effectively prevents independent references from competing successfully for physician attention and use" (93). With no effective outside regulatory system (the FDA notwithstanding) or nonpartisan group with the resources to rival the PDR, much information about drugs and disorders comes to physicians and patients with a definitive corporate influence. Denise's book may be consulted by objectively minded physicians, but it has not been written by them.

To Market, to Market, to Sell a New Drug

The point here is that Dylar is not some beneficent medical/scientific project untainted by ulterior motives. The corporation that can develop a drug like Dylar stands to make an immense profit, and the pharmaceutical industry is one of the most profitable industries in the United States: as late as 2002, "the combined profits for the ten drug companies in the Fortune 500 ($35.9 billion) were more than all the other 490 businesses put together ($33.7 billion)" (Angell 11). Thus, drugs are a major commodity and are carefully developed for certain markets. The race to create new wonder drugs, like Dylar in *White Noise*, is one driven purely by profit motive, not goodwill. As Joel Lexchin writes, "the industry ... is looking for drugs that will generate annual sales in the order of at least US$500 million and preferably US$1 billion" (12).

Although the public is not the true, literal shareholder in the pharmaceutical industry, it nonetheless has its health and lives invested in it. Yet, in truth, it is the shareholders of Wall Street who hold the real stake in the industry. Their investment is pure capital, and they expect a like return on such an investment. With capital leading the way, drug research, development, production, and advertising must all be viewed with a critical eye. Furthermore, since markets are heavily influenced by the media and its promotion of fear and death, *sometimes markets can be created for certain drugs.* Babette is right: it *is* all a corporate tie-in and a knotty one at that.

In *The Truth about Drug Companies*, Marcia Angell, a former editor in chief of the *New England Journal of Medicine*, exposes many of the ethically dubious practices of the pharmaceutical industry (or "big pharma"). When drug companies create new drugs, for instance, a majority of them are "me-too" drugs (74–93). "Me-too" drugs are copies of other companies' blockbuster-selling drugs, as Zoloft and Paxil are to Prozac. Companies develop these drugs not because there are people suffering from disorders that only these drugs can alleviate but because the markets for these kinds of drugs are enormous, and there are huge profits to be made by tapping into them. Moreover, since "the market has to be large to accommodate all the competing drugs,... me-too drugs usually target very common, lifelong conditions—like arthritis or depression or high blood pressure or elevated cholesterol" (83). Thus, the pharmaceutical industry's interests lie primarily in feeding more of the same sorts of drugs into the biggest markets and promoting them with aggressive marketing (more than $3 billion a year in advertising), rather than in developing drugs that might truly help fewer people but that will not ultimately be as profitable. Considering that Gladney and many people in the West see death as a lifelong disease, Dylar is a drug that, like Prozac, could reap billions of dollars in profit. It also represents a true condemnation of life. Life or the fear of "losing" it, in effect, becomes the disease. It is a *lifelong condition* that requires medication, and that is something the pharmaceutical industry likes to see. This is one way of laying the foundation for the professional patient.

This reminder that the pharmaceutical corporations are beholden first of all to their stockholders, and not to the general public or its health, is sobering. Not only is research and development of new drugs skewed, but so is the direct-to-public advertising as well. Angell points out that "once upon a time, drug companies promoted drugs to treat diseases. Now it is often the opposite. They promote diseases to fit their drugs"

(86). Ray Moynihan and Alan Cassels make a similar point in *Selling Sickness*, stating, "Sometimes . . . the most natural and normal processes of life are being sold as medical conditions to be treated with drugs" (40). Thus, the pharmaceutical industry is in the habit of medicalizing what are common ailments of life or aging (the most recent and amusing is "restless leg syndrome") as "lifelong conditions" by expanding medical definitions, by promoting sales of brand-name drugs over generics or older drugs that may work just as well, and by sometimes outright creating a "new disorder" and "educating" (marketing) the public about it.

This is precisely the allure that Dylar has in *White Noise*: it is essentially an anxiety reducer that is in part a response to the very anxieties it seeks to assuage but that it also helps fuel. Perhaps the pharmaceutical industry's biggest triumph regarding such anxiety medication is GlaxoSmithKline's Paxil, a me-too version of Prozac that was advertised as a treatment for "social anxiety disorder." But this disorder, while severely disabling to some people, was advertised as a common and widespread one. As Paxil's product director told Barry Brand in an interview for *Advertising Age*, "Every marketer's dream is to find an unidentified or unknown market and develop it. That's what we were able to do with social anxiety disorder" (qtd. in Angell 88). Thus, it is quite clear how a drug can tap into people's fears; define, medicalize, and treat them; and further exploit them against newer and greater fears. Paxil was an enormous success and stands as the perfect example of how social and cultural anxieties are carefully tapped, channeled, marketed, administered to, cashed in on, and sent back through the spin cycle. The resulting escalation of "patient-customers" also raises questions as to the legal status of any drug and the subsequent moral dilemma and confusion among users. For instance, in *White Noise*, after Denise learns that Babette is taking Dylar, Gladney must tell her on two separate occasions that Babette is not a "drug addict" (210, 250). The issue as to the legality of certain drugs is complex, but clearly DeLillo calls attention to the fact that any *dependency* on a drug, whether it is regulated or not, is alarming when the prescription for such a drug is promoted by capital.

In the confusion and fear of a media-infused world, like the one depicted in *White Noise*, it seems near impossible to pin down where such problems are manifested. In pharmaceutical corporations' marketing of drugs and disorders such as "social anxiety disorder," write Moynihan and Cassels, their "suggest[ion] that the 'cause' of this condition lies within the individual, whether for biological or psychological reasons, clearly distracts all of us from a broader understanding of the complex sources of social anxiety—whether it is defined as a mental disorder or not.... The messages coming from the pharmaceutical industry's marketing machinery try to keep the public focus on a narrow range of chemical *solutions* to health problems. But they also keep the focus on a narrow range of *causes*" (137). In promoting drugs that easily "solve" problems such as anxiety (or, extrapolated, anxiety of mortality itself), the pharmaceutical corporations cover up their own manipulation of fears and social and cultural beliefs (about medical science and death), which is part of the problem. *White Noise*, however, in its playful juggling of "causes" allows us to see the way the spheres of culture and capital overlap and inform each other. The novel's exploration of the larger cultural and social forces at work in creating certain problems strips away the promise offered by such simple, cause-and-effect solutions as popping a pill to cure one's ills.

This dubious nature of the pharmaceutical industry and its motivations for the development of certain drugs is most prevalent, in *White Noise*, in the figure of Willie Mink. Mink is termed "a controversial fellow" by Winnie, who relates to Gladney Mink's dismissal from the company that created Dylar and his subsequent illicit research (299). Furthermore, Mink's sketchy research methods and his peculiar insider/outsider, marginalized status also makes him perhaps an early figure for the rise of biotech companies, which now conduct much of the research and development once carried on by big pharma, in response to the changing structures of the pharmaceutical industry during the 1970s and 1980s (Kaplan 41–47). In any case, Winnie believes that the industry's problems are singular (Mink's fault), not systemic, telling Jack that the multinational corporation Mink once worked for has a "code of ethics, just like you and me" (300). These "ethics," however, are no more than the corporation's covering itself legally due to Mink's irregular research techniques (his tabloid ads and hotel interviews). At first, Mink is "reprimanded," and "they [the corporation] put all their resources into computer testing"; yet even after Mink "is kicked out, the project goes on without him" (300). Mink's illicit research can be conducted at the edges of legitimacy in an industry that may well want to keep such potentially dangerous research at arm's length, putting its energies into marketing, production, and distribution instead—the business side of pharmaceuticals.

Corporate "ethics" are hardly concerned with the effects of a drug that, as Winnie puts it, "is totally ... untested and unapproved, with side effects that could beach a whale" (300), unless it entails the testing of a dangerous prototype on a human subject who has recourse to the legal system if something goes wrong. Premature testing leads to lawsuits, and that is what the company is most concerned with, though many companies find ways of sidestepping such unfavorable results.[5] The "further computer testing" on the fear of death combined with the "death profile" that Mink creates for each of his subjects can easily account for SIMUVAC's electronic "file" on Gladney: "I wondered what he meant when he said he'd tapped into my history. Where was it located exactly? Some state or federal agency, some insurance company or credit firm or medical clearinghouse?" (140). There is a fair possibility that SIMUVAC is (part of) the corporation that has been researching Dylar. As Douglas Keesey reminds us, SIMUVAC is also a company with commercial interests invested in disaster and death (143–144). Just as the company researching Dylar is interested in creating "death profiles" to assist its research and plot its marketing strategies, so too is SIMUVAC engaged in inputting the profiles of its potential "customers" (victims). To suggest that the companies are one and the same would not be too fantastic. Regardless, the Dylar project is ongoing, and Mink's premature and failed prototype is not the last that will be seen of this type of drug. And when the breakthrough is finally achieved, when Dylar 2.0 hits the pharmacist's shelves and thirty-second spots on television, it will not be long until the copycats, the me-too drugs, abound.

Gladney's refusal near the novel's end to respond to Dr. Chakravarty's calls represents both the continuation of his fear of death and his refusal to play the perpetual patient that modern medicine demands: "He [Dr. Chakravarty] is eager to see how my death is progressing.... He wants to insert me once more in the imaging block.... But I am afraid of the imaging block. Afraid of its magnetic fields, its computerized nuclear pulse. Afraid of what it knows about me" (325). To resist becoming the permanent patient is in a sense symbolically to resist reification, but it is far too late to reverse the process. Nor can this process be reversed if one still holds the belief that "every death is premature'" (283), for then it is subject to medical science's machinery, which ultimately blurs the distinction between health and illness, turning life into a neo-Kierkegaardian "sickness unto death." By now, Gladney has already become a computer image, and the machine boasts the very qualities of human life that technology denies him—knowledge and "a pulse." Screaming in horror like Ivan Ilyich, as Murray mentions early in the novel, would do Gladney no good either. That would mean believing in the terrifying otherness of death and its power to shock, when such is not the case with a preprogrammed death. Besides, what else are the bracketed stars next to one's name on the computer printout if not the indication of an electronic scream?

Postmodern death for Gladney is ineffable in the end, and rightly so since it is computerized, a binary code of ones and zeroes, as he recognizes at the novel's conclusion: "The terminals [at the supermarket] are equipped with holographic scanners, which decode the binary secret of every item, infallibly. This is the language of radiation, or how the dead speak to the living" (326). Tom LeClair reads this ending as "uncertain," even though Gladney's "words imply he may be ready to accept the uncertain activity below the surface of our perceptions, activity that may—and only may—mean that the world of the living and the world of the dead are not wholly separate, closed off" (229). As we have seen, however, the dead and the living are completely separated not because of the imposition of any subjective belief system about death but because of the structures of late capitalist society itself. The scientific, technological, and economic principles that mediate lives also mediate deaths. Modern medicine, because it cannot "heal" death, must turn life into a constant preparation for it, essentially killing life before death can. If Gladney were to believe in the interconnectedness of life and death, it would be yet another faith he has "bought into." Perhaps this is what Gladney finally learns in the supermarket: that his choice of death can be purchased too. Whatever conclusion Gladney may reach, however, it can have no effect on the fact that his death is technologically accounted for, nor can it promise him that when the next Dylar comes along—extensively tested, safe, and FDA approved—he will not reach for its bottle on the nearest supermarket shelf.

5 / Family Incorporated: William Gaddis's *J R* and the Embodiment of Capitalism

The chaotic and discordant world portrayed in William Gaddis's *J R* is one against which not even the family can offer comfort or safe haven. In a novel composed mainly of fragmented speech, in which people break promises, ethical codes, and hearts, it is hardly surprising to discover the various families in *J R* frequently broken or breaking up as well. While novels published after *J R* (1975), such as *White Noise* (1985) and *Gain* (1998), have had time to absorb and adjust to the shocks of a thoroughly postmodernized family, the family structure in *J R* appears to be fractured beyond repair. Indeed, Dan diCepahlis's crumbling house is an apt metaphor for all the "houses" or families in the novel. Their construction is tenuous, and they are all either falling apart or in danger of doing so.

The only family that truly thrives in the novel, regardless of its ultimate disassembly, is eleven-year-old J R Vansant's—not, of course, J R's actual family but the "Family of Companies" that flourishes after he starts a corporation from a phone booth at his elementary school. Because Gaddis closely ties the fortunes of families to family "fortunes," however, a curious relationship develops between the growth of J R's Family of Companies and the dissolution of the "traditional" nuclear family in the novel. By adopting the discourse of the family and family relations, J R's business model effectively conflates the "public" world of business with the "private" world of the family. This intertwining of business and family is hardly new to capitalism—it is vital to it—yet young J R's crossing of the discourses between these two usually separate spheres indicates something remarkably new in capitalism's ongoing expansion at the dawn of the neoliberal age. For through the discourse of the family, capitalism is given a metaphorical body in the figure of the multinational corporation, granted all legal rights pertaining to it, and is subsequently adopted into a newly imagined global family. What begins, then, as a diversification or decentering of capital itself, a telling instance of its flux and tendency to destabilize various institutions, is later recaptured by the comforting image and discourse of the family, which recasts such potentially troubling revelations under the signs of stability (the family structure) and autonomy (individual family members).

The invention of J R's Family of Companies, then, is one of J R's most innovative capitalist strategies because it radically "capitalizes" on the structural changes occurring in the American economy during the 1970s, which demanded a more dynamic and fluid mode of production than earlier economic and business models allowed for. In response to the stagnation of a Keynesian model of capitalism, which had been in place since the New Deal and demanded strict monetary policy, careful regulation of business and financial markets, and active government spending, proponents of a new mode of capitalist production, neoliberalism, argued for, and eventually won, the liberalization of capital through massive deregulations in industries and financial markets and a weakening of government in its ability to spend and to oversee business as usual. J R resurrects an older corporate image construction (the family) at this key transitional moment in capitalism and revitalizes it. Just as an increasingly unfettered capitalism continues to give rise to greater social instability, J R seizes on an image, perhaps *the* image, of "traditional values" that promises to stabilize and counteract this crisis.

J R ultimately suggests that the use of this family discourse by corporations is a way in which capitalism incorporates or embodies itself and that this incorporation comes at the expense of not only nations but individuals and individual social relations as well. At the same time that capitalism is embodied in and imagined as a transnational corporate family, individuals themselves are disembodied, and social institutions, such as marriage and the family, find their bodies or structures transfigured and transformed—and not so much consumed but increasingly *produced* by the irrepressible flow of capital.

(Dys)functional Families

J R's absorbing family drama can be placed firmly within the tradition of novels centered on troubled families, in which the family often holds a metonymic relationship to the larger nation and world it inhabits.

Similar to how William Faulkner, in both *The Sound and the Fury* (1929) and *Absalom, Absalom!* (1936), mixes the Compson family history with that of the South and antebellum America itself in the petri dish of Yoknapatawpha County, Gaddis situates the families in *J R*, whether they realize it or not, at the heart of debates regarding democracy, free enterprise, and national identity or, as one refrain in the novel puts it, "what America's all about." In this focus on complicated family history, *J R* shares something with the sweeping works of Dostoyevsky and Tolstoy too—in particular *The Possessed* (1872) and *War and Peace* (1869), respectively—in which families find themselves imbricated in the pressing historical and political struggles of czarist Russia. *J R*, however, in its sketch of transnational corporate power, necessarily steps outside such national boundaries, thus opening up an increasingly confusing and entropic American experience to a global perspective. That the family ties in Gaddis's *J R* are even more complex and far-reaching than in the aforementioned novels comes, perhaps, as no surprise since it is the first novel to emphasize the crucial connection between the family and an emerging late capitalist world-system.

What is so unique about *J R*'s fractured families, therefore, lies much deeper than the mere representation of various dysfunctional family models. To be sure, the novel has its share of absentee fathers, adulterers, questions concerning paternity, and even quasi-incestuous relationships. The plot, for instance, begins with the death of one father, Thomas Bast, and the absence of another, James Bast, who, as long-bickering brothers, held equal shares in the General Roll Company, the ownership of which is consequently in dispute. One potential heir, Edward Bast (the "bastard" product of James's affair with Thomas's second wife), may be able to lay claim to parenthood with Thomas instead of James due to his parents' dubious marital status at the time of his birth. This "paternal shift" would entitle Edward to half the shares in General Roll that his cousin/sister, Stella, is eager to secure after Thomas's recent death. However, the "Law of the Father" founders here as the lawyer Coen's exasperated efforts to settle the matter with James's sisters, Anne and Julia, fail to assert the legal status of Edward's paternity. As Coen tells one of the sisters, "The law seeks order, Miss Bast. Order!" (8). But without James's physically being present to "defend" his half of the company, and with Edward's paternal ties in question, the state of General Roll and the Bast family is thrown into complete disorder.

Joining James Bast in the ranks of absentee fathers are Monty Montcrieff, the head of Typhon International, and the young J R Vansant's unnamed father. Montcrieff has rarely given his time and attention to his daughter, Amy, or his mentally disabled son, Freddie, whom he has shunted away in some kind of hospital. Amy says to the family lawyer, Beaton, regarding her father, "he couldn't take a moment to speak to me to, even to ask how I am there's always a meeting an important meeting he hides in meetings" (211). As for young J R Vansant, the implication is that he may never even have met his father. His mother, he tells Bast, is a nurse working irregular hours (134), and J R's disheveled appearance and threadbare clothing indicate a less-than-satisfactory home life. As Amy tells Jack, "[He] . . . looks as though he lives in a home without, I don't know. Without grownups" (246).

What truly distinguishes the most compelling families in the novel, however, are their significant relationships with big business, the Basts in General Roll and the Montcrieffs in Typhon. This, perhaps, should not come as a surprise since roughly 80 to 90 percent of all businesses in the United States are "family owned," which generally means "that decisions about their [businesses'] management or ownership are influenced by family" (Dyer 3). Gaddis's choice, then, to bring together family and business in *J R* is shrewd, intended in some degree to uncover the relationship between social and economic structures in an explicit way.

This connection, moreover, frustrates an easy condemnation of capitalism in the novel because a social and human face is offered in addition to the faceless and monstrous economic forces that capitalism unleashes. *The Octopus* and *The Crying of Lot 49* offered some not-so-friendly human faces supposedly in charge of such forces, and *J R* has its share of those; but the novel also introduces us to the case of Norman Angel, who Christopher J. Knight argues "is a good man" (99). Along with the co-owner of General Roll, Thomas, Angel "never lost interest in what they were doing, so that profits were never the first interest, especially for Angel" (Knight 99). With regard to family-run businesses, Angel represents the second generation (not by blood but by marriage) that must take over after the passing of the first generation. This is a common occurrence in family businesses and a time in which the business finds itself in a moment of crisis. W. Gibbs Dyer writes that "the founder's departure from active participation creates a power vacuum in the business and in the board that family and nonfamily members eagerly rush to fill" (81). In *J R*, this power vacuum is made all the more intense by the absence of James. The race by several characters to fill this void, though it may seem motivated purely by greed, is a necessity if the business is to survive this crisis. Understood in this context, Angel's explanation to

Coen of his motivations in securing as many shares as possible to prevent General Roll from going public appears legitimate: "Can't you see this is what's going to happen right here, after all it took to put all this together? Can't you see you go public and all these people owning you want is dividends and running their stock up, you don't give them that and they sell you out, you do and some bunch of vice presidents . . . , they spot you and launch an offer and all of a sudden you're working for them" (359). Angel's fears are well founded, for what is really at stake is the passing of the private family business to the public arena, or turning the private into the public.

Angel wants, echoing the sentiments of the would-be artists in the novel, "to keep it [the company] doing something that's, that's worth doing" (359). For General Roll is not a multinational corporation, and Angel and other family members have invested not only capital but also creative energies into making the business a success. Angel's experience of the family business is one in which social (family) relations are a key aspect, and the making and exchange of commodities is less important than are the autonomy to make decisions and the immediate gratification of creative labor. Certainly, Angel, in his role as capitalist entrepreneur, perpetuates the exploitative capitalist system as a whole, but not nearly to the same degree as a ruthless multinational corporation, such as Typhon. More importantly, he still retains a sense of ethics in business, as many small-business owners and family-run businesses are able to do. To go public with the company, however, is to open up the General Roll Corporation *exclusively* to the bottom line.

This explanation does not let Angel off the Marxist hook, however. It could be that his plea for keeping the business "in the family" represents merely a rhetoric of sentimentality and nostalgia that masks self-serving ends (which is precisely how J R employs such rhetoric of the family, as we shall see). While Angel appears to hold the belief that what he and the business stand for is more than profit, he may well have reduced Stella and himself to commodity status by their very marriage. This marriage, a proven failure, could well have been initiated in order to "keep the business in the family," a central concern of Angel's.[1] Nor can Angel's ethical stance toward business ensure the fair treatment of others. Since businesses' leaders and objectives change over time, and capitalism itself is amoral, there is nothing to ensure that today's benign company cannot become tomorrow's Enron, just as the "family-run" Callahan Auto Parts may become the next Zalinsky's in *Tommy Boy*. Indeed, if one does not ascribe to the "play to win" philosophy of capitalism so prevalent in *J R*, then the only remaining options for a growth-stalled company are bankruptcy or being purchased and incorporated into another. As the arch-capitalist Pierce Inverarity puts it in *The Crying of Lot 49*, the trick to capitalism is to "keep it bouncing, . . . that's all the secret, keep it bouncing" (148).

Typhon, unlike the smaller, privately owned General Roll, is a publicly traded multinational corporation, and those who run it make sure to "keep it bouncing" purely by a tenacious pursuit of profit. Montcrieff sums it up, telling J R and his classmates, "as long as you're in the game you may as well play to win" (*J R* 107). Typhon has, to pluralize an Adam Smith term, its "invisible hands" in the government and has gone so far as to incite a revolution in Gambia. Yet Typhon International, while wielding much more power and influence than General Roll does, nonetheless retains some features of a family-run business, though this appears to be the result of nepotism and cronyism. Outside of blood relation, even Zona (a chief executive), although she is not blood related, is an old friend of the family and holds a top executive position because of it. She is basically "part of the family," as is Beaton, the company's lawyer, whose father once worked for Cates.

Not surprisingly, Typhon's and the J R Corporation's business strategies also involve the exchange of people as goods. Montcrieff and Cates encourage Amy to marry Dick Cutler solely for business purposes. Early in the novel, Amy claims, "that would be like, like marrying your issue of six percent preferreds" (214), but Cates and Beaton imply, probably rightly, that Lucien married Amy for her financial assets (102). Yet even Amy submits and marries Cutler in the end for financial and emotional stability. And J R, not to be outdone by his teachers, tries (unsuccessfully) to convince Bast to marry Boody Selk, Zona's spoiled daughter, for her holdings, in a merger-marriage that would ironically wed J R's Family of Companies to Typhon International (657).

As human beings are reified and exchanged in marriage as a means to financial ends, it becomes impossible to distinguish genuine human emotion from calculated business strategy. As Amy complains to Beaton, who tells her not to "make an emotional issue" of Typhon's using her for a tax avoidance scheme, "Well it is! It is an emotional issue it simply is! because, because there aren't any, there aren't any emotions it's all just reinvested dividends and tax avoidance that's what all of it is, avoidance the way it's always been" (212). Amy's statement here unveils how capitalism promotes the idea that the domestic sphere is separate from the economic sphere, while in reality the two are inextricably bound up with each other.

Knight identifies this attempt to separate social institutions from one another as a key problem in capitalism, which the novel lays bare: "It is the belief that society's components can be bracketed, so that its ethical and religious beliefs are assigned one space, its culture and arts another space, and its laws of business a third. . . . [Yet] the consequence is that one order—exchange value—begins to hold sway over others" (86). Thus, what *J R* does, in part, is challenge the concept of the family as a "natural" social institution where members can share genuine feelings of love and support—and which is supposedly a separate sphere from the world of capital—by showing how it is ultimately subject to the rules of the market itself. The "private" world of the family and human emotion is always already subordinate to the public world of capital. Gaddis, by focusing on families that are involved in building companies and corporations (and not merely working for them), is able to gain a more complex and nuanced view of capitalism's merging of these spheres and its disavowal of doing so. In regard to representing the family, then, Gaddis is concerned with the ways in which ideas of the family are socially constructed, in addition to how and why those constructions fail. Marx and Engels once claimed that the bourgeoisie had "torn away from the family its sentimental veil, and . . . reduced the family relation to a mere money relation" ("Manifesto" 476). The same could be said of *J R*'s treatment of families, though it also heralds the arrival of a new kind of family on the block.

From Family to Family Inc.

In creating his Family of Companies, J R realizes the socially constructed aspect of a family and applies it directly to the world of capital. J R, in one sense, creates the J R Corporation because he has no real family. J R's early interactions with Edward Bast show him searching for a kind of father figure, a potential relationship that by the end of the novel has been somewhat inverted, with J R playing a more paternal role to the hapless Bast. J R constantly strings Bast along with promises of future gains and by playing on his sense of guilt: "I mean like I have to do practically everything myself, like I set all this up to try and help you out so you can do your work and all and you don't even . . ." (466; ellipsis in original). Davidoff, a corporate PR man, tells Bast, J R "really looks after you" (538), and while one can construe this paternal metaphor as entirely ironic, it nonetheless contains a degree of truth. Although J R is always looking to use Bast to his advantage, he attempts to keep him happy in more ways than just throwing money at him. Setting up a foundation so that Bast can pursue his music shows at least some thought and affection on J R's part.

J R soon comes to understand his paternal role as founder of the J R Family of Companies, expressing a certain pride in fatherhood to Bast: "the paper's always saying the parent this the parent that I mean that's me the parent!" (653–654). Earlier in the novel, J R hears the lore surrounding Cates during his class's visit to Typhon, where Davidoff proclaims that Cates is "one of your country's outstanding Americans," whom "presidents come to for advice" (91). This image apparently sticks with J R, and after recognizing his new fatherhood, he borrows another page from the business playbook of Montcrieff and Cates by hiring Davidoff to create an image of J R-the-Man. Always canny when it comes to business, J R realizes the importance of creating an image of the company's founder that projects the kinds of qualities he wants associated with the J R Family of Companies as a whole. Building the image of a founder, then, constitutes the first step in building an image of a corporation.

The image of J R that Davidoff constructs is precise and is tailored mainly to J R's specifications. J R highlights some of its features as he reads articles about "himself" to Bast. J R is "a man of vision" with a "bulldog jaw" (650), and "men who have worked with him ... for years say his chief characteristics are enormous powers of concentration and dogged persistence in attacking a problem" (651). Yet he also embodies "a mysterious thing which is hard to identify, the vital creative force of the whole J R Family of Companies" (651). In a women's magazine, he embodies "this masculine image for this here feminine reader" (651). Such mythologizing successfully deifies J R by emphasizing traditional masculine and paternal ideals—ruggedness, determination, physical strength, virility, and potency—and melding them with suggestions of mystical and seminal energies.

Davidoff's creation is highly indebted to the popular understanding of various wealthy industrialists, from Carnegie to Ford, who, in their Horatio Alger–like tales of triumph, seem to radiate such hard-nosed and God-given "American" qualities. In typical fashion, however, J R reverses the established order of such mythologizing. As Davidoff says, J R "thinks his own success story may rub off on the company and vice versa" (516). A captain of industry of old would have, so to speak, *made* a name for himself through his business success—first the triumph, then the recognition and retro-mythologizing/whitewashing. Take Pierce Inverarity from *Lot 49*, once again: he refers to himself as a "founding father" (15), yet this distinction is troubled by the "whitewashed bust of

Jay Gould" that he keeps over his bed (1). J R, intuitively aware of how such images of founders have functioned in the story of capitalism (and needing a fictional body to serve as a founder, since he is literally a child), completely fabricates an image that will function, ideologically, *as part of the corporation itself*. True, J R's dealings have been lucrative, and he has created a formidable (though dangerously leveraged) corporation, but he is hardly a well-established, venerable name in the business world. Yet, in an America increasingly obsessed with images (especially of success), there is an audience hungry for such reassuring and inspirational stories of personal triumph.

More importantly, the audience for such stories is composed not merely of the American public but of the business world as well, which has increasingly come to rely on a CEO's "image" as a kind of barometer for the fortunes of the corporation itself. As Robert B. Reich notes in *Supercapitalism* apropos of the changes in the role of CEOs since the 1970s, "Annual shareholder meetings were [in the 1950s and 1960s] perfunctory affairs where CEOs offered well-scripted little presentations, took a few questions, and departed. Today's CEO engages in an ongoing effort—in person, on the phone, in meetings and formal presentations—to reassure major investors, impress Wall Street analysts, and assuage any worries of bankers and credit-rating agencies" (75). In a postmodern world where the sign often trumps what is signified, *J R* heralds *the importance of a CEO's image to the corporation itself*, anticipating the sort of superstar CEO of the past twenty-five years or so, from Steve Jobs to Ken Lay and Michael Eisner.

This particular masculine-gendered construction of J R-as-CEO is the perfect image not only because it projects a charismatic figure more and more essential for investor confidence but also because J R needs this figure to be perceived as a "father" of a "Family of Companies." As Davidoff remarks to Bast at one point, "Boss [is] pushing the family image" (538). What J R hopes to "rub off on the company" is the image of a strong and virile patriarch in charge of his family and able to increase and maintain it. For the family image—modeled after the "traditional" nuclear family in its patriarchal hierarchy—is the *overall* image J R strives to create for his corporation. Thus, while the image of a driven and trustworthy CEO suggests a company's toughness and reliability, retaining these qualities while allying them with the warmth and security of a family offers something else entirely.

J R is not the first to use the rhetoric of family to create an image of the corporation as a kind of paternal and benevolent being, however.

In *Creating the Corporate Soul: The Rise of Public Relations and Corporate Imagery in American Big Business*, Roland Marchand traces the genesis of corporate image construction in advertising from the end of the nineteenth century to the beginning of World War II. As Marchand demonstrates through a close reading of an array of advertisements and corporate propaganda, the twentieth century saw corporations being more image conscious than ever, eager to sweep away the negative reputations they had rightfully earned during the previous century by creating a "soul" for what the public perceived as a soulless institution. Indeed, images, such as the monstrous one Frank Norris appropriated in *The Octopus*, appear to have been on the minds of corporate leaders during this period. For example, one GM executive asked, in 1922, whether it was possible to represent the company "not as resembling an octopus, but as being the parent of a large and creditable family" (qtd. in Marchand 103). The GM executive's question makes clear the prevalence of the family image that corporations chose to put forth around this time. The family image, however, found an equal competitor in military or army metaphors that stressed the efficiency, discipline, and collective effort of both a company's business strategy and its relationship with, and constitution of, its workforce (Marchand 103). Not surprisingly, in response to the growing social unrest and labor disputes of the 1930s, the military metaphors in corporate rhetoric became scarce. In their place, the family metaphor spread as "public relation officers began to cultivate a new kind of family image for the corporation—one that stressed identifiable individual employee families, real or fictional" (107). Ultimately, "the family's relations were more intimate than a team's, and its bonds of loyalty deeper and less situational, while the father's moral authority was greater than that of any coach" (107).

In regard to image making, then, J R is one step ahead of Cates, Montcrieff, and Typhon International. Montcrieff, whom Davidoff earlier fashions into an "an aggressive competitive team player" (*J R* 95) in a bio piece, relies on a sports metaphor to convey his image. In the "play to win" business world of *J R*, a sports metaphor stressing teamwork and competition seems quite apt, but J R goes out of his way to avoid using this metaphor in his company's rhetoric. Davidoff instructs Beamish not to "try the team player image no play with this family of companies angle divisional autonomy" (529–530). By promoting a family image, J R keeps the companies he buys and controls feeling a certain (false) sense of autonomy, as well as a sense of security in relation to the Family of Companies as a whole. A "family" of companies headed by a reliable patriarch creates a far more alluring image than does the sports metaphor, with its potentially negative aspects of overcompetitiveness and victory at all costs. A team can be held together by familial-like bonds, but it is always fighting another team, whereas a family can forever grow and extend itself, incorporating others not by beating and humiliating them but by "wedding" them.

Moreover, J R's use of the family image is no mere resurrection of an earlier advertising strategy. Just as the family image that corporations once projected was subject to change amid shifting economic conditions in the 1930s, so too do the economic particularities of the 1970s (*J R* was published in 1975) affect the *kind* of family image that J R constructs. For instance, when pre–World War II corporations employed the images and rhetoric of the family, there was often a kind of commitment to a paternal ideal behind the obvious façade. In an age in which "welfare capitalism" sought to atone for much of the brutality of nineteenth-century industrialism, corporate benefits, such as pensions and stock-sharing programs, became the norm. Such paternalistic ideals lasted, in one form or another, into the decades following World War II; though combined with a new age of American prosperity, the corporate family dream seemed a much realer possibility to many people (Reich 25). Under such conditions, labor was able to work with business, in a way hitherto unparalleled, to establish secure jobs, wages, and benefits for many workers—concessions that corporations saw as ultimately benefiting their own stabilized business expectations. Thus, corporations often functioned as if they were citizens somewhat beholden to the communities in which they existed—they not only employed entire towns but paid a fair amount of taxes that benefited the communities in which they put up stakes. Corporations could use the rhetoric of family and strive to create a family image, and, in a limited sense, there was still a kind of reciprocity and paternalism in the relationship between business, on the one hand, and labor and the public, on the other.

Thus, when the upheavals in social and economic conditions during the 1970s—such as the failure of Keynesian economics, the rise of "stagflation," and the Arab oil embargo in 1973—drastically changed American businesses, corporate paternalism (whatever its actual merits) became largely a thing of the past. As David Harvey argues in *The Condition of Postmodernity*, a new kind of economic structure arose during this period—which Harvey calls "flexible accumulation" (essentially his term for the shift to a postindustrial, global economy)—marking the end of mass production, or "Fordism," in "developed" nations, such as the United States and Great Britain.[2] Harvey links this transition from Fordism to flexible accumulation with certain resulting "postmodern" social and cultural formations. In short, as flexible accumulation (we might comparably say globalization or neoliberalism) took hold, a further fracturing and fragmentation of various social and cultural structures resulted, such as the decline of working-class labor movements, the growth of suburbs, and the decentralizing of corporations and capital from nations (175–179). This left a large amount of people without the safety nets of earlier decades—jobs that were well paid, secure, and provided good benefits, for instance—and gave rise to anxiety and fear for the future. Yet, Harvey writes, "as [Georg] Simmel . . . long ago suggested, it is also at such times of fragmentation and economic insecurity that the desire for stable values leads to a heightened emphasis upon the authority of basic institutions—the family, religion, the state" (171). In a postmodern world, however, *images* of such "basic institutions" function even better than the changing institutions themselves. As Harvey writes, "Corporations, governments, political and intellectual leaders, all value a stable (though dynamic) image as part of their aura of authority and power. The mediatization of politics has now become all pervasive. This becomes, in effect, the fleeting, superficial, and illusory means whereby an individualistic society of transients sets forth its nostalgia for common values" (288).

In this context, it becomes clear that J R's Family of Companies is not merely another example of a grand narrative trumpeting the triumph of laissez-faire American capitalism but a specific example of a company responding to, and benefiting from, the constantly evolving capitalist system. J R's Family of Companies succeeds at this crucial moment in capital's restructuring because it, too, is dynamic and malleable: it both responds to the new fluidity of the emerging neoliberal economy and projects a nostalgic and comforting image as an ideological cover for the drastic changes in social, cultural, and political life that are a major result of these economic changes.

J R's purchase and dismantlement of Eagle Mills in the aptly named town of Union Falls, for instance, is entirely symbolic of both the economic shift from Fordism to flexible accumulation *and* the resulting shift in the rhetoric and image of the corporation as a family. Eagle Mills is "one of the oldest textile mills in the region and mainstay of the Union Falls economy for more than a century" and has been run by men such as "president Fred Hopper, who has . . . served on Eagle Mills' Board of Directors since nineteen twenty-eight" (*J R* 293). The town also holds

148 / FAMILY INCORPORATED

picnics on company property, and the company softball team's weekly games constitute one of the town's favorite social functions. Union Falls represents the classic one-company town that, as we have seen in *Gung Ho*'s Hadleyville, has had a long and involved relationship with a corporation.

Thus, when J R institutes the first of several measures aimed at gutting the company to increase profits and cash flow elsewhere, which leads to the destruction of the town (660), Bast chastises him: "These are real people up there. . . . A lot of them who owned the stock still can't believe it's not worth anything and even the ones who owned bonds, a lot of them are old and when they first bought the bonds it was almost like they were lending money to, to someone in the family" (296). Bast's defense of the people of Union Falls uncovers the assumptions that honest people could, at one time, make about companies they believed were trustworthy and ethical in their goals. For the sense of a company being a family is one that capitalism has always perpetuated at the local or community level, where smaller businesses stay in touch with their clientele (not to mention the more "paternal" corporations noted by Marchand [pre–World War II] and Reich [mainly post–World War II to the 1970s]). What is remarkable about the people in Union Falls is their capacity to believe that a large corporation was looking out for their best interests and nothing more.

For these people, Eagle Mills *is* like a family. But believing a company is *like* a family is not the same as its actually being one, as the employees tragically learn after J R's takeover, which is itself representative of the predominance of the new economy stressing flexible accumulation. Sleepy Union Falls, still dreaming of post–World War II prosperity, receives a rude awakening at the dawn of a new era of deregulated capitalism. Ironically enough, Bast's speech may be the moment that the perceptive J R realizes the power of the family metaphor, and this "almost like" is what J R will exploit in his Family of Companies in a way that no corporation before the 1970s could have imagined.

Considering that J R will, as a sign of the times, utterly destroy many of the companies he "adopts" into his Family of Companies, he cultivates the family image to assuage any fears of such an occurrence *at the corporate level itself.* To be sure, J R's business tactics are as brutal as Typhon's, but they are well disguised. The family image actually helps win J R support from Mister Brisboy and his mother, owners of a chain of funeral homes. Mister Brisboy confides in Bast, "it's all so exciting . . . , being asked to join your family of companies Mother feels that's what we need and she's never really been one for family" (544). For the Brisboys, the allure of independence and familial safety clearly woos them to "join" J R's family. Hence, J R's use of the family image projects a warm and friendly image not only to a confused and frightened public but also to an increasingly guarded and suspicious business world, wary of just the kind of hostile takeovers regularly engaged in by corporations like J R's and Typhon International.

Furthermore, the case of Eagle Mills illustrates how, as deregulation and privatization increasingly became government policy, the resulting tsunami of capital fostered the kind of cutthroat capitalism of the 1970s and 1980s (so meticulously depicted and predicted in *J R*), wherein companies began to swallow one another up in an age of increasing corporate monopolies spurred on by corporate raiding, LBOs (leveraged buyouts), and megamergers, all of which played a part in triggering the S&L crisis and stock-market crash of 1987. Poised at the onset of this new age of corporate cannibalism, *J R* shows that old advertising strategies take on new and ever more dynamic and troubling facets in the age of global capital. Thus, whereas earlier corporate images of the family may have had some modicum of truth to them, J R's is *wholly* an image. And whereas corporations once projected such images mainly to change *the public's* perception of business and to ensure worker loyalty, *J R broadens* his audience to include shareholders and other companies too.

Corporate Imagi-Nation

By offering companies, employees, and customers the image of a Family of Companies, J R is creating an "imagined community" in Benedict Anderson's sense of the term. In *Imagined Communities*, Anderson argues that the nation is "an imagined political community," and such imagined communities "are to be distinguished, not by their falsity/ genuineness, but by the style in which they are imagined" (6). J R's Family of Companies, as false and abhorrent as it may be, can be seen to function in a similar way to such a community. It is surely an imagined community/family for the companies it owns (as seen in Eagle Mills and the Brisboys' funeral homes), as well as for its employees, which even Eigen, a struggling writer, acknowledges when he complains that "these companies are so damned paternalistic with their deferred stock options retirement plans insurance medical benefits they finally have you tied hand and foot" (*J R* 261).

If corporations can foster an imagined family relationship with their employees, entire towns (such as Union Falls), and other companies too, then the potential of J R's imagined family could be or, according to the logic of capitalism, *must* be limitless. And the remaining element in such an expansion is the consumer, whom Davidoff considers a stockholder or stakeholder (even if he or she actually holds no stock) in the company. Davidoff mentions how affixing each of J R's companies' goods with the "parent company logo audience knows it's dealing with a reliable dependable outfit builds your stockholder relationships see it someplace and they feel a nice warmth like somebody in the family just died" (536). His reasoning here is telling in that logos and brand building do as much ideological work, if not more so, on consumers as they do on stockholders.

The implied conflation of consumer and stockholder here recalls the booming lecture given in *Network* by the CEO, Arthur Jensen, in which he describes a utopian capitalist world composed of "one vast and ecumenical holding company, for whom all men will work to serve a common profit, in which all men will hold a share of stock." Davidoff's vision, like Jensen's, conveniently mystifies the (purse) strings of power. In this case, the "stock" that all men hold is not of the common or preferred variety; it is a *figurative stock*, meaning the stockholders/public must "serve" by necessity a system or corporation that has complete influence over all aspects of society—it is a "holding company" indeed—but against which they have no individual say in any decision-making process, socially, politically, or culturally.

The direct appeal to these potential consumer-citizens underscores this point. One of the ads for a J R company reads as follows: "Alsaka Development working day and night to bring the American family its full share of the world's energy. Alsaka. A proud member of the J R Family of Companies. When you see a product. A service. A promise of human betterment for all. If it's J R. It's Just Right. J R. An American family of American com . . ." (578; ellipsis in original). The conflation of nation and corporation here rightly signals the growing power of corporations like J R's that now proclaim their nationality (to a specific national audience) in a global context/market and make themselves appear necessary for the allocation of basic goods and services, which government, that toothless, old, flag-waving patriot, cannot properly ensure.

Thus, when Major Hyde (the Endo corporation man attempting to capitalize on grammar schools via implementing closed-circuit television) asserts, "the only place left for loyalty if you got any's the company that's paving your way, when my company says jump I jump!" (455), he indicates that the conflation of nation and corporation that J R's Family helps to bring about is perhaps mainly a *replacement* of national identity with corporate identity, unbeknown to the consumer-citizen. Here, then, arises another dynamic aspect of J R's family image amid the mutation of global capitalism: imagining America becomes imagining J R's Family.

In other words, *J R* represents an early fictional representation of the apparent power of corporations eclipsing that of nation-states. This notion is given a fresh turn in Michael Hardt and Antonio Negri's *Empire*, in which the authors theorize "Empire," a concept tracing the decline or changes in the sovereignty of nation-states that "has taken a new form, composed of a series of national and supranational organisms united under one single logic of rule" (xii). They contend that "the activities of corporations are no longer defined by the imposition of abstract command and organization of simple theft and unequal exchange. Rather, they directly structure and articulate territories and populations. They tend to make nation-states merely instruments to record the flows of commodities, monies, and populations that they set in motion" (31). This is certainly true of the corporations in *J R*, with Typhon International leading the way. The J R Family of Companies, in contrast, never quite reaches the status of a multinational by the time it collapses, but its advertisements and business strategies are clearly treating America itself as a map on which to record various potential economic flows. Moreover, the movement of the J R Family by the novel's end is toward a complete control over life and death. Hardt and Negri, employing Foucault's notion of biopower, explain how economic powers, such as corporations, "within the biopolitical context ... produce needs, social relations, bodies, and minds" (32). So deep does biopolitical production run that "the whole social body is comprised by power's machine and developed in its virtuality.... Power is thus expressed as a control that extends throughout the depths of the consciousnesses and bodies of the population—and at the same time across the entirety of social relations" (24).

The tendency toward biopolitical production can be seen in two ways in the J R Family: first, in the J R Family's scheme to create, in Davidoff's words, "A Personalized Plan from Nave to Grave" (519); and second, via the extension of the imagined J R Family onto an imagined America. One of J R's last business deals is to acquire a string of nursing homes, which he hopes to tie in to the Brisboys' Wagner Funeral Homes (516–517). Davidoff calls the plan a "Health Package," evidently because the pharmaceutical company Nobili will be brought on board to supply prescription drugs to customers. Davidoff sums up the package as a "funeral right through the cemetery with the drug line nursing home tie-in" (519).

J R's "health package" is even more insidious in its cool calculation than is the pharmaceutical industry's influence on people's concepts of life and death in DeLillo's *White Noise*. Such an all-encompassing scheme takes corporate power and applies it *directly* to the bodies of individuals, but in such a subtle way—it is for the care and benefit of one's own body and life—that it makes the individual's "choice" to join the plan a "necessary" one.

If this were not chilling enough, J R reveals to Bast the full implications of his plan: "I mean like banks we could have these different kind of banks like this regular bank and these blood banks these eye banks these bone . . ." (654). The dismemberment of bodies, and subsequent investment of them in a sort of bio-economy, illustrates, once again, the desire of capitalism to commodify life itself. Gaddis, however, takes the idea of the commodification of life even further than Pynchon's play on capital's literal *consumption* of life (and death, via Beaconsfield Cigarettes) in *The Crying of Lot 49* by stressing the commodification of the *production* of life itself. This notion goes further than the idea of human beings being replaced by the inanimate, as evidenced in Governor Cates's various surgeries, because here blood *is* capital, and it must be made to circulate in a bio-economy that will *produce* life-as-commodity. Bodies will be banked on, invested in, loaned out, and financed. From birth to the grave, the J R Family of Companies will father and take care of its own. The institution of such a health package, therefore, would represent the J R Family of Companies' final conversion of the citizen to the citizen-consumer. In such a case, the care of the individual body is sustained not by the body of the state but wholly by a corporate body.

But since the corporate body is concerned only with the expansion of capital, individual bodies must become capital as well. This is where the literal and figurative elements of a corporation come into play. Corporations have been legally treated as persons since Justice John Marshall declared, in 1819, that a corporation is "an artificial being, invisible, intangible" (qtd. in Donaldson 3). Thomas Donaldson summarizes the outcome of this legal declaration, writing that "with the passage of the Fourteenth Amendment to the Constitution, U.S. corporations acquired full status as abstract persons, complete with rights to life, liberty, and state citizenship. (Most U.S. corporations are citizens of the state of Delaware.)" (3).[3] Thus did the invisible hands of Adam Smith find an invisible body in the corporation.

Corporatizing is, in *J R*, a way in which capitalism incorporates or embodies itself in the guise of a person/body. So too is this a "healthier" body than the novel's representation of the human body, which, as Stephen H. Matanle notes, "is incoherent, fragmented into a variety of parts, deprived of stability and balance" (109). *The Crying of Lot 49* similarly calls attention to this merger of the corporate body with the human body in the figure of Pierce Inverarity, but Pynchon's novel focuses its critique of capital mostly on America, and the massive global economic changes in the 1970s have yet to occur. The emergence of a "tighter," more interconnected global economy allows Gaddis to take this notion of capital's embodiment and *extend it through the family metaphor*. With the adoption of the family metaphor, an incorporated capitalism in *J R* clothes its supposedly invisible body (and the bodies it now encompasses), which retains similar rights to the ones American citizens are granted. Through incorporation—literally, the creation of a corporeal being, a body—capitalism creates an imagined body (or the bodies/members of the J R Family), which is then mapped onto the social body (citizen-consumers), thereby incorporating the social itself.

Incorporation, from the point of view of investors, is a way of ceding personal liability or responsibility in a capitalist enterprise to a fictional body (as the law sees it). As J R explains this process to Bast, "Getting incorporated all it is is then you don't get screwed on taxes like everybody else and like for this here limited reliability and all if something happens" (*J R* 345). As Donaldson notes, "Modern corporations are created by persons, but they are created in the image of their creators" (3). The result is that the corporate body appears to transcend its creators' control, but it is driven by the *same desire* to increase capital that governs its creators' and investors' actions. So whereas for Justice Marshall, writing in the early nineteenth century, this invisible body exists "only in the contemplation of law," in the latter half of the twentieth century, the era of multinational capitalism, this invisible body not only finds metaphorical and imaginary weight but exists literally "outside" the law, and with drastic consequences for many people. Once America itself has become synonymous with J R's Family (or that of any corporation), composed of a "nation" of consumer-citizens, this imagined corpora-nation attempts to replace the less and less stable structure of the nuclear family (traditionally capitalism's basic unit of production) with one at the global level. Nations are like families in the global community, and since nations are increasingly eclipsed by corporations, corporations have no trouble presenting themselves as the default families of the future.

Same as It (N)ever Was

Considering the success of the family image for J R's Family of Companies, occurring as it does amid great economic and social shocks, it should be no surprise to discover that so many of the families in the novel are crippled or broken apart. Gaddis's interplay between family and capital is strategic, intended to call attention to the inverse relationship developing between the two spheres—the expansion of capital and the relative "fractionation" of the family. The ideology of the nuclear family, which a corporation like J R's perpetuates, eventually falters as the private and the public merge in the imagined J R Family of Companies. J R's corporation is able, literally, to produce blood ties (through biopower) between the social body and its own Family, while it helps to sever the (older forms of) kinship and blood ties that constitute such constructions as the nuclear family. Thus does Gaddis call attention to the fact that, as Pauline Irit Erera writes, "the family is not simply a social institution. It is an ideological construct laden with symbolism and with a history and politics of its own" (2)

As we might expect, then, Gaddis's fractured families are also indicative of actual changes in family structures around this time. The rapacious capitalism emerging during the 1970s found its counterpart in the radical changes occurring in "traditional" families. In *The State and the Family*, Anne Hélène Gauthier writes that, since World War II, "fertility, marriages, cohabitation, divorce, and the participation of women in the labor force, have all been on the increase and have changed the dynamics of family formation and dissolution" and that "if the 1960–75 period witnessed the onset of some of these transformations, the period from 1975 witnessed their deepening and extension to all countries" (146). Undoubtedly, many of these changes in family structures were a direct result of the social and cultural movements of the 1960s, the legalization of abortion, and the popularization of the birth-control pill, but economic factors played just as much a role in these changes as social ones.[4]

J R's critique of the global capitalist dream—a world united as one harmonious family—makes sense here considering that changing familial structures since the mid-1970s are an *international* phenomenon. In a similar fashion to the way that nation-states used (and still use) constructions of the family (the basic unit of production) to perpetuate various ideologies, capitalism adopts the family mantle in an effort to subsume even the nation-state's image of the family. After all, writes Paul Gilbert, "the social agents responsible for the family's discursive formation are those who hold political power—the power to control government in their interests" (141). Since corporations, like Typhon, often influence government decisions, they also have the power to affect how the family is constructed discursively, as J R's company shows. Hence, when capitalism's myth of the separate spheres of business and family breaks down (as Gaddis especially demonstrates in the Bast and Montcrieff families), the rhetoric of family merges with capital's master narrative, and the "play to win" capitalist ethic gives birth to a new kind of family and new kinds of social relations. We have only to look at the behavior of two of the children in the novel to find evidence of the effect of capital's ethic on some of this new breed: J R Vansant's (trans)actions, of course, and the actions of Eigen's son, David, who, as Moore notes (76), expresses his love for his mother in quantitative, monetary terms and who cheats at children's board games (*J R* 263, 267).

It is important to understand that Gaddis's portrayal of families in crisis is no mere nostalgic and reactionary call for "family values." For such radical and abrupt changes in family structures and values at the time led to the perception that the family was in "crisis" (a perception that still persists). Gauthier remarks that "it is evident that family issues have received increasing attention [since 1975], and moreover, that support of families has emerged as a major political winner" (148) and that "initiatives launched by governments since 1975 have revealed an increasing interest in family issues" (150). In America, for instance, 1980 saw the "White House Conference on the Family," which had to be changed to "Conference on Families," writes Gauthier, since "there was no longer one single family type but a plurality of family types" (153).

Such politicization, however, while a response to a perceived "crisis," further legitimatizes this perception through the very nature of politicization itself. The resulting crisis of the family, of course, was the despair at the dissolution of the nuclear family, often considered the "traditional" family structure by many people in the West. Yet as Caroline Wright and Gill Jagger point out in discussing a century's history of the discourse of family values in Britain, "there is nothing new in today's talk of a crisis in the family" (18), and "the narrative of family crisis accompanies a primarily 'moral' or 'moralising' state, concerned with inculcating the 'right' sort of values and cultivating individual responsibility to meet needs" (22). Thus, whenever family configurations are radically altered, a familiar *discourse* of crisis concerning these changes arises. As Stephanie Coontz notes in *The Way We Never Were: American Families and the Nostalgia Trap*, "Historically, Americans have tended to discover a crisis in family structure and standards whenever they are in the midst of major changes in socioeconomic structure and standards" (257).

What such alarmists of this perceived crisis fail to take into account is that the nuclear family is not a "natural" familial structure. Many critics of the nuclear family (Cheal 18–23, Thorne and Yalom 1–20, Gilbert 141, Jagger and Wright, "Introduction" 10–14) have called attention to its historical specificity and constructedness. As Edward Shorter argues in *The Making of the Modern Family*, "The nuclear family is a state of mind rather than a particular kind of structure or set of household arrangements," and "what really distinguishes the nuclear family . . . from other patterns of family life in Western society is a special sense of solidarity that separates the domestic unit from the surrounding community" (205). Gaddis, for example, is no alarmist per se and acknowledges the socially constructed nature of the family through Eigen, who defends his sorry actions as a husband and father to Marian by asking, "How many husbands do you think come home from work all smiles come on Marian, it's the oldest God damned story there is putting up with the same crap day after day trying to make a living and then coming home to I've been slaving all day over a hot stove while you've been down in a nice cool sewer" (*J R* 269–270). To be sure, Eigen's gripe is self-serving (artistic failure has embittered him), but his story nonetheless constitutes a critique of the entire history of work under capitalism—where the traditionally gender-determined public-work sphere and private-domestic sphere are separated—in addition to a critique of the supposed "happy" nuclear family. Hence, Gaddis anticipates the call for "family values" that became the rallying cry of many politicians and pundits (mostly conservatives) during the Reagan era, which he later addresses in *Carpenter's Gothic*.[5]

For *J R* fits Gilles Deleuze and Félix Guattari's description of capitalism, in *Anti-Oedipus*, as a "twofold movement of decoding or deterritorializng flows on the one hand, and their violent and artificial reterritorialization on the other" (34). In some sense, then, the "decoding" of older family narratives and their "recoding" in a global capitalist enterprise unleashes vast amounts of energy and capital, yet much of this energy is immediately rechanneled into the "imagined family" of J R's corporation. For, as Deleuze and Guattari write, "capitalism institutes or restores all sorts of residual and artificial, imaginary, or symbolic territorialities, thereby attempting, as best it can, to recode, rechannel persons who have been defined in terms of abstract quantities. Everything returns or recurs: States, nations, families" (34). Indeed, in *J R*, everything returns, from the faux global family to the corpora-nation to the "failed" ideal of the welfare state.

If families and the nuclear family structure are irreparably fractured in *J R*, so, in the end, are the individuals who try to make these families. The novel's final image is exemplary of this, although the image is of no image at all: it is merely J R's voice incessantly speaking from a dangling telephone receiver. This completes, as one critic writes, "the process of his [J R's] abstraction from a person to a corporation" (Wolfe 159). Likewise, it also completes capitalism's incorporation from abstract entity to social body. If all speech in *J R* involves, as John Johnston contends, "not a human being talking, but money itself [and] not just the language of money but the speech of money, the flux of capital as it enters into and becomes part of verbal communication" (*Carnival* 204), then the construction of J R's Family of Companies is the perfect social body for that voice. J R, a natural spokesperson for capital, is not so much speaking for capital as capital is speaking through him. Not really an orphan after all, J R is capitalism's child and a grim reminder of the consequences of the breakdown of any kind of family or social structure that, however it may be composed, promotes values based on love, trust, and understanding, values that find their worth in human interaction and not in the marketplace.

6 / Your Loss Is Their Gain: The Corporate Body and the Corporeal Body in Richard Powers's *Gain*

While *J R* traces the way the corporation's fictional personhood can be marshaled into a familial structure, thus not only granting capital a body but placing a potential "global family" within its reach, Richard Powers's *Gain* engages directly with the legal and fictional aspects of the corporation—that it is legally considered a "person"—by exploring the corporation qua corporation and analyzing corporate history in the light of American history. It is the first novel to do so explicitly and rigorously, and thus it differentiates itself from works that are either too "vulgar" in their outright condemnation of capitalism or simply do not grapple with the peculiarities of its most powerful and influential invention. In this way, *Gain* outdoes even that great critique of corporate power, Frank Norris's representation of the Railroad Trust in *The Octopus*, by offering a full anatomy of the corporation at the end of Norris's nascent twentieth century, dissecting its organizational structures and decoding its "genetic" makeup. Whereas Norris, appropriating popular representations of the Trust, depicts the railroad corporation as a kind of beast or monster, Powers, after extensively researching corporate history, takes for granted the legal construction of a corporation as a kind of person and treats it as such with compelling results. In other words, Powers's novel explicitly *historicizes* the corporation itself as a kind of corrective to the fact that the corporation has become so *naturalized* that it appears as if it has always existed and, therefore, always will. What we end up with from Powers, a writer always interested in the aesthetic and practical possibilities of science and technology, is a thoroughly scientific account of corporate evolution and the simultaneous devolution of the individual, who finds him- or herself instead subject(ified) to the emerging biopolitical regime of the neoliberal era. At stake is the (in)ability of human bodies to resist the sway of corporate bodies, the accountability of contemporary America's balance sheet of "gains" and losses under capitalism, and the kind of future that is possible as we approach corporate capitalism's bottom line.

Anytown, USA™

Powers's *Gain* introduces us to a world beholden to multinational corporations, typified by the Clare Soap and Chemical Company, whose entire two-century history Powers recounts in detail. Yet in contrast to a novel such as *J R*, in which William Gaddis emphasizes the entropy and confusion of a world where unfettered, free-market capitalism entails devastating consequences (even reproducing such chaos at the narrative level), *Gain* introduces us to the humdrum life of the suburban Midwest in the mundane town of Lacewood, Illinois, a quiet and modestly growing suburb, a place of well-tended gardens, communal bonfires, and town picnics. Worlds apart from, say, the besieged suburbia of DeLillo's *White Noise*, a novel which itself takes on the glow of the hyperreal in its re-presentation of Simulacra, USA, the suburb of Lacewood, in *Gain*, is rendered as uneventful and as "normal" as we might expect to find it. There are no near plane crashes, Airborne Toxic Events, or famously photogenic barns. Moreover, the amusing exposure of Jack Gladney to Nyodene Derivative is replaced, in *Gain*, by the sobering diagnosis of Laura Bodey's ovarian cancer.

What *Gain* does differently than these other novels is examine the seemingly calm and ordered surface of late capitalist society in search of its hidden cracks, its spackled and slipshod repairs. Gone is much of the mirth and play with which Gaddis and DeLillo inform their views of postmodern life, and this allows Powers to concentrate on drawing the complex and multifaceted relationship between corporations and individuals. The people of Lacewood live mostly unexamined lives, and yet, Powers's narrative makes clear, they are still worth living.

Indeed, Lacewood's unassuming qualities are precisely what Powers needs to trace the almost invisible presence of corporate America. Similar to Eagle Falls, which J R devastates in *J R*, the dying Hadleyville in *Gung Ho*, and the precarious Sandusky in *Tommy Boy*, fast-growing Lacewood (it is "dying" by the novel's end; Powers 354) fits the classic image of the one-company town: "The town cannot hold a corn boil without its corporate sponsor. The company cuts every other check, writes the headlines, sings the school fight song. It plays the organ at every wedding and packs rice that rains down on the departing honeymooners. It staffs the hospital and funds the ultrasound sweep of uterine seas where Lacewood's next of kin lie gray and ghostly, asleep in the deep" (6). Such an all-encompassing influential power might well merit attention, but the corporate presence has become so *naturalized* in Lacewood that it seems hardly worth a second thought to the townspeople since it appears to pose no threat: "There must have been a time when Lacewood did not mean Clare, Incorporated. But no one remembered it. No one alive was old enough to recall. The two names always came joined in the same breath. All the grace shed on Lacewood flowed through that company's broad conduit.... And Lacewood became the riches that it made" (4). History here is subsumed by capital and the corporation, much as it is in *The Octopus* and *The Crying of Lot 49*, as the existence of Clare becomes synonymous with the birth of Lacewood. What came before Clare, therefore, is of no interest and has been swept away by capital, "the riches" that have replaced it. The insistence that "there must have been a time" before this corporate time—despite the novel's chronicling of Clare's history—becomes merely an ironic echo of the failure of individual memory and collective history in the Janus face of late capitalism.

Even the town's story about having "tricked its way into fortune" when it convinced the "fifth Mr. Clare" to choose Lacewood for the construction of his newest plant is nothing but a self-serving myth (4). The image the town tries to project—that of being a homely but bustling community—by setting up plaster façades on Main Street and fixing up an old train engine is seen by the visiting Douglas Clare Sr., for the cheap cosmetic job that it is. Clare, who "glowered throughout the length of the inspection" and "shook his head continually," is in complete control of the negotiations all the while. He is revealed to be the huckster par excellence as he agrees to build the plant just before returning to Boston: "Sighing, he accepted the massive tax concessions proffered him in perpetuity, and closed the deal" (5). Excited by the prospect of joining the industrial age's daily grind instead of having "dozed forever" and "stayed a backwoods wasteland until the age of retrotourism," Lacewood enters into a true devil's bargain without considering the future costs of its endeavor (5).

This Faustian union between Lacewood and Clare serves as a microcosm of America's relationship with business as a whole and allows Powers to investigate this relationship dialectically. By further refining the terms of this dialectic down to the history of Clare's birth and growing pains as set against Laura Bodey's declining health and eventual death due to cancer, Powers calls attention to the extent to which corporations and individuals are entangled in the era of late capitalism. It is the complexity of this dialectical relationship that makes the novel more than a mere condemnation of corporate capitalism.

On Company Time

Clare's history is rigorously recounted throughout the book in a linear fashion that doubles as a history of American capitalism itself, similar to what Immanuel Wallerstein has called, borrowing the term from Fernand Braudel, the *longue durée* of capitalism. Wallerstein, adapting Braudel's views on time as both "the *longue durée*, or structural time, long but not eternal, and that of the *conjoncture*, or cyclical, middle-range time, the time of cycles *within* structures," applies these concepts specifically to the history of capitalism ("Heritage" 236). Such a history is further complicated since Powers presents Clare's maturation as an analogue of an organism's or person's growth, which bolsters the view of capitalism as a time-bound, historical economic system with a beginning, middle, and, at some time in the future, "end" or transformation. As Wallerstein writes, "The world is in transition. Out of chaos will come a new order, different from the one we know. Different, but not necessarily better" ("ANC" 33). Indeed, *Gain*, by its end, is caught up in the uncertainty of what the capitalist world system will bring next or what new system might succeed it.

Clare's *longue durée* is traced back to Jephthah Clare, who flees England and comes to America in 1802 after some insider trading puts him afoul of a business associate, which leads to Jephthah's house being burned down in retaliation. Jephthah quickly secures himself a ship and begins a shady trading business with both Britain and France, which are at war, until Jefferson's Embargo Act of 1807 bans any such trade in foreign ports. Turning smuggler, Jephthah makes a steady income, eventually trading in Oregon furs and Cantonese teas, for "Clare was, from the first, transnational" (Powers 8). Thus, early on, Powers registers an even longer view of capitalism than the early "birth" of Clare will allow, for, as Wallerstein points out, "in the real world of historical capitalism, almost all commodity chains of any importance have traversed ... state frontiers. This is not a recent innovation.... Moreover, the transnationality of commodity chains is as descriptively true of the sixteenth-century capitalist world as of the twentieth" (*Historical Capitalism* 31).

Such transnational trading affects Jephthah's imagination in a telling way: "The world had to be circumnavigated before the humblest washerwoman could sip from her ragged cup. The mystery of it all sometimes visited Jephthah at night.... He, the Oregon trapper, the Chinese hong: everyone prospered. Each of them thought he'd gotten the better end of the deal. Now, how could that be? Where had the profit come from? Who paid for their mutual enrichment?" (10). Jephthah's mystical (and already global) vision of capital—essentially Adam Smith's wonder at the magic of enlightened self-interest—is interesting in its simultaneous expression of awe and confusion at the economic workings of capitalism. The question as to how this seemingly contradictory endeavor works to the benefit of all is never answered and instead is forever deferred. To be sure, Jephthah's industry creates jobs for workers and forges connections with other industries the world over that, in their turn, do the same in stimulating job and economic growth, yet it also helps to establish the hierarchical structure and antagonism between capitalist and worker that subsequent generations will have the endless task of attempting to reconcile. For it would be naive to believe that anyone making a deal always thinks he or she has gotten the better end of it (as Jephthah's soured sugar-beets deal in England proves) or that "everyone" prospers equally. Indeed, Jephthah prospers to the degree that he can afford to tithe to charity as a kind of spiritual insurance, but the very fact that he enlarges his consideration of the system to the point of asking, almost despite himself, "Who paid?" is a tacit admission that someone has to foot the bill. Of course, the traders in commodities that Jephthah deals with may be as wealthy as he is, but the people doing the actual trapping or picking of tea leaves are certainly not.

In this sense, Jephthah's amazement at the breadth of the capitalist system doubles as a mystification of production. The profit (Marx's concept of surplus-value never seemed so obvious) clearly comes from the backs of those whom Jephthah need not see or deal with as he walks around the exchange floor and views figures and prices instead of people and things. His wonderment at how the system works is, if anything, frightening in its disclosure that the forces that men like Jephthah wield—with influence the world over—are not only merely assumed to be beneficial to all but are even misunderstood by those who attempt to wield them. Such sublime, though essentially mystifying, visions punctuate the first half of the novel (the second half offers more disconcerting visions), occurring when various characters have epiphanies in some way related to the scope and power of capitalism, as seen when Jephthah's son

Samuel ponders the transformational forces of industrialism (155) or the anonymity of his workers as Clare grows (165–166) and when his other son, Ben, conceives of a link among chemistry, nature, and capital (79).

Powers, however, as he indulges the philosophy of free enterprise in this way, simultaneously works to historicize it and show its tenuous underpinnings. Jephthah, the representative capitalist, is, from the start, an unethical and rapacious businessman, given to delusions of the grandeur of his works. It might seem easy at this point in the novel simply to claim that Jephthah is a morally corrupt man and thus creates a morally corrupt company (much as the film *Executive Suite* argues for a good-versus-bad capitalism through individual agents), but this is far too facile a defense of the capitalist system. Powers quickly moves past the founder of Clare to the second generation of owners, Resolve, Samuel, and Benjamin. This tripartite ownership immediately undercuts the temptation to vilify one figure for the business's wrongdoings. The three brothers become different facets of one company, foregrounding the structure of the corporation that Clare will eventually become. Resolve represents the pure business aspect of profits and company growth; Samuel embodies the concern with God and morality as it pertains to the work(s) the company is doing; and Ben, through his love of botany and lack of interest in business, is an early figure for research and development, the power that science (specifically chemistry) will come to have in transforming the world. Yet however individually uninterested (Benjamin) or interested in business (Samuel partially, Resolve fully), the three collectively show how free enterprise marshals different forces or fields to do capital's bidding.

Three more essential keys to Clare's success come in Resolve's wife, Julia; Anthony Jewitt, the British mechanic; and Ennis, the industrious Irish immigrant. Julia is essentially an early public-relations representative. Once again, as in *Network* and *Michael Clayton*, it is a woman who is the figure of deception and illusion (later it will be the less ideological prototype of today's PR/ad man, Hiram Nagel).[1] Julia's work as a political propagandist is key to Clare's profiting through several wars. Her fanatical propagandistic tracts and boosterism of britches-itching Expansionist America is delivered via the vitriolic rhetoric of Manifest Destiny. Her work views American history—past, present, and future—from the steely eyes of industry, even helping to instigate the Mexican-American War and taking political stances on issues such as abolitionism (in this case pro), not out of moral or ethical considerations but only according to whether it will be beneficial to the business (93). Jewitt, in the meantime, stands for the mastery of technology and engineering that will construct the machinery needed for the mass production of commodities. Similarly, Ennis's toil and ingenuity as a soap maker pays off in the free-enterprise system and proves the superiority of capitalism and democracy, which allow the conditions from which anyone with determination and perseverance, regardless of class and ethnicity, can become a success—that is, so long as capital decides to back you, as the Clares do Ennis. Ennis's story might have been penned by Horatio Alger (although its grisly end by Norris; *Gain* 142).

It is this "extended family" that brings Clare through tough economic times into "the Fiduciary Age" (Powers 166), in which, flush with capital, it is incorporated under Peter Clare, the last surviving offspring of Julia and Resolve. The rest of Clare's history marks the Clare Corporation as outgrowing its "familial" roots. CEOs come and go, and Clare weathers financial storms during various panics, the Depression, and even the social movements of the 1960s and 1970s through a combination of careful and prescient management and pure luck. With the passing away of the second Clare generation, however, the history of Clare turns from an exciting venture with a leading cast of characters to a whirlwind tour of the history of capital, with an electric, but ultimately cold and inhuman, charge.

Much like the family firms in Gaddis's *J R*, *Gain* thus charts the falling away, or impossibility, of continuing familial ownership of corporations as they grow. Clare begins as a family-run business that goes through the "humiliations" of turning from a merchant company into a manufacturer (70), of becoming incorporated (154), and finally of taking its stock public (238). Despite some of the family members' being disturbed by these changes in business, they find themselves compelled to follow capital's logic, which eventually leads to Clare passing out of the family's hands altogether. For *Gain* is the story of the corporation, to which capital, not so much a particular family, gave birth. A similar point is made regarding such an outmoded ownership schema (in addition to showing how individuals are merely cogs in capital's self-perpetuation) in William Gibson's *Neuromancer* (1984). In the novel, Gibson figures the decaying Tessier-Ashpool family (one of whose members, Lady 3Jane Marie-France, is a clone and whose patriarch, Ashpool, is cryogenically frozen and "resurrected") as Victorian and portrays as anachronistic its attempt to hold onto power (which the family correlates with life) in a world where multinational capital and new informational systems have given rise to AIs, computer systems that can essentially run themselves—self-referential or autopoietic systems. These systems, like capital, outreach and outlast their human creators (the Tessier-Ashpools develop the AIs that eclipse them). It is the AIs that are "evolving," while the humans, seemingly "devolving" by contrast,[2] have no choice but to become posthuman by adapting to a more fluid and less physically important "world" through technological means, such as bionic body parts or subcutaneously embedded microchips. Family ownership and management, in both novels, is shown to be merely a phase in a corporation's growth, a phase that must fall by the wayside as economic and technological systems continually expand.

Powers, without engaging in future shock, shows that capital's self-perpetuation—itself the very trigger of technological innovation that leads to advanced information technologies—and freedom from human control have long since occurred. The mechanism that has made this possible is the concept of limited liability, which, as we saw in *J R*, frees investors from being held liable for a corporation's actions. Powers even goes so far as to claim that incorporation was the most powerful invention of the nineteenth century, as he sums up the wonders of the Chicago World's Fair: "It compiled an anthology of those inventions that had cracked open the globe's buried wealth: steam, electricity, telegraph, telephone, chemistry, internal combustion, dynamo: and surpassing them all, the limited liability corporation" (247). Here Powers invokes Henry Adams's dynamo a hundred years after the fact, suggesting that today it is the corporation that inspires the true awe and dread of the twentieth century. Thus, "here, in Chicago, four hundred years after Columbus's landfall, America could see itself for what it truly was: less a nation than a collective outfit for the capitalization and development of its endless hinterlands" (247). The true dynamo is the limited liability corporation, that new machine which will drive the hitherto most dynamic economic system known to man, since, as David C. Korten writes, "the marvel of the corporation as a social innovation is that it can bring together hundreds of thousands of people within a single structure and compel them to act in accordance with a corporate purpose that is not necessarily their own" (74).

In this manner, the limited liability corporation is released from a large amount of responsibility for its actions. At the same time, investors and shareholders are the actual beneficiaries of limited liability since it absolves them from individually being held accountable for a company's debts. Yet it is this very "protection" that simultaneously directs, by chartered fiat, the corporation to pursue its sole purpose of amassing profits and thus increasing its worth. The limited liability corporation, once it has been set free of human responsibility as such, becomes the perfect vehicle for capital's perpetuation through a very special kind of body—a body that is no *one's* body and aspires to a kind of immortality. Powers, therefore, is careful to leave Samuel as the last remaining "original" core family member running Clare. Not quite as devoted to, or savvy at, business as his brother Resolve, Samuel, a religious fanatic (he is a Millerite, at one point selling his shares in the company to stand on a hill with his wife and other believers to await the apocalypse; Powers 82–83), demonstrates a dedication to work that reads like Max Weber's classic diagnosis of the Protestant work ethic and makes him more *prophet* oriented than *profit* oriented (Powers 80). Thus, it is he who oversees Clare's incorporation, which seems to Samuel, at first, to entail a loss of status for the company. But soon Samuel's once-deferred rapture becomes the rapture of incorporation, since "incorporation could live forever. It carried on beyond the span of any owner's life. It passed itself down through the generations of those assembled thousands who would, in time, work its engines. Its dynasties surpassed the longest family" (156–157). Samuel's speech to the workers is telling. He calls incorporation "the beast that gave them all eternal life. They heard him speak of an aggregate giant, one that summed the capital and labor of untold Lilliputians into a vast, limbered Leviathan" (158). Caught up in the ecstasy of "eternal" corporate life, Samuel forgets that such a heaven comes paired with apocalyptic destruction. Ironically, then, while he misses the end of the world, his part in the Clare Corporation helps to end the world as it was before the industrial revolution: "The world's end had come after all, invisible, secret, snickering, some time after that promised night when he had stood waiting for it" (154). So it is that Samuel, against his better religious sentiments, comes to unleash "the beast" on America.

Bodies That (Don't) Matter

As in Gaddis's *J R*, *Gain*'s depiction of capital as attaining a body through incorporation is explicitly tied to people's disembodiment through the loss of rights and "individuality," a critique that is extended to its fullest as Powers traces the onset of disease and death in Laura Bodey. Regarding the financial rhetoric that Powers uses to describe characters and their feelings, Paul Maliszewski writes, "If people in *Gain* resemble small corporations, companies in turn become like people" (179). Moreover, as in *White Noise*, medicine and the pharmaceutical industry come into play in regard to the pressing problem of adequately treating serious, terminal illnesses such as cancer. By foregrounding both the disembodiment of the individual and the difficulty of obtaining effective and affordable drugs to treat serious illness, *Gain* offers a troubling assessment of the corporeal being versus the corporate one.

The Clare Corporation is described throughout the novel in terms of an evolving organism. Even from the first description, Clare's genetic makeup is key to understanding it: "Business ran in the Clares' blood long before one of them made a single thing" (Powers 8). This business-driven blood leads the family to settle near "ports, always ports. They thrived in tidal pools, half salt, half sweet. Brackish, littoral. They lived less in cities than on the sea routes between them" (8). Clare's genesis evokes the first form of life crawling out of the sea or tide pool, suggesting that the beginning of the corporation is just that—the emergence of a new form of life. Clare's second-generation owners mark its adolescence, which is characterized by awkward growth and incorporation: "The law now declared the Clare Soap and Chemical Company one composite body: a single, whole, and statutorily enabled person" (158). After this embodiment, the second generation runs the company until it "turned fifty in 1881, to great public fanfare of its own generating. As a corporation, it was but a scant teenager" (221).

Passing on to the third generation of ownership, Clare experiences yet another maturation: "Its revenues now solid, the firm prepared to take its inevitable next step into young adulthood. A national firm, with national advertising, fighting national competitors, required nation-sized capital. There was but one place to secure the needed sums: America herself. In 1891, Peter, Douglas, and their families, and associates took Clare public" (238). And thanks to Hiram "Hy" Nagel's advertising schemes, Clare even develops a "look" in its Clara logo: "In this, her first incarnation, Clara simply gazed gratefully at the golden cake [of soap] that let her recapture an unblemished purity" (223). Thus begins Clare's long obsession with its public "body image," as one of its modern-day advertisement illustrates: "As corporate bodies go, ours has grown beyond belief in this short century. But however big a body gets, there's still no place like home" (140). Yet this adulthood also marks a "monstrous transformation" (238). Around the same time that Clare is embodied and reaches adulthood, its body mutates significantly, as does Powers's representation of it: after employing the governing figure of Clare the fictitious person-as-corporation for a time, *Gain* returns to the familiar array of corporate figurations—such as the beastlike (Leviathan, octopus) and mythical (Colossus, Frankenstein)—for the rest of the novel.[3]

Having, for the first time, self-consciously presented the corporation as a legal person, *Gain* also self-consciously sums up all prior representations, constituting a kind of catalogue or cabinet of metaphor oddities. A massive restructuring of the company, for instance, is described as a "revamping [that] simultaneously strengthened the core nervous system and increased the number of [Clare's] limbs" (273). After such reorganization, "Clare had become a vast man-of-war, if not a small armada" (274). The metaphor of the corporation as a man-of-war, with its hierarchy of crew, serves not quite so well here as the "small" armada of semiautonomous agent boats still answerable to a flagship.[4] The corporation is slowly becoming more decentralized with each metaphor. Samuel conceives of the corporation as a Leviathan (Hobbes's sort, in which the State is composed of a number of individual bodies) binding together numerous Lilliputians, but increasingly, as Clare "grows up," these separate beings find partial autonomy. Moreover, the man-of-war metaphor cannot help but recall the Portuguese man-of-war, a poisonous jellyfish-like sea creature whose tentacles average around 30 feet in length but can reach up to 165 feet. In a strange way, then, we return to Norris's figure of the octopus, but with an improvement: the Portuguese man-of-war is not actually a single animal but a siphonophore, a creature composed of several organisms working as one (*National Geographic*). With its truly monstrous proportions, poisonous nature, and constituent parts that work together toward one goal, the Portuguese man-of-war seems an even more insidious metaphor than Norris's. In short, after creating Clare's corporate body, Powers returns to the typical "monstrous" and inhuman metaphors to suggest that the evolving Clare has become something much more than a legal person. Hence, when "ever-larger institutions began to spring from the corporation's brow, giving birth to one another: the Federal Reserve System. The Consumer Price Index. The first national income tax" (Powers 290), we recall Athena springing from Zeus's head and recognize the godlike power of the corporation.

The maritime metaphors continue, however, in a more horrifying cast later on. The price of having so many limbs in times of financial troubles, thinks Clare's modern-day CEO, Frank Kennibar Jr., could be amputation: "Chopping up the firm will horrify the board; it may choose any other fate over such an end. Sprinkling the bloody pieces on the waters may make the sharks even hungrier. Or the move may prove a kind of starfish solution: each severed limb regenerating a whole new body" (350). Corporate dismemberment has been one of Clare's driving fears since its incorporation, turning it, too, during the era of megamergers and leveraged buyouts, into the very kind of predator over which Kennibar now worries. Yet the Hydra-like "starfish solution," and the possibility of regenerating limbs, seems the more likely outcome of Clare's dilemma. Indeed, as a kind of legal person dedicated to the endless accumulation of capital and the endless "expansion" of itself following the creed of "enlightened self-interest," the Clare Corporation is incredibly solipsistic. If capital begets capital, then Clare begets Clare. Or, as Kennibar imagines it in the final, and perhaps most apt, image of the corporation, "in reality, there is nothing but a series of little Clares, each with its own purpose, spreading down the fiscal quarters without end" (349). Such an endless succession of "selves" underscores the fiction of the corporate self and personhood for what it is—an endlessly deferred identity contingent on an endless accumulation of capital.

Powers, however, challenges this smoke-and-mirrors conception of the infinite expansion of corporate capitalism. Without directly hitching tenor and vehicle together, he suggests that corporate capitalism is a kind of cancer. Clearly, the details of Laura Bodey's struggle with cancer could double as a description of the Clare Corporation's and capital's expansion throughout the novel: "Something is loose in her system, a runaway growth. They can try to gun down the criminal, but not without firing into the innocent crowd" (229). Laura's body has been "invaded," in a sense. As one specialist tells her regarding the possible causes of her cancer, "There's also some evidence that provoking agents, either combined with or inducing an alteration in the immune system . . ." (99; ellipsis in original). The suggestion is that chemicals from the Clare Corporation have "invaded" Laura's body/system, infected her, and turned her own immune system against itself/herself. In turn, these descriptions eerily fit the way that the Clare Corporation and capitalism have been mapped throughout the novel, as runaway, monstrous, "cancerous" growths that cannot be stopped by anyone, even those who are deeply involved with assuring their success, and certainly not without the entire economic system coming to a halt.

At first inspection, this seems to be a peculiarly American problem. As per Norman Mailer's diagnosis of America's "disease" during the Vietnam War era in *The Armies of the Night* (1968), the system is endlessly perpetuating itself "in the cells, the cells that traveled, and the cells [that] were as insane as Grandma with orange hair" (152). With its "cities and corporations spread[ing] like cancer" (189), America has become an Establishment that Mailer calls "The Corporation" (189) and that *Gain* describes as "less a nation than a collective outfit" (247). In this view, the system, endlessly perpetuating itself like cancerous cells, has long ago infected an America that appears not to be spinning but multiplying out of control. Mailer traces this fundamental rupture, which *Gain* explores through the contradictory mission(s) of Samuel, and emphasizes the irreconcilability between the (corporeal) body of Christ and the corporate one: "For the center of Christianity was a mystery, a son of God, and the center of the corporation was a detestation of mystery, a worship of technology" (188). This update of Henry Adams's Virgin and Dynamo dialectic also recalls John Winthrop's "A Model of Christian Charity," in which Winthrop sermonizes the Christian-body-eclectic from Christ to Church ("Christ and His church make one body"; 153), stressing the bonds and ligaments of love among its members ("love is absolutely necessary to the being of the body of Christ, as the sinews and other ligaments of a natural body are to the being of that body"; 155) while sailing on a chartered, thus "corporate," ship "boarded" by some people as equally interested in the business of goods as the business of salvation. Clearly the irritation between the corporeal and corporate body began when the *Arbella* set sail. Thirty or so years after Mailer's initial diagnosis, however, a second, and broader, opinion is needed.

Since that time, "America's" disease has spread worldwide, and the global expansion of capital further complicates the notions of "America" and even nationhood itself, as Laura's ex-husband, Don, recognizes on visiting Clare's headquarters: "Ropes click against the four flagpole stands.... The Stars and Stripes in position one. It strikes Don as a bit of handy nostalgia. How transnationals love to play the citizenship card whenever they're looking for a protective break. But Clare is just like elites everywhere: the company keeps so many residences that it has no fixed abode" (Powers 253). Thus, while Powers shows us the historical union of American Industry and its "Democratic Vistas," he also calls attention to the corporation's ability oftentimes to transcend national borders as well as the regulations and restrictions on its powers.

Powers's figuration of capital as cancerous should come as no surprise, and not simply because of Mailer's use of cancer as metaphor. As Susan Sontag points out in her analysis of representations of disease in *Illness as Metaphor*, "Early capitalism assumes the necessity of regulated spending, saving, accounting, discipline—an economy that depends on the rational limitation of desire. TB is described in images that sum up the negative behavior of nineteenth-century *homo economicus*. Advanced capitalism requires expansion, speculation, the creation of needs . . . ; buying of credit; mobility—an economy that depends on the irrational indulgence of desire. Cancer is described in images that sum up the negative behavior of *homo economicus*" (62). But, as Sontag reminds us, such rhetoric can trivialize the disease, pain, and suffering of those who are ill. Sontag hopes that, with the advent of new treatments, the metaphors of cancer will change and become "partly de-mythicized" so that one day "perhaps it will be morally permissible, as it is not now, to use cancer as a metaphor" (84). Powers avoids merely exploiting the cancer metaphor, however, not only by indirectly suggesting that corporate capitalism is a sort of cancer but by directly dealing with the disease in his dignified and unromanticized depiction of Laura's rapid deterioration and death.

Powers ultimately takes up the cancer metaphor in order to draw the Clare Corporation and Laura together in the most intimate, if devastating, of fashions. Part of Powers's point here is to explore the deep ties that people have to corporations in the age of late capital. Laura realizes, at one point, that "every hour of her day depends on more corporations than she can count," and "wasn't she born wanting what they were born wanting to give her?" (Powers 304). Laura eventually comes to accept this relationship as symbiotic, though Powers is careful to show that while this appears true from one vantage point, a larger view (the novel itself) shows a kind of parasitism that is much more one-sided.

If the Clare Corporation has "invaded" Laura's life, Laura is complicit in corporate America too. Early on, she is buffered from the destructive elements and painful facts of the world around her. She is a "woman who has heard, yet has not heard" (8). Moreover, she is a successful real-estate agent at a realty company ironically named Next Millennium, recalling both the early messianic edge to Samuel's and Julia's vision of capital, as well as the (im)probability of a "next" millennium, since the imminent, religious apocalypse has been replaced by an immanent, secular (environmental) one. Laura's work is directly tied to capitalist expansion through land ownership, development, and the American Dream/myth of home ownership.[5] And so she is very much part of the answer to the questions that her ex-husband asks himself as he drives through Lacewood: "What happened to that manageable, mid-sized town they used to live in, where everything still worked the way it was supposed to? The one with the intact tax base, where they fixed the potholes, where you could drive anywhere in ten minutes?" (62). The ideological stock of small-town nostalgia is a sure bet in a world where capital must abolish the long-trumpeted Main Street either through growth or dereliction and most likely through a combination of both.

Furthermore, the fact that Laura has "heard" suggests, à la Max Weber, that venerable Protestant work ethic, according to which one "hears" one's calling. As Weber puts it, "The idea, so familiar to us today and yet in reality far from obvious, that *one's duty consists in pursuing one's calling* . . . and that the individual should have a commitment to his 'professional' . . . activity, whatever it may consist of, irrespective of whether it appears to the detached observer as nothing but utilization of his labor or even of his property (as 'capital'), this idea is a characteristic feature of the 'social ethic' of capitalist culture" (13). Yet what Laura has not yet heard—and later literally cannot "hear" when she is unable to help her son, Tim, with his homework assignment (a gloss on Walt Whitman's "Crossing Brooklyn Ferry")—is any narrative counter to late capitalism's. Unable to comprehend Whitman because he is "long-winded, a total mystery" (Powers 88), Laura remains, early on, deaf to the poet's "barbaric yawp," a yawp that, even in "Crossing," frequently champions American industrialism (the constant evocation of trade in the poem's descriptions of ships, the "white-sail'd schooners, sloops, lighters! / Flaunt away, flags of all nations"; Whitman, "Crossing" ll. 117–118) and ingenuity with an idealism that seems, in hindsight, almost naive today in its unquestioned assumption of the inherent goodness of such growth, especially considering the outcome of such "democratic" expansionism.

Laura's failure to understand Whitman comes with another price: the death of the sovereign, embodied individual. Whitman's pluralistic vision always meant *e pluribus unum* and *e unum pluribus* and was attendant on a radical idea of the body put forth in "Song of Myself"—"I have said that the soul is not more than the body, / And I have said that the body is not more than the soul, / And nothing, not God, is greater to one than one's-self is" (*Leaves* ll. 1262–1264)—and that "Crossing" stakes out as well: "I too had receiv'd identity by my body, / That I was I knew was of my body, and what I should be I knew should be of my body" (ll. 63–64). But the body and identity are at odds in Laura's world. As the junk mail Laura receives daily illustrates—"She's not being singled out. It's the same old list. The master database. The mass mailing to everybody" (Powers 283)—"individuality" is a mere marketing scheme, spawning "a whole new art form: the protectively disguised bulk envelope" (283). Under these conditions, Laura's inability to understand Whitman takes on symbolic resonance. Her presentiment that "at day's end . . . we'll all be disembodied. Mobile microcomputer puppets doing our shopping and socializing. Human heads pasted onto modem bodies. Insert your face here. Like those billboards that Next Millennium posts everywhere around town" (30) is truer than she realizes.

Mild Luddite-like concerns with technology and disembodiment aside (MySpace and Facebook have surely triumphed as electro-appendages to the social without ending it, in this respect), Laura's grueling battle with cancer shows the very real, physical toll of the Clare Corporation's actions. Of course, the link between Laura's ovarian cancer and the contaminants from Clare's factory can never be fully proven (something akin to the missing scientific link between cigarette smoking and lung cancer), but Clare's eventual settlement (even if it is merely because it is "cost effective," as Laura realizes; 333) is still an admission of sorts. Yet the effect of Clare's poisonous chemicals on Laura's body is telling. After several chemotherapy treatments, Laura expresses a kind of painful alienation from her own body, which "scares her now. Alien infestation. A pink, bare, cave newt, bald down to her plastic pubes.... No one can tell her how much of the changes come from the cancer, how much from the chemo.... Whatever the cause, she no longer recognizes the scraps of person left to her" (227). Laura's disembodiment is far from the free-floating, "fun," postmodern kind offered by technology and computer systems. It is, instead, a harsh reminder of the limits of mortality.

Clare's line of products, however, has always shown a concern with the body, from the company's early obsession with cleanliness and the "natural" healing properties of its "Native Balm" soap (116–118, 131–132) to its late expansion into all areas pertaining to the body, as one of its advertisements clearly shows: *"Are you the unwitting victim of harmful B.O. (Body Odor)? You may not be able to detect it yourself. And your closest friends may be too polite to tell you.... Science tells us that a full 83 percent of all cases of detrimental B.O. can be cured by simple preventative hygiene. Don't let your body tell people more about yourself than you want"* (313). Clare perpetuates the idea, at an unconscious level, that one is divorced or alienated from one's body. The body is *something else, not me*, and it will embarrass you if you do not take the appropriate steps to keep it in check. Your body needs the products developed by science and technology in order for you to control it because it is something that you *own*, something that requires upkeep, as would a garden or a house.

Thus, "owning" your body comes with a certain "responsibility." This responsibility requires the costs of maintaining one's health in the face of death/expiration. Whereas in *White Noise*, Jack Gladney yearns for an unmediated, authentic death that is *his own*, *Gain* demonstrates that, in the wild world of privatization, life and death are not existential conundrums so much as financial obligations. You will thus be held personally accountable for your life, because, no matter what troubles you may encounter, the social is no longer a space that accepts or cares for the individual—hence the success of self-help healing books that promise recovery through the power of positive mental thinking. In *Gain*, when the ailing Laura takes to reading one of these books, she reflects on its message: "Even now, she is responsible for her own, ultimate cure. And if she dies it'll be her own fault. It'll be because she doubted, took her eyes off the road, let negative thoughts poison her" (317). Laura does not become a true believer here, but her halfhearted attempt to buy into this brand of New Age spiritualism shows the allure of these kinds of books and how they tap directly into the ideology of late capitalism's world of indiscriminate privatization.

Such privatization also leaves one at the mercy of the health care industry, something *White Noise* takes for granted in Gladney's obsessive testing for the effects of exposure to Nyodene D. In *Gain*, Laura's dwindling savings show the toll that a for-profit health care industry takes on its patients/customers, particularly those with incurable or chronic diseases. The treatments for Laura's cancer are expensive, and though she is lucky enough to have excellent health insurance (189), she learns, at one point, that there are better drugs she could be taking to deal with the intense pain caused by her treatments but that, due to their higher costs, she is barred from using (152). The hospital nurses and orderlies alert her to these facts about the health care industry, as well as tell her about the benefits for someone in her pain of (illegal) marijuana. As in *White Noise*, the business aspect to drug development comes off as shady at best: "The ingredients multiply without limit, most of them less than a month and a half old. How we live, now: a new set of doses every day. From experiment to established practice, even before the first round of guinea pigs can sicken or get better" (113). The coup de grace comes when Laura learns that the Clare Corporation provides many of the raw materials (thanks to its earlier vertical, as opposed to horizontal, integration)[6] that the pharmaceutical companies use to make the drugs that treat Laura. Clare, then, very likely gives Laura cancer and, in turn, helps to provide the costly drugs that will futilely fight it.

The structure of a for-profit health care sector also affects the actual quality of the care, the novel suggests, since doctors are worried about malpractice suits. When the teenage Ellen, Laura's daughter, learns over the phone that the doctor is "ninety-eight percent sure" of her mother's diagnosis, her anger details the problem. She "can't explain to him [her father] why doctors stoop to saying such crap. They say it because they think it comes across as some kind of professional reassurance. Cheerful, meaningless, and unprosecutable. That's what you get when your whole health care business is driven by fear of malpractice. They can't say *Shut up and relax*, as in the old days, because Suzy Homemaker has become Susan Health Care Consumer, and won't accept a professional's word as answer" (38). Thus it is that only the nurses, orderlies, and other patients seem to form a supportive community while Laura is in the hospital. The doctors and specialists, those who fear being sued in their role as doctor/provider, must keep a "professional" distance, which can easily become an emotional distance as well (the same is true of the experts Gladney encounters in *White Noise*). The thing to fear, for the patient who "owns" her disease and for the doctor who treats it, is the acceptance of *personal* responsibility—the very thing that the limited liability corporation is able to elude thanks to its clever legal structure.

As David Harvey sums up in *A Brief History of Neoliberalism*, the latest phase of late capitalism, neoliberalism, means that "we live ... in a society in which the inalienable rights of individuals (and, recall, corporations are defined as individuals before the law) to private property and the profit rate trump any rights you can think of." This entails the championing of "individual responsibility and liability; independence from state interference ... ; equality of opportunity in the market and before the law; rewards for entrepreneurial endeavour; care for oneself and one's own; and an open marketplace.... This system of rights appears even more persuasive when extended to the right of private property in one's body (which underpins the right of the person to freely contract to sell his or her labour power ...) and the right to freedom of thought, expression, and speech. These derivative rights are appealing. Many of us rely heavily on them. But we do so much as beggars live off the crumbs from a rich man's table" (181). Whereas corporations are not liable for certain actions, people are, and yet the rights of individuals also apply to corporations, the rights of which, when contested, are brought before the rule of law, the legal decisions of which often favor businesses and industry in general. If one is lucky enough even to secure the financial resources to follow through on a lawsuit with a company that can endlessly spin out litigation for a mere pittance of its holdings, the legal system is still weighted against him or her.

The only resistance to the corporation, nevertheless, is through legal recourse.[7] Ironically, this is also the only element of collective action that seems to have any effect, since the class-action lawsuit that Laura joins affects Clare to a greater degree than the protests outside its factories in the 1960s. But even when the company agrees to settle, as small an admission of guilt though it may be, Laura realizes it only "means that the common stock has fallen to unacceptable levels. It means an offer is the more cost-effective solution" (Powers 333). Corporations merely see such legal battles, like the nearly settled lawsuit in *Michael Clayton*, from a cost-ratio perspective. From their point of view, innocence or guilt is never really an issue. The bottom line is how little it will cost to make the problem go away.

Don's reflections on Laura's first refusal to join the class-action lawsuit bring together neoliberal hegemony and the hopelessness of the individual in the face of its most vaunted institution. At first, Don is near evangelical in his attempt to persuade Laura to join the suit and earn justice, but soon he realizes that "she is due nothing. No more than anyone else with a body. No more than anyone who will get sick, which is everyone. As bad as she has it, millions will have it worse. She is on her own. She has always been on her own. Everyone who lives here is on her own. And anyone who promises otherwise is selling a bill of goods" (286). This pessimistic vision of alienation and isolation, with an attendant "market" responsibility, is disconcerting. The "individual" here is thrust into a hostile marketplace, where, instead of Adam Smith's notion that "enlightened self-interest" will rule the day for the benefit of all (as it does in Jephthah's utopian vision early in the novel), we encounter a marketplace based on mistrust and fear, one composed of individual agents out to bilk the next rube out of his or her life/savings. Yet some of these "individuals" are massive business organizations.

Don keeps pushing Laura to join the class-action lawsuit, however, because he realizes it constitutes the only way to fight Clare—that is, before the law, the neoliberal way. He has already recognized the true decenteredness of multinational capitalism and the Clare Corporation when he visits the company and ironically notes its "citizenship" (253). In this scene, we also find nineteenth-century "anarchist" violence (the kind registered in the poet-hero Presley's failed attempt to blow up the Trust's representative S. Behrman in Norris's *The Octopus*) to be a mere fading memory from a high school history class: "One bomb, it occurs to him. One little envelope of plastic explosive slipped into a portfolio while court was in session. The anarchist's dream: fifteen feet away from being able to change things forever. Then the imaginary dust settles, and it dawns on him. The board? The board's not even close to ground zero. Nor is the CEO's office, or the CFO's, or the majority stockholder's, or any other target that Don will ever be allowed to walk past" (256). The system is too widespread. It is everywhere and nowhere, unchartable, unmappable: "real commerce went on ebbing and flowing, out there, scattered, pressed thin past finding, in the shape that shared life has taken" (257). Worse yet, unlike the ambiguous Tristero-in-waiting in *The Crying of Lot 49*, even the dream of resistance in *Gain* appears to be dead: "The truth of the matter is: there is no ground zero. Nothing the anarchist could ever hit, even in imagination" (257). As Slavoj Žižek puts it in *First as Tragedy, Then as Farce*, "In contemporary global capitalism, ideological naturalization has reached an unprecedented level: rare are those who dare even to *dream* utopian dreams about possible alternatives" (77). Thus it is that due to the failure of the imagination to conceive of any different world to the capitalist one in which we find ourselves, we are only able to replay the same old fables, as Laura's son, Timothy, illustrates in his incessant playing of simulated computer games in which players build up ancient and modern civilizations with the sole intent of dominating the world (Powers 200–202) or, as the novel's final paragraphs suggest, when Timothy takes the never-touched and maturing settlement from his mother's lawsuit to help launch a corporation with some friends in order to develop a cure for cancer, a move that takes Timothy and Co. into the future of bioengineering.

Laura's coming to terms with her dying also constitutes a version of the familiar and homegrown ideology of American transcendentalism. Laura experiences "a weird dream of peace. It makes no difference whether this business gave her cancer. They have given her everything else. Taken her life and molded it in every way imaginable, plus six degrees beyond imagining. Changed her life so greatly that not even cancer can change it more than halfway back" (320). Laura accepts the "deal" that she and Clare have struck, though, of course, she has had no actual say in it at all. Her initial refusal to join the class-action lawsuit against Clare because she wants a "real" apology, not monetary compensation (which is to continue capital's game), changes when she considers her children's future. Thus, Laura, if not the text, expresses another naturalizing discourse—a kind of "family preservation" motherhood gene—a "natural drive" to which Laura submits, against her stubborn, and arguably truly Whitmanian, refusal to take part in capital's zero/tidy-sum game. As Joseph Dewey writes, "Laura evolves into an organic creature who finds, finally, her way to union within the process that keeps the system around us in motion. The vaster Clare becomes, the deader it grows; the deader Laura becomes, the vaster she grows" (126). As such, Dewey argues, "Powers nevertheless fashions a difficult act of affirmation, one that echoes what transcendentalists in their giddiest moment declaimed: only dying confirms humanity's oneness and justifies the greedy embrace of every moment" (114).

That being said, Laura is no simple throwback to the romanticized, heroic individual. As Charles B. Harris argues, Powers's reclamation of the individual "is not the nineteenth-century Romantic egoist or Modernism's existentialist hero or even quite the Habermasian post-Enlightenment individual" (104). Instead, the individual "achieves a horizon of authenticity when in dialogical exchange with other individuals . . . thereby preserving the idea of the individual but only in collaboration with other individuals" (104). Thus, at the novel's end, the "woman who has heard and not heard" gains her own peace that comes with a renewed relationship with herself, her children, and her ex-husband. Ursula K. Heise, moreover, points out that "the self-assurance of the narrator's command of the global and his transparent (though complex) language remain in tension with the scenario of individual powerlessness vis-à-vis the global power networks that the novel portrays. In this respect, the novel's formal accomplishment lags behind its conceptual sophistication" (773). Heise's point is crucial here, not merely for suggesting the "powers" of the novelist to make some kind of sense and order of a chaotic world but also for reminding us that the text, with respect to Powers's project in *Gain*, is always (un) equal to the task.

The final "transcendental vision" in *Gain* is therefore Laura's, not necessarily the text's: "Life is so big, so blameless, so unexpected. Existence lies past price, beyond scarcity. It breaks the law of supply and demand. All things that fail to work will vanish, and life remain. Lovely lichen will manufacture soil on the sunroofs of the World Trade" (344). Laura's transcendental vision, quite Whitmanesque after all, requires an incredible *longue durée* of the imagination. But the literal deification of "Life" here hinges on conceiving of it as a better producer, or "manufacturer," than is capitalism itself. What, we may ask, about the potential of economic catastrophe? Moreover, nature-as-producer eventually falls to the same logic as the conquering "force" as the Wheat in *The Octopus* is: it is only the possibility of an emergent market (the global/India in Norris and bioengineering in Powers) that, as David Harvey puts it in *The New Imperialism*, creates "spatio-temporal fixes that absorb the capital surpluses in productive and constructive ways" (135). Such transcendental visions do little for the here and now of capital, or even for conceiving of a future for *human beings*. Lichen will do just fine, we are assured, but this vision does not bode well for human life.

Calls for these kinds of conceptions—imagining a reality / possible world outside the current system—seem even more absurd when confronting the expiration of human life and the continuance of nature. All such visions paradoxically require us to imagine that which, by definition, cannot be imagined and, worse, to imagine a world in which observation and imagination themselves no longer exist. It brings back the throes of Bishop Berkeley's kind of Idealism—the tree falling in the forest becomes the earth free of humans. But this impossible imagining is never the intention of these kinds of visions. Instead, one is secretly supposed to imagine that one is the sole perceiver/survivor in such a world. The horror induced by this image is then meant to inspire people to change their wasteful habits and/or to inspire environmental protectionism in the world. The transcendental vision, however, sinks into quietism if it only seeks to assuage the problems of human reality by subsuming them under the indomitable force of nature, which is imagined to be eternal and positive. The conception of nature as Nature or a godlike force itself is a human projection. The challenge, instead, is to imagine a world not of silence, exhaustion, and devastation but of voices, intensities, and creativities.

Conclusion: Corporate Hegemony, Cubed

If Richard Powers's *Gain* can be said to be as thorough and compelling as any fictional representation of a corporation could possibly hope to be, how then might corporations be dealt with in the future? Certainly, there will always be the familiar morality-play representations of corporations, as many popular films demonstrate. There has been, however, another trend in corporate figurations, one that has taken a more inside-out approach, though always with the feeling that there is no way out of such a maze of cubicles. The postindustrial shift of the U.S. economy to white-collar and service-sector jobs, and away from blue-collar jobs, has created a large workforce/audience susceptible to this type of corporate critique. Much like the disgruntled Stanley Koteks in *The Crying of Lot 49*, there have been a number of texts that have prodded the soft insides of the corporate underbelly in a rather benign fashion. Chief among these are some of Matt Groening's *Life Is Hell* comic strips (particularly those strips of the 1980s and early 1990s collected in *Work Is Hell*), the Dilbert comic strip and now-defunct animated cartoon, and the British and American television series *The Office*. Concentrating on the cubicle-prisons of the office, these texts probe issues of boredom, resistance, and the existential meanings of being a white-collar professional in a postindustrial society, even if they ultimately lack the sharpened teeth of focused critique and tend to remain soft in registering complaint at the ubiquitous enemy, often called "corporate."[1] Rage or anger is bypassed for the ennui of Post-It note complaints. The popularity of such texts, however, has been recently appropriated by literature as well, especially in Joshua Ferris's bestselling *Then We Came to the End* and Ed Park's *Personal Days*. These novels, while playing off the soft corporate critique of popular texts, deepen their explorations of corporate life in compelling ways that highlight the expanding scope of the pseudocommunities that white-collar life gives rise to and the formation of their supposedly collective voices.

Appearing in the early to mid-1980s, Matt Groening's *Life Is Hell* comic strips satirically skewered Reagan's America, conservatism, and corporate capitalism. The strips collected in *Work Is Hell* are one of popular culture's early instances of cataloguing the dreariness, conformity, and anonymity of (mostly) office life through the ever-suffering bunny character Binky, evidenced in "chapters" such as "The Nine Types of Bosses," "The 81 Types of Employees," "How to Get Along with All the Jerks at Your Crummy Job," "Just How Bad Is Your Job?," "The Game of Work," and "How to Kill 8 Hours a Day and Still Keep Your Job." As these titles suggest, the comics depict Binky's office life as one of alienation, fear, paranoia, and complete unease. In the ironically titled "How to Tell Everyone Off and Go into Business for Yourself, Be Completely Fulfilled, and Starve to Death," for instance, Binky's expression hardly changes in each of the nine panels as he fantasizes about rebelling, quitting his job, and starting anew (a couple of "worry lines" appear in panels three and four, and a very slight expression of anger/dissatisfaction appears in panel five), subtly reinforcing the idea that nothing ever changes in the day-to-day of corporate life. The time must be filled and wasted, as Groening's other strips humorously advise, by office gossip, coffee breaks, and fashioning an eraser into a "pig" with the addition of several pushpins.

While *Work Is Hell*'s critique of corporate life might hit a dead end of sorts, it hardly panders to the world it is lambasting. Scott Adams's *Dilbert* (begun in 1989), however, was able to capitalize on the white-collar world's burgeoning dissatisfaction with office life by focusing on one office drone, Dilbert, who is essentially an office conformist (unlike *Work Is Hell*'s Binky, who is desperately isolated and clearly out of place in the office). Dilbert's success was partly a matter of timing, for although "insecurity was creeping into the office by the mid-'80s," as Nikil Saval points out in "Birth of the Office," "on or around October 19, 1987 everything changed" (114). The market crash ushered in a new economic climate in which even office workers' jobs were at risk. Apparently this worried white-collar audience helped to ensure *Dilbert*'s rise to fame, which included a spin-off television cartoon and plenty of merchandise. Dilbert's corporate "critique," however, is harmless to nonexistent. Pointing out the little absurdities of office life through one of its worker-drones leaves little room to expose the futility and despair underlying much of the corporate life, which Groening did so well. In the end, Dilbert's success is dependent on the very corporate life it pretends to make fun of—the strip is less humorous than humoring, including such tired gags as a talking dog, Dogbert.[2] Dilbert, for instance, has appeared on several *Fortune* magazine covers, something it would be hard to imagine Groening letting happen to his *Life Is Hell* characters.[3] As Norman Solomon points out in *The Trouble with Dilbert*, Adams is merely pandering to the corporate world he appears to be lampooning. Citing several interviews in which it becomes clear that Adams, a business-school alumnus, lauds the benefits of downsizing for the good of productivity, Solomon points out the paradox of the cartoon strip: "Dilbert has become schizoid by design—both a cherished mascot of oppressed office workers and a valued marketing tool for companies oppressing them" (ch. 1). The gentle pokes at mismanagement and corporate carelessness that make *Dilbert* a champion to many office workers were easily co-opted by the system.

Somewhere between these two poles of corporate critique stands the Ricky Gervais and Stephen Merchant British television program *The Office*, which ran for two seasons and a Christmas special and spawned an American version of the show that I will address here. Following the "straight" couple of Jim and Pam, *The Office* plays on the "family" aspect of the workplace (Dunder-Mifflin, a paper company), which is full of quirky characters working under the continual threat of downsizing. In order for the American *Office* to eclipse its British counterpart in length, however, the show, which ran for nine seasons, had to make some strange plot twists. The ever-troubled paper company somehow keeps growing and allows a cast of characters in and out of its doors and even provides room for advancement for Jim and Pam, the show's central characters. The truth of the protagonist couple, however, is that they are the safest and most boring characters on the show, as their near-interchangeable and "normal" names suggest. Their average lives, confined to the office, belie the aspirations they obviously had to surrender to keep working for such a modest company in stifling small-town Scranton. At one point, Pam drops out of a graphic-design program she attends in New York, and Jim leaves a bigger branch to come back to the smaller Scranton one. The two are only "released" on the series's last episode (when it is safe to do so) after Pam accepts Jim's desire to move to Austin to help run his now-successful start-up. While earlier in the series Jim and Pam's practical jokes and time wasting appeared to be mildly rebellious, their sudden advancement in position shows them to be less interested in resistance than in a better-paying job and a quiet family life. The show, in order to continue beyond the point of the British version, must make the two more comfortable in what initially was supposed to be a workplace/life from which to escape. In short, all corporate critique, even at the existential level of the nine-to-five meaninglessness, is completely lost. Instead, the show is now arranged around the protagonist couple who give the viewer a shared vantage point from which to watch the ridiculous, yet ultimately frail and human, co-workers whom the couple is meta-aware of (through dry looks at the camera at key moments) and must daily suffer. In this respect, it is not unlike the Super Bowl commercials from some years ago depicting a man in an office working with a bunch of screaming and violent monkeys. Everyone is an idiot, except me, such ideology suggests.

Mike Judge's *Office Space* (1999) takes this soft critique a step forward by indulging in a kind of "revolutionary" fantasy regarding corporate life. The film depicts three friends who are stuck working at a downsizing Silicon Valley–like company in an office park, living in cookie-cutter apartments, and eating lunch in strip malls at TGI Friday's–like franchise restaurants that boast "flair" and a simulacra fun-time entertainment atmosphere. The protagonist, Peter Gibbons (Ron Livingston), hates his dead-end job updating code for the upcoming Y2K nonapocalypse, has relationship problems with his girlfriend, and consequently indulges in a good amount of self-loathing. Peter's self-hatred arises from the fact that he plays the perfect lackey, unable to stand up to his dreary and annoying boss, who constantly requests that Peter come in on weekends. In addition, Peter is repeatedly harangued for small oversights by two other bosses, who treat him as if he were a little child. Like Milton Waddams, his unhinged and muttering co-worker, who eventually burns down the company, Peter cannot adequately articulate his dissatisfaction and frustration with the system, finding himself powerless against the excruciating boredom and blandness of corporate life. In short, he is unable to resist the corporate hegemony in any fashion.

Yet Peter and his two friends are filled with rage at the stupidity of office protocol, malfunctioning equipment, low wages, and their suddenly fragile job security. Resistance to this corporate and suburban nightmare, however, comes in the release of pent-up anger via the relatively newly popularized music genre gangsta rap. The film humorously points out that it is an inauthentic appropriation by a (mostly) white middle class of legitimate black anger at social conditions when one white friend of Peter's blasts rap in his car while stuck in bumper-to-bumper traffic, until he rolls up next to a person of color selling flowers, after which he quickly shuts his windows, locks his door, and sinks down in his seat. Yet the film goes on to endorse this view of the "resistance" of gangsta rap itself, playing the Geto Boys' "Still" in the film's most famous scene, in which the three friends take a baseball bat to a recalcitrant fax/copy machine. White "corporate" rage needs to be registered by popular culture's current system-smashing music of choice, which, at the time, could hardly be the ultimately apolitical grunge of Nirvana and its ilk but the newly outrageous gangsta rap groups, such as the seminal N.W.A., which boasted such songs as "Fuck tha Police."[4] Indeed, when Peter begins to rebel against the system, he comes in to work to the tune of the Geto Boys' "Damn It Feels Good to Be a Gangsta."

However, Peter and his two friends, true to their white-collar roots, engage in an accounting scam, lifted from the plot of *Superman III* (1983), that will potentially make them rich. Resistance to the system in this case merely reinforces the system, for no fundamental value or values are questioned here. The primary "value" of the system, capital, is embraced. Only the means for obtaining it, those that the system deems illegal, have changed. This is also why gangsta rap seems so appropriate to many of the scenes of "resistance." Just as in mob films from *Scarface* (1932) to *Scarface* (1983), gangsta rap (though it may, at times, raise issues of social [racial, ethnic] justice) ultimately argues that the way to "equality" is through an inverse and spectacularly violent pursuit of the American Dream. The fundamental system is fine, but because of structural disadvantages, illegal means must be pursued in order to partake in it.

The real possibility of resistance, however, is played out through Peter. Peter begins the film as a spineless and unimaginative office flunky, enticed only by a waitress who works at a restaurant he and his friends eat lunch in and by a construction-working neighbor who offers Peter both sympathy for his white-collar troubles and a potential life of freedom outside the office (such as fishing). This all changes with the film's key plot twist. When Peter visits a hypnotherapist with his soon-to-be ex-girlfriend, he is hypnotized to believe he can do anything he feels like, no matter the consequences. When the psychologist who has hypnotized him dies of a heart attack before waking Peter from his fantasy, Peter remains in this state of euphoric hypnosis. Under such influence, Peter decides he will do whatever he feels like doing, such as sleeping in the next morning, skipping work, and finally asking out the waitress he has been quietly eyeing for months.

That Peter's new cavalier "I'll do whatever I feel like" attitude is a psychologically induced state and not a deeply considered personal choice to change is telling. In one sense, of course, Peter's new attitude is a deep wish fulfillment, not just for Peter but for the film's entire audience—he comes into work dressed in casual attire and flip-flops, tells the boss he does not feel like working, tears down one of his cubicle walls, and admits to the consultants hired to lay off workers that he has no motivation or desire to work harder. Who would not like to follow such whims with complete self-assurance, composure, and contentment? Peter has become pure pleasure principle here, flowing on with endless unimpeded access to happiness, and we go with him, enjoying his newfound power to tell the boss off and not give a damn about the consequences, as if we too were able to do so if we simply *felt* like it.

Yet we "know" that such a wish fulfillment really *is* a fantasy. Peter has been hypnotized to believe *his* fantasy is reality, whereas we all "know" that it is the other way around. Could we find a better definition of ideology even in Marx? The film suggests that the "real" world consists of dull, corporate slavery. Since, moreover, it would be impossible to imagine Peter's kind of resistance (a classic Thoreauvian self-reliant individualism with a twist of California cool and gangsta swagger) occurring in our "real" lives, the resistance must be staged as fantasy—both Peter's fantasy and the fantasy of the film that we watch. Yet the "real world" we live in, of course, is ideological as well. Capitalism asks that we get up, go to the office, follow orders, earn a paycheck, leave work, purchase commodities, watch TV, go to bed, and repeat. The well-oiled system promises a slickness unto death. At a much deeper level, it asks that we accept this as the way things are, have been, and always will be.

But to release the force of the pleasure principle means to release, also, that other drive, the one set toward disintegration and annihilation. This comes, of course, in Milton Waddams, Peter's co-worker and secret Other. It is Milton's murmured, yet ignored, threats and continual dispossession (his ever-missing stapler) and alienation (as he is moved from smaller office to smaller office and finally to the symbolic basement, where he sits under a sign warning, "Danger: High Voltage") that eventually causes him to erupt in a way that Peter's anger, due to his hypnosis, will not allow. Milton stands not so much for the bottled-up rage of the dispossessed proletariat (or bourgeois 1990s increasingly insecure office worker) but as the "real" of Peter's anger that psychoanalysis/therapy is unable to master. Milton's weird and incessant mumbling literally enters into Peter's head at one point, as his cubicle neighbor calls him on the phone to complain about the way he is being treated. His burning down the office is no revolutionary statement (indeed nobody even knows he has done it since he is, and always was, invisible) but the fulfillment of the death drive, the darker underbelly to Peter's wondrous and dream-like pleasure principle.[5]

The problem with the film, however, is that the fantasy never ends. It seems as if the hypnosis effect eventually dissipates as Peter shows concerns for his friends' jobs after they are fired. But the truth is that Peter is *never actually brought out of his state of hypnosis*; he is enthralled by it. By the end of the film, Peter has shrugged off the corporate life for a blue-collar job. We see him in his own Hollywood ending, happy, the girl gotten, wearing a hard hat and engaged in construction work with his romanticized neighbor. This return of the repressed, to a nostalgic vision of authenticity via blue-collar labor, is the most fantastic element of Peter's and the film's dream of resisting capital, akin to the portrait of the disciplined workers at the end of *Gung Ho*. In other words, Peter never snaps out of it, and neither does the audience. The film merely replaces one ideology with another. While *Office Space* thus remains a cult classic for its canny and engaging anticorporate fantasy, it ultimately indulges in as much capitalist ideology as it challenges.

Two recent literary examples of this corporate "inside-out" trend offer a different dynamic to popular culture's soft critique, suggesting and exploring the possibilities of a collective "we" or, more troubling, a corporate collective "we." Joshua Ferris's *Then We Came to the End* and Ed Park's *Personal Days*, like the aforementioned comics, television shows, and film, present an office world of quirky, bored "characters" given to gossiping and worrying about the instability of their jobs in an era of downsizing. Each novel charts the slow disintegration of a business/office while showing the absurdity of white-collar office life in the style of *Catch-22* (1961; or like Joseph Heller's darkly comic and lesser-known office novel *Something Happened* [1975])—each story circles around a core of "sadness" (in Ferris's book it is one character's secret cancer, in Park's it is one character's secret crush, and in both it is the fleeting relationships formed in an ever-changing environment) meant to legitimate its cataloguing of the employees' petty bickering, time-wasting activities, and prank playing. As for the characters (who are truly "characters" or "types"), they could easily take a metafictional romp from one novel to the other (or for that matter into *The Office* or *Office Space*) without upsetting the tone, atmosphere, or ontology of each world. In a sense, the characters do just this. As the layoffs in each story increase, characters disappear, many are eventually forgotten by the dwindling few, and some are never seen again (the latter more so in *Personal Days*), which gives each text a mildly despondent feel, a kind of melancholy halo to the aforementioned core of sadness. As one character complains to a co-worker in *Personal Days*, "you're all interchangeable," and it is markedly true (238).

The prominence of these interchangeable character parts explains, to some degree, the curious narrative voice employed in each text. Both Ferris and Park adopt a third-person-plural point of view, an impossible "we" form of "limited" omniscient narration, for the majority of each novel. This point of view suggests that the company's employees form a collective, a kind of family, and that the "we" speaks for their universal experiences and feelings. As the "we" says in *Personal Days*, "you form these intense bonds without realizing it" since "you see co-workers more than you see your so-called friends, even more than your significant others" (14). Yet the point of view is impossible to defend at the narrative level since it cannot be pinned down to any one individual, which creates a very special sort of "we," one very much defined, confined, and refined by the corporate structure out of which it arises.

At first glance, the use and formation of a "we" would seem to be apt for Ferris's and Park's novels because of the small social worlds they construct—that of the office or, to be more precise, a certain department or floor of an office. In such a reduced environment, the collective "we" appears to make sense. The incessant watercooler gossip, time wasting, e-mails, and socializing would answer to how this impossible "we" seems so omniscient. Park's *Personal Days* uses the "we" until its final section, offering a possible answer to its impossibility if one were to reduce the "we" to the character of Jonah. At the novel's end, Jonah remains inside the corporate whale, so to speak, awaiting rescue in a stalled elevator and typing a "tell-all" letter about the company to a former co-worker and crush, Pru. Told in the first person, Jonah's letter allows Park to escape formalistically the limiting and impossible "we" of the novel. Moreover, as the Jonah/Ishmael prophet-survivor (everyone else has been fired by this point), his intimate knowledge of the company's recent changes, spearheaded by the imposter and clinically insane corporate restructuring officer Gordon Graham Knott (aka Grimes), makes him the sole character privy to all the information that Grimes gathers en route to his corporate restructuring. Since Jonah uncovers the mystery of Grimes, he is the only real survivor/writer/detective able to write the "we" sections. But Jonah's letter feels more like a cop-out, a sudden Patricia

Highsmith twist that offers a truly insane Ripley-esque Grimes (who, like Milton Waddams in *Office Space*, Tom Mota in *Then We Came to the End*, and, to a certain degree, Ted Warburton, the "Mad Memo-ist" in Don DeLillo's *Americana* [1971; 21, 99–100], represents the now-familiar unhinged, disillusioned employee) to mop up the attenuated mystery running throughout the novel (that is, whether there is a conspiracy to fire certain people). This ultimately serves as the excuse for the cold corporate hatchet decisions, even though the new Californian owners would have probably implemented a fairly similar restructuring plan to Grimes's. The "irrational" Grimes is a figure of capital's irrationality, but it is a figure that needs no literalizing in this context. The switch to first person in the final section/letter remains not only dissatisfying but formally suspect.

Ferris's *Then We Came to the End* raises even greater concerns with its "we" point of view. As in *Personal Days*, when characters are laid off or quit, we begin to wonder who will be left, or who could be possibly left, to tell the story. Yet we are not left with a Jonah/Ishmael survivor as a potential narrative candidate. Ferris's "we" is also an ideological sleight of hand, making more generalized pronouncements revealing the class makeup and assumptions of this "we": "We believed that downturns had been rendered obsolete by the ingenious technology of the new economy" (18); "We were corporate citizens, buttressed by advanced degrees and padded by corporate fat. We were above fickle market forces of overproduction and mismanaged inventory" (19). The novel, a supposed wake-up call for these comfortable "corporate citizens" during harsh economic times, is largely muted because of the privileged position of such individuals, whose sufferings are cushioned at best.

As Ferris acknowledges, the title of his novel, *Then We Came to the End*, is an allusion to the first line of Don DeLillo's *Americana*. To compare the two novels' portrayal of corporate life and the advertising industry, however, leads to radically different conclusions. In fact, the conclusion of each novel might offer a good starting point in the analysis of each. *Americana* ends with the narrator, David Bell—who has stopped in Texas on his way back to New York after a rollicking and unfulfilling cross-country road trip through America and as far west as Arizona (falling short of the symbolic Phoenix)—engaged in a violent and sordid orgy. He emerges from this dark encounter and finds himself at a racetrack, where he watches the cars looping endlessly around before making a symbolic trip down Elm Street in downtown Dallas (the site of JFK's assassination) en route to the airport, where he books a flight back to New York. The linearity of the supposed soul-finding road trip ends symbolically in the closed circular track of boredom, violence, and decadence.[6] *Then We Came to the End*, though its title suggests what DeLillo's novel enacts, ends with the remaining employees of a company that has seen an economic downturn trigger a mass of firings. Seeing a company through tough economic times, however, merely leaves the reader caught up in capitalist business cycles.

Then We Came to the End attempts to transcend this cyclical trap through art itself in the figure of a onetime employee, the forgotten Hank Neary, who publishes a novel some years after he has been let go. At the novel's end, the company's employees, current and erstwhile, gather together at a reading of Hank's novel. In a mild metafictional move, the chapter that he reads appears to be an earlier chapter in *Then We Came to the End*, the sole chapter that explores an individual character, the boss, Lynn Mason, through third-person omniscient narration, temporarily abandoning the impossible corporate/company omniscient "we."[7] Art, then, is able to bring together this onetime "family," many of whom have lost contact with one another. The metafiction lite also suggests that Ferris's novel, as art object, is able to transform and transcend the meaninglessness of white-collar corporate life through the structure and forms of literature. But, again, this is dishonest. DeLillo's "ending" is apocalyptic, Dante's day at the races, but Ferris's ending is more the Marx Brothers' *A Day at the Races* (1937). We, like Groucho, end up getting a fine tutti-fruitsying, as in Ferris's novel the same old cycles of capital, like that of Chico's nearly endless sales of code books to the hoodwinked, horse-betting Groucho, softly reestablish themselves: many of the once-anxious employees get new and similar jobs to the ones they lost, and nothing much changes. As the narrator states regarding the former employees' new jobs once their company has gone under, "the colors of the corporate logos were all new and different, but the song and dance remained the same" (359). *Americana*, while its ending might appear cyclical, is redeemed by the fact that David Bell, the narrator, tells his story from a desert island, suggesting a possible space outside the known and disintegrating world. In other words, we never really "come to the end" in Ferris's novel. Capitalism's *longue durée* still happily rules the day, whereas in DeLillo, it rues the incipient end of it.

Not surprisingly, American-style transcendentalism makes a small appearance in *Then We Came to the End* as well, through the character of Tom Mota, an older, disgruntled employee who is fired. Aware that he is close to being axed, Mota mourns the changing business climate—"Didn't

General Motors, . . . IBM, and Madison Avenue establish postwar American might upon the two-martini lunch?" (116)—and takes to sending cryptic and violently suggestive e-mails to his co-workers, as well as quoting Whitman, and especially Emerson, to them. After being fired and sending a few more e-mails suggesting a possibly deranged mind, Mota returns one day wearing a clown suit and pelting his former co-workers with a paintball gun, which leads to his jailing. Mota sees himself as a tough, self-reliant individualist, but while in jail, he confesses to his former boss and nemesis, Joe Pope, that he was wrong. He calls Joe the arch individualist, who is somehow able to rise above the corporate life: "I thought *I* was up there, but no, that whole time, I was down *here*, with everybody else—churning, spinning, talking, lying, circling, whipping myself into a frenzy. I was doing everything they were doing, just in my own way. But you . . . , you stay here, Joe. You're up here" (344). Thus, the novel would seem to offer the possibility of the sovereign individual transcending the mundane world just as Norris, Pynchon, and Powers have suggested. Pope, as Mota says, ignored the catty gossip and insults hurled his way and concentrated on his work, the very reason he survives being laid off. This casts the novel's heroic epigraph, an Emerson quotation from "The American Scholar," in an ironic light: "Is it not the chief disgrace in the world, not to be a unit—not to be reckoned one with character;—not to yield that particular fruit which each man was created to bear, but to be reckoned in the gross, in the hundred, or the thousand, of the party, the section, to which we belong. . . ." In *Then We Came to the End*, the Emersonian individual need not abandon his white-collar roots for a blue-collar utopia, as in *Office Space*, because, apparently, the office worker—more specifically the committed corporate ladder climber like Joe Pope—*is* the neo-Emersonian self-made man. If the rest of the corporate drones could simply be as serious and responsible about their work as Joe Pope is, they too could truly taste the Emersonian fruits of their labor, instead of grumbling with Willy Loman that a man is not a piece of fruit.

While *Personal Days* eventually escapes the awkward and tiresome "we" by shifting to the first person, *Then We Came to the End* irritatingly hangs on to its impossible narrative voice throughout the novel. Thus it is that "we" arrive at the curious last line of the book: "We were the only two left. Just the two of us, you and me" (385). Suddenly the reader is also implicated in this "we," which apparently has been assumed all along (and correctly, judging by the novel's sales success and National Book Award nomination). Such a cloying narrative switch feels unearned here.

Then We Came to the End makes the jump from an impossible "we" to an impossible "you." In short, you, the reader, have been part of the "we" all along. You too are part of the family.

In the 2007 Back Bay paperback edition of *Then We Came to the End*, a "Conversation with Joshua Ferris" records his answer to the question about the use of the narrative "we." Ferris's response is interesting:

> Companies tend to refer to themselves in the first-person plural in annual reports, corporate brochures, within meetings and internal memos, and, in particular, in advertising. What used to be the "royal we" might be thought of as the "corporate we." It's not just a company's way of showing unity and strength; it's also a way of making everyone feel as if they're a member of the club. . . .
>   In *Then We Came to the End*, you see who this "we" really is—a collection of messy human beings—stripped of their glossy finish and eternal corporate optimism. It returns the "we" to the individuals who embody it. (4–5)

But it is the "corporate we" that ends up having the final say. The workers who sometimes consider themselves a "kind" of family are only brought together under the aegis of the corporation. In other words, contra Ferris, individuals (if we can still call them that) do *not* embody the corporation; *the corporation embodies them*. The fact that the employee "family" loses contact with its "members" once they are terminated or leave to do other things shows that the bonds created under such conditions—corporate capitalism—remain more contractual than social. The analogy that Ferris would like to make between a family and a "family" of co-workers is thus: we do not pick who the members of our family are, but we have to learn to tolerate and live with them, just as, since we do not pick who our co-workers are, we similarly have to learn to tolerate and work with them. Therefore, both are, in a sense, families, communities that can voice their beliefs, histories, and hopes for the future.

But if the bonds holding the company-family together are in no way social but are contractual, then it is the corporation and capital that keeps this "family" together, as *J R* clearly shows. This does not mean that coworkers cannot become good friends, date, perhaps even marry and start families. Indeed, these kinds of relationships emerge from workplaces all the time, although based on the literature's and popular culture's representations of officer-worker life, this is a rarity and something to be avoided. What this does mean is that the communal "we" has no basis outside the bonds of capital. It can only be the corporate body, and thus corporate voice, that survives its rotating cast of "family members." The "collection of messy human beings" proves itself, by and large, incapable of having a communal voice because it *has no space or body of its own.*

In the decentered, no-place of corporate capitalism, on what stable ground can such a communal "we" be based outside the advertising and "corporate we" that Ferris mentions? Who, we might ask, is speaking? I would suggest that the answer is the corporation itself, surely not the monological, if highly scripted, voice of its advertisements but the dialogical one that emerges from Ferris's attempt to give the impossible voice back to the privileged, "oppressed" office workers. What results is a corporate voice that *seems* to speak to corporate capitalism's irrationality yet is merely a co-opted version of it. In the end, this "we" is little more than an esprit de corporation.

The literature of the inside of the corporation becomes merely a vehicle for capital's voice. Since capital cannot truly "have" a voice, it compels those who work for and within it to speak for it, seemingly as a ventriloquist does the dummy; but, somewhat like the famous *Twilight Zone* episode, it is now the dummy controlling the ventriloquist, only the ventriloquist is completely unaware of this and chatters mindlessly on. The petty complaints about management, the gripes about labyrinthine and mindless corporate bureaucracy, the anxiety experienced during economic downturns, even the desire to escape into a life of "real" blue-collar work—none lodges an effective critique of corporate capitalism itself. The "we" is not so much those employees, who, one by one, are laid off or fired, but the "immortal" voice of the corporation itself, that which survives its individual owners or employees, as Samuel Clare realizes in *Gain*. Such literature gives a voice to the corporation in the guise of its workers, the same corporation that has, through incorporation, been granted a body, a set of rights based on the law, and an "ethical" position based on limited liability and its commitment to its shareholders. So it is that this voice is even more disturbing than the "voice" the corporation has gained through advertising. Rather than speak for itself, the corporate "we" now compels others to speak it, to speak for itself. Thus it is that such "inside" views of the corporation are ultimately even less able to offer an effective critique or resistance to corporate power.

Selling (Out) Futures

If the neoliberal project ever wholly rights itself again, it would not be too hard to imagine how quickly the widening gap between rich and poor would continue to grow, finally squeezing the last juice from the once-lush pulp of America's middle class. In the introduction, I drew from Giorgio Agamben's characterization of modern politics as instituting a permanent "state of exception" to argue that neoliberalism, particularly after capital's latest crisis, has initiated an "economy of exception," wherein those institutions that helped to instigate the 2008 financial crisis are, by and large, exempt from having to answer for it. There I pointed out how average Americans have been essentially abandoned to the market forces unleashed during the neoliberal financialization of the economy. Partly because of predatory lending, securitized debt obligations, high-interest credit cards, student-loan debt, and the taxpayer bailout of the banking system, Americans have found themselves deeper in debt and more uncertain about their futures than ever. At the risk of tolling the dystopian bell too loudly, I would like to consider the ramifications of this economy of exception in regard to the concept of biopolitics that emerged in the chapters on *J R*, *White Noise*, and *Gain*.

There are essentially two major tributaries to biopolitical criticism that, though each contains its own methodological interests, share a common concern with the status of "bios" or life in the contemporary world. Roughly put, the first of these is preoccupied with life as it is transformed by the comingling of science, technology, and capital, while the second is focused more on the role of nation-states and governments in managing populations, what Foucault once called "governmentality" in his late lectures on biopolitics.[8] We might reformulate this equation as a biopolitics of capital and a biopolitics of the state, although the two mutually inform each other and are never entirely distinct. On the whole, the novels in this study express biopolitical concerns of the first kind in their consideration of the commodification of life, the business of medicine, and the medicalization of everyday life. Indeed, these texts recognize that as capital seeks out new markets to offset the falling rate of profit, it finds itself having to commodify more and more hitherto-unimagined aspects of life—and eventually life itself.

This is no longer mere dystopian speculation, however. Recent breakthroughs in genetics—human, animal, and plant life—have made it necessary, following the logic of capital, for companies to patent their "discoveries." As a result, corporations now own patents on genes, the DNA of life itself.[9] This takes things a step further than even the everyday medicalization of life as it relates to the pharmaceutical industry witnessed in *White Noise*. Genomics suggests that disease can be dealt with at a genetic level; thus, medicine becomes even more "personal" and necessary than ever. The potential for developing such genetic therapies, however, is attendant on building a database of personalized genetic information. The database that Gladney finds himself included in when he talks to the SIMUVAC technician may appear relatively benign in the end (Gladney eventually turns his back on the doctors), but it heralds the fact that many subjects in the biopolitical age are unlikely to have any choice in the matter of how their genetic information is used or stored.[10] In short, we can see the ways in which neoliberal capitalism has been able to capitalize fully and to unprecedented levels on life itself in an age of biopower—and not necessarily by way of some deliberate corporate or plutocratic conspiracy but as the inevitable result of capital's influence on the still relatively young biotech industry.

This is surely a disturbing trend, but this more publicly visible example of biopolitics, which can often stoke sensational fears of genetic engineering or organ harvesting, should not eclipse the less spectacular, yet thoroughly widespread, biopolitical character of the modern state.[11] In *Homo Sacer: Sovereign Power and Bare Life*, Agamben extends Foucault's ideas on biopolitics to theorize about what happens to life itself when politics and the law are given over to "the state of exception." Modern biopolitics, for Agamben, means that "today a law that seeks to transform itself wholly into life is more and more confronted with a life that has been deadened and mortified into juridical rule" (187).[12] Life is thus reduced to what Agamben calls "bare life" or "naked life," particularly as captured in the ancient Roman juridical conception of *homo sacer*, or "sacred man," who, in his ambiguous status, "can be killed [by anyone with impunity] but not sacrificed" (94). *Homo sacer*, then, can stand for the numerous marginalized bodies that are defined at the edges of, or outside, the law, thus constituting exceptional cases of peoples who are included in contemporary society through their very exclusion, such as migrant workers, immigrants seeking asylum, or the "enemy combatants" (still) held at Guantánamo Bay. Stripped of rights and reduced to "bare life," *homo sacer* is abandoned in, quite literally, a no-man's-land. Moreover, with the turn toward biopolitics that a never-ending state of exception facilitates, *homo sacer* comes to serve not only as a figure for the "exceptional" body reduced to "bare life" without rights—a body that simply does not count—but also as a figure for its seeming opposite, the normal(ized) body that is increasingly made docile, as Foucault might put it, and produced in accordance with the "rule(s)."

This dual mode of *homo sacer* can be seen in the film *Children of Men* (2006), which depicts a dystopian, totalitarian future in which humanity can no longer reproduce through natural or scientific means and civilization is collapsing.[13] The film shows the relative "freedom" enjoyed by certain British citizens, themselves subject to the tyranny of biopolitical control (ironically the subject cannot reproduce life, while the state, in fact, (re)produces it in biopolitical fashion), as well as the suffering of those who are excluded, the many illegal immigrants seeking asylum who have no place in such a society and are rounded up in internment camps. My point here is that both kinds of *homo sacer* can simultaneously exist in a society. The immigrant detention centers dotted along the wall being constructed across the U.S.-Mexico border, for instance, and the civil liberties lost in the Patriot Act (still in place) illustrate that the "state of exception," the endless War on Terror, and *homo sacer* are integral to America's current social and political livelihood. Indeed, the recent revelations of the federal government's surveillance of Americans' phone and e-mail records underscores how the exceptional (government surveillance) has become the rule (a permanent safety precaution) that the American public, for the most part, dislikes but has apparently been conditioned to accept.

Taking into account today's permanent state of emergency does not, however, preclude the fact that a disaster of major proportions—whether environmental, natural, war related, or financial—could easily exacerbate the divide between the haves and have-nots in America into a further (class-based) division between the haves and yet another version of *homines sacri*. Naomi Klein's *The Shock Doctrine: The Rise of Disaster Capitalism* makes clear that neoliberal capitalism does not just initiate various crises but has learned to capitalize on them: "Now wars and disaster responses are so fully privatized that they are themselves the new market; there is no need to wait until after the war for the boom— the medium is the message" (13).[14] When Klein discusses the failures of the government and FEMA in responding to the victims of Katrina in 2005, and the ways that private industry stepped in (Wal-Mart delivered supplies to some victims), the outlines of the true danger begin to appear (408–413). In the midst of such a disaster, in which the federal government, long since crippled by neoliberal economic policy, failed to assist many of its poorer citizens and to establish order, private companies came to people's aid instead, although often only to the aid of wealthy residents. One such company was the right-wing-run Blackwater (now called Academi), the private military "contractors" (by definition, they are mercenaries composed of U.S. veterans and dubious types, such as former El Salvadoran death-squad members) active in Iraq at the time, who arrived on the scene to help reestablish order *before* the government actually hired them (Scahill 324).[15] Blackwater, a paramilitary group acting under its own authority, defended the neighborhoods of the rich, while poorer neighborhoods remained in turmoil. Katrina shows that after a disaster of major proportions, already-existing class divisions are brutally exposed for what they are, and people in need of help are essentially abandoned to their fate unless they can afford to purchase assistance. Many who were unable to pay for such services eventually ended up living in FEMA trailers or were herded into the Louisiana Superdome (now, ironically, the Mercedes-Benz Superdome)—a better example of *homines sacri* would be hard to find. Furthermore, the reconstruction and gentrification of once-poor New Orleans neighborhoods has aggravated the class and racial divides that preexisted the disaster, as poorer residents have been left out of the city's tourist-based reconstruction plans (see Gotham; and Venkatesh).

That the images of Katrina struck the American public as eerily reminiscent of disasters in the so-called third world, the kinds of disasters that could never occur in America, illustrates that the line separating citizen from *homo sacer*, first from third world, is more precarious than it seems. The global perspective of capital that results from this comparison is critical to keep in mind, not so much because it gives a portrait of capital's older mode of exploitation (indeed, it reveals that mode is ongoing) but because it offers a paradigm of a possible future one. In reality, corporations' labor policies and business practices in developing countries, while they appear to be draconian and backward, are simply more basic and ruthless forms of corporate exploitation that poverty-stricken nations are compelled to accept. Already, as corporate capitalism reaches its territorial global exhaustion, corporations are finding it difficult to tap into cheap labor sources by threatening to pull up stakes and move elsewhere—thus indulging in a lowest-common-denominator wage game with its prospective new homes (countries)—and are subsequently engaging more and more in what David Harvey calls "accumulation by dispossession" (essentially taking resources from peoples unable to defend themselves, whether through military or economic muscle), in which "regional crises and highly localized place-based devaluations emerge as a primary means by which capitalism perpetually creates its own 'other' in order to feed upon it" (*New Imperialism* 151). Considering the various global environmental crises, catastrophes, and the growing scarcity of natural resources, such as oil and water, there is fair reason to think that the right mixture of economic crisis and governmental policy, as Katrina suggests, could create the tenuous social and political conditions in America that often exist in developing countries. For it is not only wealthy individuals but also wealthy nations that are invested in a world economic system which ensures that such declining resources will be allocated only to the few who can afford them.

Capital's "othering," however, means that corporations create, despite their increasing decenteredness, a figurative, if amorphous, "self" or body that can serve as a target for those who attempt to battle neoliberal capitalism as it transitions into a truly unique and hitherto-unparalleled biopolitical stage of late capitalism. To date, small groups of farmers have begun to fight, legally and with varying success, against Monsanto's patent-infringement suits over genetically modified seeds that spread to some farmers' fields and affect their crops.[16] Legal victories against corporate power, however, are few and far between, as corporations have enormous resources with which to prolong legal cases, thus making sustained challenges from small groups or individuals next to impossible. Armed resistance, like the kind seen in America during the industrial age and early twentieth century, today appears to be the only feasible strategy for fighting corporate power available to the very poor in developing nations. Bolivia's Cochabamba, for instance, fought a successful, though costly, victory against Aguas del Tunari and the privatization of their water (Bakan 164–166), and the Zapatista movement has similarly fought against the privatization of the land of the people of Chiapas, Mexico. These kinds of material resistances toward neoliberal capitalism and privatization may have to be adopted more and more in Western states too, where the preferred method of opposing the corporation is by legal challenge. If nothing else, these examples show that a small yet localized form of resistance against corporate power can be highly successful. As the anarchist collective The Invisible Committee writes in *The Coming Insurrection*, "The new economy cannot be established without a ... selection of subjects and zones singled out for transformation. The chaos that we constantly hear about will either provide the opportunity for this selection, or for our victory over this odious project" (72). Perhaps a constellation of these micro resistances could add up to a macro one, though it is difficult to see how such a large-scale transformation could actually occur. So what more can be done?

The Socialist Corporation: Utopia Ltd.

Is there, then, the possibility of reforming the corporation? Can a corporate body be tamed by regulation or even transformed by a business vision that includes the pursuit of the social good as much as it does profit? Considering the lack of economic reform after the 2008 financial crisis, as well as the Supreme Court's 2010 *Citizens United* decision that grants corporations even more of a political voice via unlimited campaign contributions, that answer would appear to be a resounding no. Putting aside the question of corporate reform, however, what of the corporate form itself? Can we detect a nascent utopian corporate form within the corporate structure as we know it today? Indeed, Fredric Jameson asks that we do just this in *Valences of the Dialectic* when he ponders the value of one of America's most notorious corporations, Wal-Mart. Not content with simply writing the company off as a capitalist monster, Jameson also examines Wal-Mart's business innovations as possibly outlining the "shape of a Utopian future looming through the mist, which we must seize as an opportunity to exercise the Utopian imagination more fully" (423). Further, Jameson's analysis of Wal-Mart is exemplary of a greater method requiring the "prodigious effort to change valences on phenomena which so far exist only in our present; and experimentally to declare positive things which are clearly negative in our own world, to affirm that dystopia is Utopia if examined more closely" (434). Surely the corporation is impressive in its ability to gather people and capital together and to imagine, organize, and build often large and vast enterprises that affect the world in significant ways. Is the corporate form itself thus neutral? Could it be used to produce the common good for all more than goods just for profit? And what would such a corporation look like?

Kurt Vonnegut's *Jailbird* (1979) offers a model of a potentially "socialist" corporation in its depiction of the multinational conglomerate RAMJAC. The novel is narrated by the recently released ex-convict Walter F. Starbuck, a onetime idealistic communist who, after a series of personal and political mishaps in life, ends up halfheartedly working for the Nixon administration before ending up in prison as a result of Watergate. After his release, Starbuck, through a series of serendipitous events, is reunited with a former lover, Mary Kathleen O'Looney, from his communist days. Mary, though living disguised as a homeless woman for fear of her life, is actually the majority stockholder in charge of the multinational RAMJAC corporation. Still committed to her communist ideals, she is disgusted by RAMJAC's dealings but justifies them because the company's profits will one day be redistributed to those whom she believes are RAMJAC's rightful owners, the American people. After Mary dies, Starbuck secretly keeps the corporation running until word gets out. As a result, he is sent back to jail, and the corporation is sold off by the government. Despite the obvious contradictions of Mary's vision, it nevertheless constitutes a utopian dream of the redistribution of capital through the means of capitalism itself, a utopia achieved through dystopia. The corporate form can be used to serve all, the novel suggests.

Always skeptical of utopian visions, however, Vonnegut, like his hero Starbuck, is well aware of the limitations of Mary's plan, which manifest themselves at the moment the corporate legacy is bequeathed: "For one thing, the federal government was wholly unprepared to operate all the businesses of RAMJAC on behalf of the people. For another thing: Most of those businesses, rigged only to make profits, were as indifferent to the needs of the people as, say, thunderstorms. Mary Kathleen might as well have left one-fifth of the weather to the people" (272). Here Vonnegut shows how the longstanding and tense relationship between government and capital would remain unchanged despite the more socialist business plan, since government is not adept at running businesses, and businesses are run solely for profit. Redistribution as a policy is not so easily mastered. In addition, "foreigners and criminals and other endlessly greedy conglomerates were gobbling up RAMJAC. Mary Kathleen's legacy to the people was being converted to mountains of rapidly deteriorating currency, which were being squandered in turn on a huge new bureaucracy and on legal fees and consultants' fees, and on and on. What was left, it was said by the politicians, would help to pay the interest on the people's national debt, and would buy them more of the highways and public buildings and advanced weaponry they so richly deserved" (280). In the end, the capitalist game continues; RAMJAC has just cashed in its chips. Mary's vision would have to be a global one to have a true effect, but as the fear of "foreigners" shows (as well as the fact that the multinational RAMJAC belongs to Americans only), this communist plan is hardly "international" in any way. True, Vonnegut, through Starbuck, self-consciously indulges his nostalgia for the welfare state throughout the novel, yet Vonnegut also realizes that this redistributive vision of corporate welfare harks back to a past, which, as we have seen in *J R*, *Gung Ho*, and *Gain*, has long come and gone.

Vonnegut's troubled socialist corporation, moreover, should serve as a warning for those who today distinguish "good" corporations from "bad" ones. Starbucks is "good" because it pays its workers well, offers benefits, and deals in Fair Trade coffee. Nike, in the late 1990s, was "bad" because of the revelations of its involvement with sweatshops. In this sense, Target and Wal-Mart can be seen as constituting a kind of dialectic of "savings stores," with Target as the democratically run "good guy" and Wal-Mart as the conservatively controlled "bad guy" that runs mom-and-pop stores out of business.[17] The truth, however, is that all such distinctions are specious. Underneath the stores' surface differences, the goal of each remains essentially the same—to earn capital. Both Target and Wal-Mart remain popular with shoppers for their affordable goods that undersell and drive away most of their competition. Wal-Mart, even if it does destroy Main Street competition, ends up offering rural communities—which have been much harder hit economically in the neoliberal era than have their urban counterparts—the only outlet for affordable goods and (dead-end) nonunion jobs. Target (also nonunion) and even the "socialist" Ikea do the same to their competition and provide similar unpromising, low-level jobs. Even the large corporations of today that actually espouse a philosophy of being good are still involved in the messier details of production costs and profits. Google's slogan "don't be evil" has been called into question since its agreement to allow the Chinese government to censor its search engine, and Apple's socially conscious and hip image continues to suffer as its labor practices have turned out to be as dubious as those of any other multinational corporation. From this vantage, the choice between a "good" or a "bad" capitalism attendant on a coalition of "good" or "bad" corporations is, according to the underlying logic of capital, no choice whatsoever. Actual democracy, then, is supplemented by a consumerist politics, in which shopping at the "democratic" or "republican" store constitutes a vote for a way of doing business, if not a way of life. What the "political shopper" belies is that shopping is *not* political in the way that it seems and that spending one's dollar as a kind of "vote" for a certain kind of capitalism does nothing to change the fact that this is merely a vote *for* capitalism that, in the last instance—and as this study of the figurations of corporations has been at pains to show—can *never* have a human face.

This specious difference between the good and bad corporation illuminates perhaps the most troubling aspect of even the redistributive socialist corporation. Because it still retains the hierarchical divisions and structures that corporations require to function—no matter how much more open or fluid these organizational structures are today than in the past—it is not directly subject to democratic political processes. A corporation is not a democratic entity, even if it claims to listen to its semiautonomous divisions, flexible teams, or networks of workers. Management is not elected (indeed, in *Jailbird*, Starbuck and his friends are appointed to their executive positions). The socialist corporation governs its citizen-subjects via a different kind of biopolitical control than neoliberalism's commodification of everyday life—and that is through technocratic means that preclude any true democratic debate over means and ends. Again, as Foucault notes, in such instances, "one must govern for the market, rather than because of the market" (*Birth* 121). Such a corporate style of governance would demand leaders who hold the specialized knowledge to which only certain experts and technocrats can lay claim. A true politics, in this case, comes to be replaced by biopolitical management.

In the confrontation between corporate and individual bodies, the corporate body, whether socialist or not, remains a threat to democracy. The capitalist utopia that CCA president Arthur Jensen envisioned in *Network*, one delivered by multinational corporations under the auspices of global capital, may not be so different in the end from the socialist corporation that promises the redistribution of wealth for those who commit their lives to it. Perhaps the true differences between these corporations, then, are merely formal ones that leave untouched the fundamental content, or antagonism, of capital itself.

The Coming Incorporation

Jameson's call for a dialectical view of the corporation and capitalism notwithstanding, I would like to shift the analysis away from the question of the ways in which the corporation might hint at the utopian through its contemporary forms and practices to the question of how *incorporation itself* might be questioned and reconceived in a more utopian light. Perhaps what is needed instead of a more utopian corporate form is a different concept of incorporation altogether, one that challenges the integrity of the corporate body by reimagining what the collective social body, or individual body, can be. That is, if the corporation through its legal standing constitutes a certain kind of fictional or figurative "person" whose "body" and personhood mimics that of the human individual, perhaps the time has come to reconceive what a body can be. For if the corporation is a sort of posthuman figure piggybacking on outdated notions of the human, then perhaps a more positive embrace of the posthuman and its possibilities could challenge the construction of the corporate body. Placing the sovereign individual (or not-so-sovereign subject) against the sovereign corporation means that it stands little chance of resistance. So why not change the conditions and terms of the body and the collective? Why not imagine a coming incorporation of a radically different nature?[18]

To this end, Michael Hardt and Antonio Negri's concept of the multitude, especially as elaborated in *Multitude: War and Democracy in the*

Age of Empire (2004), presents a significant attempt at reconceiving the body of a social collective.[19] The multitude is essentially a new way of understanding the revolutionary proletariat in its global manifestations, one that exchanges Marx's erstwhile subject of history for an updated, more pluralized version, a proletariat 2.0. For, as Hardt and Negri write, "the multitude . . . is not unified but remains plural and multiple" and "is composed of a set of *singularities*" (*Multitude* 99). Careful to distinguish the multitude from an anarchic mob or a notion of "the people" (who are easily unified to "speak for" anyone in power), Hardt and Negri claim that "the multitude is an internally different, multiple social subject whose constitution and action is based not on an identity or unity (or, much less, indifference) but on what it has in common" (100). What is key here is that, regardless of the multitude's abstract nature and diverse makeup, it still forms a "subject" of sorts: "From the socioeconomic perspective, the multitude is the common subject of labor, that is, the real flesh of postmodern production, and at the same time the object from which collective capital tries to make the body of its global development" (101). The multitude, although it cannot be pinned down or unified in any simple sense, constitutes a collective social body made up of actual bodies. Significantly, this kind of collective differs from Ferris's "corporate we" in *Then We Came to the End*, which, while it represents a humanistic desire to grant a voice to the forgotten white-collar worker, remains empty of revolutionary content. The multitude, by contrast, is revolutionary.

Just as importantly, the body of the multitude differs markedly from the corporate body. As we have seen, the corporation is a kind of "body" that "represents" its more limited collective—of executives, shareholders, stakeholders, and so on. Yet this collective body, having achieved a degree of sovereignty, is one that is shielded from legal liability and the greater social collective. Indeed, corporations, however fragmented their operations or fluid their workforce, have a distinct hierarchy of management and a bottom line to follow. In this sense, the fictional body that the corporation is granted by law and projects via its logo, advertising, and business model is an attempt at unifying itself, as Gaddis's *J R* shows in the family image that the J R Corporation fosters in order to embody its many holdings. Granted, the body is a figure, a fiction hiding a truly monstrous disorganized body, as Norris's *The Octopus* so keenly perceives, but this is precisely the point. The multitude stands in opposition to this kind of embodiment since, as Hardt and Negri write, "if the multitude is to form a body, in any case, it will remain always and necessarily an open, plural composition and never become a unitary whole divided by hierarchical organs" (*Multitude* 190). Simply put, the body of the multitude thus avoids becoming yet another hierarchical corporate body that replaces the old one—like the socialist corporation depicted in *Jailbird*—and only ends up reproducing the same problems it sought to bypass.

What I refer to here as the "coming incorporation," therefore, is this very possibility of the multitude's "embodiment" or "incorporation" as a collective body-without-organs. Such a body affirms the corporeal yet resists hierarchical organization, and it is composed of singularities that share what they have in common—not a profit motive. For make no mistake, the struggle between the corporate body and the corporeal body is a biopolitical battle of bodies in a real, as well as a virtual, sense. As abstract a body as the multitude can be said to constitute, it is always composed of actual bodies or singularities, irreducible as they are to "individuals." If the "fictional" corporate body has trumped the individual one, the body of the multitude presents a new and different challenge to it. The notion of a coming incorporation, therefore, is not one invested in trying to humanize the corporation through reform or in resuscitating an earlier humanist discourse to defend the "individual." Even Howard Beale's infamous humanist rant in *Network*—that he is "mad as hell and not going to take this anymore"—eventually petered out into cynical resignation. To embrace the concept of the multitude or a coming incorporation is to see the utopian and productive potential in the posthuman instead of fearing it to be simply the dehumanized detritus of techno-capitalism—in essence: go ahead, let corporations be people, but let the people become the multitude.

The task remains, therefore, to offer a more concrete example of the multitude. For this reason it would be illuminating to return to Thomas Pynchon's *The Crying of Lot 49* and the mysterious Tristero, composed as it is of America's excluded and alienated, which I left waiting in "the separate, silent, unsuspected world" back in chapter 1 (101). There I viewed the Tristero as the abstract possibility of resistance, or one perhaps engaging in a "Bartlebian" politics of challenging the legitimacy of the prevailing political system by "preferring not" to take part in it (much the same way that Occupy Wall Street refused to provide a list of set demands to authorities). However, having outlined the contours of a new sort of incorporation and social body that contests the corporate one, that of the multitude, I would like to put forth the Tristero as the paradigm of this very multitude.

The Tristero as multitude embodies several distinguishing features. First, as much as the Tristero is associated, for Oedipa, with those who are deprived of the American dream, its membership would appear to be much larger than that. The Tristero includes not just the marginalized and poor, the erstwhile proletariat, but the white-collar Mike Fallopians and Stanley Koteks, the creative class, of the world too. In this regard, the Tristero truly forms a multitude. Second, it is also a networked community that, as a result, is plugged directly into the capitalist mainframe. This means that the multitude is always already dispersed throughout the capitalist system and, most importantly, is coterminous with it. Third, the multitude is a creative, productive, and positive force. It is not simply a reactionary force, a force that must be marshaled in its own name by a revolutionary vanguard (which would merely be another representational, hierarchical body), or one that must wait for power to give way to do its work.

The Tristero as multitude is thus distinct from a Bartlebian politics because the multitude contains within itself, so to speak, the means of its emancipation. It need not wait for a prolonged crisis or a state of emergency that, anyhow, is a permanent and defining feature of the late capitalist system today. Oedipa, for instance, entertains the possible Bartlebian dimension of the Tristero when she wonders if it is "waiting above all; if not for another set of possibilities to replace those that had conditioned the land . . . , then at least, at the very least, waiting for a symmetry of choices to break down, to go skew" (150). Yet while this withdrawal and waiting can be an effective avenue of resistance, it still gives precedence to the power of the system, which must eventually falter of its own accord, if not at least helped to do so by those who "prefer not to" be a part of it. Properly speaking, however, Tristero members such as Fallopian have not completely withdrawn from the system, at least not in the same way as those "alienations" forcibly excluded by it. If anything, they are withdrawn in plain sight. Fallopian's and others' co-option of the Yoyodyne corporation's interoffice mail system to service their W.A.S.T.E. mail is a perfect example of how the means of oppression can be turned into emancipation without their being an outside agent to provoke it, or by granting power the ultimate upper hand. For the W.A.S.T.E. mail is not part of a saboteur's plan meant to jam the Yoyodyne system and bring it down from inside. Instead, it marks a reappropriation of the tools of the capitalist system by the multitude. In this sense, Jameson's point about the utopian potential of capitalist technology, corporate based or otherwise, is well taken. A mail system, or means of networked communication, is a powerful tool to have at one's disposal, no matter its intended use. And as the vital role of cell phones to coordinate protestors via text or Twitter in the so-called Arab Spring and other recent uprisings proves, such a means of communication is critical for resisting power in the new millennium.

Hence, from one perspective (Oedipa's), the Tristero appears to be the disenfranchised and depoliticized American people in need of salvation and waiting for change. From another, however, the Tristero, as a collection of singular bodies conjoining those in "the infected city" with those in the mundane suburbs, is a potential multitude primed for the coming incorporation, in which Inverarity's incorporated America will become the incorporation of the Tristero. This coming incorporation will not arrive from outside but from within the Tristero itself. The Tristero as multitude is immanent, not transcendent, and embodies the means of its own biopolitical emancipation. The multitude's ability to reappropriate something like the Yoyodyne mail system thus avoids the pitfalls encountered by the socialist idea of redistribution because there is no sovereign body, be it government or Pierce's incorporated America, that can withstand, or arise from, the multitude, which in its radical gathering of singularities can never be sovereign itself. This is also why, ironically, one of Oedipa's theories concerning the creation of the Tristero—that it is all a hoax perpetrated by Inverarity (140)—in a way turns out to be true. From the point of view of the multitude, the idea that a fully commodified world where human life has been reduced to biocapital might be turned back on itself through the once-subjected biopower of the multitude is perfectly sound.

Thus, Oedipa awaits, at the novel's end, for a transcendent meaning or divine intervention that the novel suggests will never come since the Tristero, inasmuch as it is the "excluded middle," is precisely what deconstructs the dialectic of salvation in which, as Oedipa imagines it, either all is redeemed or all must be damned: "Behind the hieroglyphic streets there would be either a transcendent meaning, or only earth" (150). The reader, however, is able to peek over her shoulder and gain a different perspective that belies her position, which leads to a resigned cynicism. For if the Tristero can stand for the multitude, then it makes Oedipa's dilemma moot. In short, it is not up to Oedipa. The Tristero is the coming incorporation that will utterly and irreversibly transform capital and its corporate bodies.

The purpose of this study has similarly been to offer particular vantage points, via the various textual figures of the corporation, from which to view the excesses of the capitalist system. Whether the texts analyzed herein pointedly critique the power and structure of the corporation, represent it as a source of economic agony and ecstasy, or indirectly call attention to its pervasive and persistent influence, each evinces, in its fashion, both a fascination with and an apprehension about capitalism that, despite the seemingly apolitical economy of the neoliberal era, is alive and well today in American literature, film, and popular culture. While the imagined solutions to the dilemmas of corporate capitalism, from endorsing a casual acceptance or renewed faith in the system to registering outrage or cynical despair at its failures, may not always convincingly address the problems they lay bare, the attempts at symbolic closure nonetheless call attention to the necessity and the difficulty of being able to conceive of any alternative to the current capitalist system. For, as Theodor Adorno reminds us in *Aesthetic Theory*, "the basic levels of experience that motivate art are related to those of the objective world from which they recoil. The unsolved antagonisms of reality return in artworks as immanent problems of form" (6). Taken together, these texts illustrate how crucial the effort is to imagine, and to demand, the seemingly impossible. In turn, this study has sought to trace the larger pattern at work in the figure of the corporation, to diagnose the dialectical trap of joy and despair that accompanies capital's boom-and-bust cycles, and to point toward the political possibilities that lie beyond the limits of the capitalist system. If and when something akin to a global multitude properly emerges, seizes the productive forces of capital, and bends them to its own ends remains to be seen, but certainly something of its creativity, positive productive power, and multiplicity will be vital for imagining and building a new world out of the crisis-ridden ruins of the old.

NOTES

Introduction

1. As David Graeber sums it up in *Debt: The First Five Thousand Years*, "The results [of the crisis] were predictable. Financiers were 'bailed out with taxpayer money'" while "mortgage holders were, overwhelmingly, left to the tender mercies of the courts, under a bankruptcy law that Congress had a year before . . . made far more exacting for debtors. Nothing was altered. All major decisions were postponed. The Great Conversation that many were expecting never happened" (381).

2. Kiel and Nguyen.

3. As David Harvey notes in *The Enigma of Capital and the Crises of Capitalism*, "There is . . . nothing unprecedented, apart from the size and scope, about the current collapse" (10). Some other notable neoliberal crises are the 1987 S&L debacle, the tech bubble bursting in 2001, the numerous Latin American debt crises in the 1980s and 1990s, and the collapse of the Asian and Celtic Tigers.

4. For a breakdown of the disproportionate recoveries of different income groups, see Emmanuel Saez and Thomas Piketty's "Striking It Richer."

5. Joseph E. Stiglitz's *The Price of Inequality: How Today's Divided Society Endangers Our Future* deflates the neoliberal arguments for tighter budgets and further austerity, which he argues will only exacerbate the crisis (207–237): "The critical point to bear in mind . . . is that the recession caused the deficits, not the other way around" (211). Stiglitz also details the Federal Reserve's bank bias and the lack of financial or banking regulation postcrisis (238–264). Paul Krugman's *End This Depression Now!* also takes aim at the folly of austerity policies (130–207).

6. However, the income gap in the United States is greater than in other highly developed countries, such as Japan, Germany, and Great Britain, which suggests, among other things, that U.S. tax and economic policy has much to do with this unequal distribution (Alvaredo et al., "Top 1 Percent").

7. Greta R. Krippner carefully demonstrates this "financialization" in *Capitalizing on Crisis: The Political Origins of the Rise of Finance* (27–57), arguing that "the turn to finance allowed the state to avoid a series of economic, social, and political dilemmas that confronted policymakers beginning in the 1960s and 1970s, paradoxically preparing ground for our own era of financial manias, panics, and crashes some three decades later," though this was "not a deliberate outcome sought by policymakers but rather an inadvertent result" (2).

8. As Randy Martin demonstrates in *Financialization of Daily Life*, "Financial self-management leaves no corner of the home untouched. Cradle to grave, dawn to dusk, the *oikos* of economics returns to its original residence where home organizes both labor and its reproduction" (194).

9. Alison Shonkwiler's excellent "Don DeLillo's Financial Sublime" reads Packer's character and the novel's aesthetics against the problem of representing finance capital in the neoliberal era.

10. In *The Return of Depression Economics and the Crisis of 2008*, Paul Krugman proposes that this rehearsal can also be seen in the various debt crises in Latin America and Asia during the 1980s and 1990s.

11. See Bethany McLean and Peter Elkind's *The Smartest Guys in the Room: The Amazing Rise and Scandalous Fall of Enron*. Although the authors argue that their book is "ultimately . . . a story about people" (vii), they identify what I would call "the financialization" of the corporation as one of the underlying factors in the firm's failure (150–152, 212–228, 380).

12. David Harvey argues that banking and corporate capital "exist in a symbiotic relation to each other" (*Limits* 319). Greta Krippner traces the financialization of onetime "nonfinancial firms," including General Electric, General Motors, and Ford, that "all created captive finance units that were originally intended to support consumer purchases" and that "eventually became financial behemoths that overshadowed the manufacturing or retailing activities of the parent firm" (29).

13. Though there are many books dealing with corporate power and abuse, I draw here on those also that trace the history and development of the corporation and that propose solutions to the problems of corporate capitalism. David C. Korten's *When Corporations Rule the World* set the basic standard of this genre by offering a concise history of the corporation, an analysis of its legal structure, a catalogue of the dangers of corporate growth, and providing some ways to resist corporatization. Thom Hartmann's *Unequal Protection: The Rise of Corporate Dominance and the Theft of Human Rights* pays special attention to the corporation in American history and specifically regarding the Founding Fathers' ideas about freedom and constitutional rights. The most creative, Joel Bakan's *The Corporation: The Pathological Pursuit of Profit and Power*, which spawned a documentary of the same name, is amusing in its Freudian analysis of the "pathological" corporate "person," though a Deleuze-and-Guattarian schizoid analysis by way of *Anti-Oedipus* would probably have been more apt. The latest addition to this topic is Jeffrey D. Clements's *Corporations Are Not People: Why They Have More Rights than You Do and What You Can Do about It*. Clements centers his analysis on what he argues was a thirty-year build-up to the 2010 *Citizens United* decision largely spearheaded by the activism of Supreme Court justice Lewis Powell.

14. Surprisingly, however, there are no studies that explore the impact of corporations on America from a literary or pop cultural perspective. The closest in this

respect is Alan Trachtenberg's *The Incorporation of America: Culture and Society in the Gilded Age* (1982), which traces the massive effects of rapid industrialization and what Trachtenberg calls "the incorporation of America" in the decades following the Civil War.

15. Some of this was Horkheimer and Adorno's earlier critique of the "Culture Industry" in *Dialectic of Enlightenment* (1944) writ, or broadcast, large. In *The Society of the Spectacle*, Guy Debord claimed that this world was constituted solely by the spectacle, which "is *capital* accumulated to the point where it becomes image" (24), wherein "spectators are linked only by a one-way relationship to the very center that maintains their isolation from one another" (22). Striking an apocalyptic tone in *Simulacra and Simulations,* Jean Baudrillard declared that the world had collapsed into mere simulacra that heralded "the generation by models of a real without origin or reality: a hyperreal" (1).

16. Martha Woodmansee and Mark Osteen's *The New Economic Criticism* (1999) gathers together several different economic approaches to texts that move beyond the simpler economic readings of the past. Roughly, these include the economics of literary production, the literary marketplace, and literary canonization; critiques of contemporary and neoclassical economists' concepts, metaphors, and assumptions about economic man; and the formalist, language-based analyses of various symbolic economies generated by a text's metaphorical and tropic exchanges. Woodmansee and Osteen's introduction provides a thorough genealogy of this type of criticism that is too long to be detailed here (3–50). Of the works they mention, my approach shares something in common with Richard Godden's in *Fictions of Capital: The American Novel from James to Mailer* (1990), though Godden looks at works from the 1920s to the mid-1960s. Godden establishes "a homology between the history of capital and the meaning of novels" from the 1920s to the mid-1960s in order "to understand how different fictions take their forms from the economic history that is their finally determining context" (7, 11).

Other and more recent studies of note in the "new economic" vein include Regenia Gagnier's *The Insatiability of Human Wants: Economics and Aesthetics in Market Society* (2000), which traces "how an aesthetics of taste, pleasure, and consumption arose with a conception of Economic Man as maximizer of individual choice" from classical to modern political economy (17). The study fulfills a "tripartite task: analyzing art objects, analyzing the aspects of everyday life that have been aestheticized for the consumption of citizens or subjects, and providing critique and alternatives" (233). Michael Tratner's *Deficits and Desires: Economics and Sexuality in Twentieth-Century Literature* (2001) explores the joining of economic theory (primarily Keynesian deficit spending) and theories of sexuality in modernist works to show how "economic and sexual theories are not merely analogous: they combine in their effects on everyday life, supporting and modifying each other" (7). Catherine Gallagher's *The Body Economic: Life, Death, and Sensation in Political Economy and the Victorian Novel* (2006) is concerned with the crossover of economic discourse in the work of political economists and novelists of the Romantic and Victorian eras. Her study "tries to explain how they were, at first, divided by common premises and then how their orientations toward each other shifted as those premises were revised in the course of the century" (3). Most recently, Michael Clune's *American Literature and the Free Market: 1945–2000* (2009) makes a striking argument for the relative autonomy of the aesthetic from the social realm. Clune examines what he calls the "economic fiction," or the way in which literature and culture embrace the self-organizing aesthetic of the unrealized and theoretical "free market" of really existing capitalism: "in the economic fiction the market ... becomes the organizing principle of a nonsocial collective" (162). Clune's notion of an emergent "nonsocial collective" is a fascinating, if unorthodox, way of revising our understanding of the social in relation to capital.

1 / California Dreaming

1. Walter Benn Michaels points out that supply and demand "sets rates in a free market, but the railroad, as a monopoly, doesn't operate in a free market" (*Gold Standard* 209), while Adam H. Wood notes the physical labor involved in building the railroad: "As is well known, the bulk of the railroad line in California was laid by a predominantly Chinese workforce" (122).

2. It is not clear if Norris actually read Marx during his life. But being alive during the late nineteenth century would have made him privy to Marxist or similar kinds of arguments about capitalism, even if he were not to have actually read a single line from Marx's own pen. However, Norris's greatest literary influence was Émile Zola, who had indeed read Marx. It is safe to say that Norris, then, gained a kind of "reading" of Marx through his reading of Zola. Thus, when I refer to Norris's "reading" of Marx, I mean "reading" in the figurative sense—the sense that he has, at least, been *indirectly* influenced by Marx and that his own work clearly puts a spin or interpretation on that "reading" itself. Indeed, if Norris never read Marx, his work is all the more startling for his essential grasp of Marx's main arguments in volume 1 of *Capital*.

3. Ironically, this is a reference to the infamous 1936 Tex Avery cartoon "The Blow Out," in which a Horatio Alger–like Porky Pig foils a bank-bombing anarchist in New York's Lower East Side.

4. Lawrence E. Hussman summarizes the negative critical response to Norris's ending(s) (both Presley's final vision and S. Behrman's death) in relation to Presley's earlier talk with Shelgrim (based on Norris's actual interview with Southern Pacific's Collis P. Huntington), which most critics argue influences Presley's (and Norris's) increasingly grim view of the world (148–159). Hussman argues, however, that the reader is unable to ascribe Vanamee/Presley's views to Norris. Hussman claims that Norris points out the fallibility of each character throughout the novel and is more of a mind with modernist despair than a regressive Romanticism, so that "at the end of *The Octopus*, Norris is still without a world view consistent with his already fully developed sense that to recognize and address the needs of others constitutes a far higher moral calling than to satisfy the self" (159). Such an argument seems strained, however, considering how directly Norris's pen tips the wheat on S. Behrman and how it so neatly "proves" Presley's earlier romantic vision. Norris may indeed remain suspicious of this vision, and even criticize it through Presley and Vanamee, but the vision nonetheless prevails, which is a semiendorsement of it, at the least.

5. Adam Wood's excellent essay also applies Jameson's concept of narrative's symbolic function, though in a slightly different way. He argues that "Norris's 'story of California' thus animates not the particular incident of Mussell Slough but the process of myth construction necessary to the conquest of California, the form of ideological construction required in early-twentieth-century capitalism. It is only by understanding this process of myth construction that the textual contradictions of *The Octopus* may be thoroughly historicized and understood as both inherent in the deterministic novel and, more crucially, indicative, perhaps critical, of capitalism's contradictory ideology of the 'forces' and 'conditions' of humankind's fate" (126).

6. Thomas Austenfeld argues that Norris's ending—"Annixter dies, but in a far distant corner of the world thousands of lives are saved" (*Octopus* 652)—reinforces a utilitarian philosophy by projecting its "cosmic" vision at the global level: "This world-wide perspective not only transcends individual human fates through the large scale it employs, it also appropriately depersonalizes the entire issue of what the right thing to do might be. We are now not talking of individuals but 'nations'" (41). Russ Castronovo's analysis reveals "how [the] conceptualization of the globe as a single geo-economic unit depends on a historically specific aesthetic formalism exemplified by Norris's fiction" and that "the contradictory nature of this project—that is, a contextual history of aesthetic formalism—captures the logic that ushers an Americanized global sensibility into being" (158). This is none other than "Manifest Destiny appear[ing] on the Pacific Rim not so much as an imperial mission but as a transhistoric return in which nationality and race pale before the great idea of a new human unity engineered by world markets" (177).

7. Both John Johnston and John Dugdale note Inverarity's importance as a corporate figure. Johnston writes that "Pierce represents an entirely secular order, for the unity of 'San Narciso' is only produced by the demands of corporate capitalism," and that "with Pierce's death ... a segment or corporate chunk is loosened from its moorings, and official reality begins to come apart" ("Toward the Schizo-Text" 69–70). John Dugdale claims that "Oedipa attempts to counteract this imminent dispersal [of Inverarity's holdings] by replacing him as a source of unity, substituting connections made by imaginative investment for those of capitalist investment" (145).

8. Stefan Mattessich points out the paradox of resistance in the novel, arguing that, "more than simply telling a story of civil society's sacrifice to the economic requirements of late capitalism, [*Lot 49*] evokes the function of that civil society as the limit on whose transgression the capitalist machine depends in order to exist at all" (65).

9. Naomi C. Reed gives a fine summation of prior Marxist criticism dealing with Bartleby's possible silent resistance, as well as offering a fresher Marxist perspective, in "The Specter of Wall Street: 'Bartleby, the Scrivener' and the Language of Commodities."

10. Of course, Pynchon problematizes communication not least by stressing the influence of entropy between sender and receiver (84) and by making us privy to one of Mike Fallopian's W.A.S.T.E. messages, which are meaningless in their content and anticipate the frivolity of today's text messages or tweets (39). Yet, as David Seed points out, "the value of the letter is as a gesture, that Fallopian's friend should be collaborating with others in their underground mail-system in a communal act" (141).

2 / "Domo Arigato, Mr. Sakamoto, for the New Non-Union Contract!"

1. Certainly this piece of Manhattan held great symbolic import, though not nearly as much as did the 51 percent of Rockefeller Center purchased by Mitsubishi Real Estate in 1989.

2. As Kahn wrote in *The Japanese Challenge*, "Some Americans are concerned that Japan's economic strength might eventually be used against U.S. interests, but as long as the world economic growth continues, the prospect that a strong Japanese economy would amount, on balance, to a threat to American interests is extremely small" (152). Published in 1979, however, Kahn's analysis does not foresee the American auto industry's mounting troubles, which popular opinion came to fuse with the "Japanese threat."

3. Inkster argues that "there is little reason to believe that the one [Japanese surplus] caused the other [American deficit] in any direct fashion" and that "the calibre of any causal link between the medium-term policy contributions on the one hand and the more underlying historical factors on the other remains debatable" (282, *sic*).

4. Clearly there are no rice paddies in Tokyo. However, the film collapses space-time in Hunt's wandering scene, so that it appears as if the two coexist.

5. This appears a curious, yet apt for the 1980s, inversion of Clifford Odets's *Waiting for Lefty*, in which the workers at one point chant, "Strike, strike, strike!"

6. In *Crash Course: The American Automobile Industry's Road from Glory to Disaster*, Paul Ingrassia places the blame on the "thirty and out" provision in UAW contracts that allowed a worker who started at eighteen to retire at forty-eight and draw pension until the end of his life—probably thirty years or so (56–57). Ingrassia never goes so far to accuse auto workers themselves of being to blame for their contracts—this he reserves for a bloated union (46–47)—but one wonders if a "forty or fifty and out" with a 401K would please him instead. Moreover, after the 2008 financial crisis, one wonders how many more years one would have to tack on to counter the damage done to such market-based pensions.

7. As Milkman writes, "GM appears to be typical of U.S. auto assembly plants in that new technology has been introduced without jobs being fundamentally redesigned or the traditional division of labor altered between production and skilled-trades workers" (159).

8. Ingrassia and White also point out that the Big Three's sales rose between 1984 and 1988, giving them a false sense of having weathered the tsunami and probably making them less interested in Japanese production methods (60). This may account, in part, for the film's ultimate optimism regarding the success of Assan Motors. Unfortunately, in 2009 NUMMI became a victim of the latest financial crisis and was closed.

9. One study of a Mazda plant, Joseph J. Fucini and Suzy Fucini's *Working for the Japanese: Inside Mazda's American Auto Plant*, details various workers' complaints about the Japanese system and presents the "better" relationship between American workers/management and Japanese management/owners as largely illusory. Yet the Fucinis' study is interesting in that none of the complaints about the Japanese Mazda plant appear any different than complaints in numerous American plants that Milkman notes.

10. Rae (170), Sobel (314), and Maynard (308) all call attention to the multinational ties between automakers in the United States and abroad.

11. Surely the quashed Dubai port-security deal in 2006 shows how nationalism, xenophobia, and nation-states still have a say in such matters, especially considering that the Bush administration pushed for the deal to go through, only caving in after relentless public and congressional outcry from across the political spectrum made it politically expedient to do so.

3 / Good Times, Bad Times . . . You Know I Had My Share(s)

1. Obviously numerous films dealing with corporations by necessity must be left out of this chapter. Perhaps the most glaring are films that deal with corrupt corporate power by representing "true" stories. Films such as *The Insider* (1999), *Silkwood* (1983), and *Erin Brockovich* (2000) tend to present the corporation as an evil institution that the individual must fight against without compromising the pursuit of "truth and justice." Thus, whatever the (Pyrrhic) victories achieved by the real-life-based characters, they are always cast as ultimately heroic in their overcoming personal doubts and problems to defeat a much larger institution. In this sense, one could replace the corporation with the government or any institution that tries to crush the never-say-die individual. The fact, again, that these films are based on "real life" only underscores their commitment to presenting "true" tales of *personal* triumph and less a systemic critique (which is simply accepted as the foundation for the individual's struggle and passed over). Such films are more "biopics" about personal struggles than anything else. The HBO film *Barbarians at the Gate* (1993), a treatment of the novel by the same name about the 1987 S&L scandal, similarly focuses on characters and their struggles.

2. I use this term generically. More strictly, "urban renewal" refers to the sort of redevelopment that brutally razed entire city blocks (Robert Moses's projects, for instance), which was superseded after the 1960s by a combination of liberal commitment to historical preservation, promoting the arts, and new local and federal policies. See the chapter "From Urban Renewal to Historic Preservation" in Reichl (21–42).

3. This is an important point and one that separates the Ghostbusters from merely being a kind of gang of superheroes. The Ghostbusters are almost superheroes, but they come with a price—literally. Whereas Gotham's three most famous superheroes—Superman, Spiderman, and Batman—all "work" pro bono, as it were, the Ghostbusters work only for cold, hard cash. The crew's, and particularly Venckman's, newfound independent spirit, moreover, is not that of the vigilante (Batman and Spiderman) working outside the law for justice and the betterment of society but of the private company out to provide the best services available for its customers. Even after the Ghostbusters "save" the city for no *apparent* charge at the end of the film, there still exists a hidden receipt for their particular brand of services that will have to be reckoned at a later date. That Gotham's populace sees them as superheroes, however, is both troubling and a telling reminder of the times.

4. The area should, by no means, be wholly representative of the different areas of New York that underwent gentrification around this time. This gentrification continues, though the recent financial crisis has stymied such "growth" and will have an interesting effect on the largely untenanted, pricey real-estate ventures that have rapidly expanded into "changing" neighborhoods.

5. This image of Times Square is so strong that it still resonates in Penny Marshall's *Big* (1988). When Tom Hanks's character escapes to the city, he books himself a room in a seedy Times Square hotel, where he cowers in fear on his bed to a chorus of sirens, gunshots, and Spanish-speaking voices screaming outside his door. The fact that Hanks is, at this point, literally a child ensconced in an adult's body and registering the typical white suburban fear of the inner city is quite suggestive.

6. Even these "objective" policies were highly suspect, writes Mike Davis, helping to ghettoize further the very same neighborhoods that politicians later backed for "renewal": "Banks and S&Ls, ... pumped capital out of the inner city but refused to loan it back, especially to Black-majority neighborhoods. Instead they drained Northeastern savings to the Sunbelt, where they stoked a massive speculating building boom" (389).

7. As reported in the audio commentary of the DVD.

8. Need it be mentioned that Coke and Cheez-It also appear to be instances of product placement in the film, a burgeoning practice in the 1980s?

9. This is where a film such as *The Constant Gardener* (2005, based on the titular John le Carré novel) distinguishes itself from *Michael Clayton* in its exposé of corporate violence. Taking place mainly in Africa, the film draws together the corrupt political ties that assist a multinational pharmaceutical company with its deadly testing of newly developed drugs on an unknowing and expendable Kenyan population. The corporate killings in the film take place in Africa, a space in which, because of corrupt political regimes and police, such violent acts do actually occur. Moreover, the film is careful to point out how the killings have been sub-sub-subcontracted out in a way that divorces direct corporate authority from the hits. *Michael Clayton*, on the other hand, has Crowder meeting with the assassins in person. Even in a world where such killings take place, *The Constant Gardener* makes clear, this is not the way things work. The subcontracted killings are thus related to the film's "message" about global capital—who is to blame? Corrupt governments and corporations? Yes, but let us remember the hostage third-world "test subjects" and how they contribute to the health care and drug benefits we enjoy in the first world. In other words, let us see how this capitalist-structured global society necessitates such a relationship. Let us rethink the fundamentals, the film suggests.

Furthermore, Clayton is drawn into the U/North case because of Edens's murder and does not appear to care so much about the case—he goes after Crowder for the murder, not so much U/North itself. Similarly, in *The Constant Gardener*, when Tessa (Rachel Weisz) is murdered by the pharmaceutical company for her activism against the dangerous testing, her husband, Justin Quayle (Ralph Fiennes), continues to work on her case. But he ultimately is drawn into the cause as much by a sense of justice as he is merely for the love of his late wife. Indeed, the film and he fuse these concerns together, and his final "suicide" is a kind of sacrifice for the cause, whereas Clayton's commitment to bringing down U/North is the fulfillment of personal revenge.

4 / A Capital Death

1. In a similar fashion, Mark Conroy explores various narratives that Gladney clings to in an age that lacks stable, authoritative narratives, in "From Tombstone to Tabloid: Authority Figured in *White Noise*." The first part of my reading of the novel is concerned specifically with particular discourses on death.

2. *Existentialism* is a slippery term, one that is often used rather broadly to denote many modernists' sense of man's isolation from God and the absence of objective values, the (consequently) utter meaninglessness and absurdity of life, and humans' ability to freely choose and determine their fate. Yet, as Jean Wahl has written regarding the definition of existentialism, "It is ... a problem to define this philosophy satisfactorily.... May we call Kierkegaard an existentialist, or even a philosopher of existence? He had no desire to be a philosopher.... In our own times, Heidegger has opposed what he terms 'existentialism,' and Jaspers has asserted that 'existentialism' is the death of the philosophy of existence" (4).

3. The Bayh-Dole Act came to be at the end of the beleaguered Carter administration. It allowed universities and small businesses to patent their National Institutes of Health–sponsored discoveries, then license them to the drug companies of their choice, thus creating a lucrative quid pro quo cycle. This led to the rise of biotech companies, which, like universities, ended up doing most of the research for drug companies. The Hatch-Waxman Act was intended to help the generic industry but, to do so, lengthened the patents for brand-name drugs for five years (with the possibility of a thirty-month extension if a drug company sues a generic company for infringement, no matter what the result of the suit).

4. Also, in 1997, the FDA relaxed its standards for direct-to-consumer advertising by the pharmaceutical industry. The result has been a deluge of drug commercials since then. As of 2005, the industry spends more than $3 billion a year on such advertising (Moynihan and Cassels 101).

5. See Lexchin (14–15), L. Weber (119–139), Angell (99–109), and Moynihan and Cassels (5–10).

5 / Family Incorporated

1. Steven Moore suggests, quite plausibly, that the opposite may be true: that Stella marries Norman for his allotment of shares (95). Nor would it be surprising if each married the other for similar reasons.

2. Nicholas Spencer similarly explores the historical particularity of 1970s capitalism as it bears primarily on the aesthetics of *J R*, in an essay employing a close reading of David Harvey's *The Condition of Postmodernity*. I use Harvey's main ideas here not only because they offer a detailed analysis of the economic sea change of the decade but particularly because they help to explain the genius and timeliness of *J R*'s image constructions—from the CEO/founder to the Family of Companies—in the novel. Spencer applies Harvey's ideas on postmodern culture and economics to *J R*, concluding that "instead of being simply mimetic, *J R* literally mirrors the attributes of postmodernity to produce a critical mimesis" and that "Gaddis's emphasis on historical transition and interconnected economic and cultural tendencies creates a narrative whole that is clear and stable" (149). Spencer uses Harvey primarily to grapple with aesthetic issues, whereas I will return to some of Harvey's main premises regarding

the economic changes of the 1970s mainly as they relate to J R's specific business tactics and corporate image building.

3. This is due to Delaware's incredibly lax corporate tax and disclosure laws. In *The Crying of Lot 49*, Pierce Inverarity is incorporated in Delaware.

4. Thus, I am not arguing that the capital/family relationship operates under a simple cause/effect model. It is clear, however, that economic changes have their counterpart in changing family formations. As Erera writes about earlier changes in American families, "In some ways, the decline of the 1950s family grew out of the trends and contradictions of the fifties themselves. The main reason for family change was the breakdown of the postwar social compact between government, corporations, and workers" (4).

5. As Nicholas Brown notes in "Cognitive Map, Aesthetic Object, or National Allegory? *Carpenter's Gothic*," such patriotic bluster and ideological rhetoric is taken to task in the hideous character of Reverend Ude, a jab at the Moral Majority.

6 / Your Loss Is Their Gain

1. Like the women in *Network* and *Michael Clayton*, who sacrifice various relationships to further their careers, Julia, after Resolve's death, "never remarried.... She needed no warm body other than the corporate one." Further, "she neglected her ... children, tending to the welfare of her youngest, William, only as a worst-case insurance policy" (*Gain* 182).

2. Admittedly, establishing some kind of evolutionary chart—from human to posthuman—risks reproducing a similarly racist, or in this case "speciesist," system of classification of "mankind" such as arose in nineteenth-century European pseudoscientific discourse. This is surely the warning that Philip K. Dick registers in *Do Androids Dream of Electric Sheep?* (1968), in which he suggests a similarity between the rogue androids' position in postapocalyptic Earth and slaves in nineteenth-century America.

3. Norris, of course, describes the Trust as an octopus, a Leviathan, and a Colossus in *The Octopus*. Justice Louis Brandeis, in a 1933 Supreme Court decision, called corporations "Frankenstein monsters" (qtd. in Bakan 19). Surely, Atlas could be added to this list, as Ayn Rand's *Atlas Shrugged* (1957) suggests that creative entrepreneurs are akin to the mythical Titan holding up the world (which in a capitalist society they surely are). From corporeal beings—entrepreneurs, CEOs, etc.—to the corporate body in which they function, and without which their abilities would be severely limited in today's world (whether a Bill Gates or a Ken Lay), it is not too much of a stretch to see such figures in metonymic relationship to corporations.

4. It would not be too far out of Nantucket to suggest that Herman Melville's *Moby-Dick* (1851), that most famous of Leviathan novels, finds its true Leviathan in another boat, the *Pequod* itself, which, as earlier critics have pointed out, can be seen as a microcosm of America in all its multifarious parts (or an ideological construction of early American nationhood, as clearly issues of race, ethnicity, and gender prove these critics' microcosm to be drastically shortsighted). The *Pequod*, however, is also a kind of corporation in this respect, from its initial economic launching as a player in the whaling industry to its owners and investors, CEO and executive officers, to its middle management and even "janitorial" staff. Its risk-taking CEO, Ahab, drives his "ship" to ends even the ship's owners (board members) and investors would balk at. The capitalist

crash, like Ahab's fate, can and cannot be avoided. Of course, *Moby-Dick* predates the limited liability corporation, instead being concurrent with its forerunner, the joint-stock company. For an excellent cultural-materialist reading of labor, capital, and the marketplace as it relates to Melville's use of language in the novel, see Paul Royster's essay "Melville's Economy of Language" in *Ideology and Classic American Literature*.

5. The recent "subprime" mortgage crisis underscores the perpetuation of the "ideology" of home ownership (Harvey, "Fictional Finance"). As an ideology, such a vision of owning one's home involves predatory lending practices and the capitalist myth that "owning" a home is an investment that will always pay off in the future (and is *always* better than renting): either you have your "own" home or you can sell it for profit later. Thus, in our current short-term-profit-oriented system, "flipping" houses has become immensely popular. The housing market is just that, a market, and thus is rife with an ideology that taps into America's collective imagination of home ownership that arose post–World War II, when a new suburbia, GI bill, and postwar economic boom time led to a record number of U.S. home owners. As Kim McQuaid writes, "In the 1930s, only about 45 percent of U.S. families owned their homes, a percentage almost unchanged since the 1890s. . . . Not until the late 1940s did over half of all American families become home owners. By 1960, that number had risen to 60 percent; and from 1970 to 1993, to about two-thirds" (80). With such visions and desires to "own" assets and investments, people are easily given credit where credit, in stauncher financial times, would not be due. In short, the cliché "home is where the heart is" might be better subscribed to than the belief that "home is where the investment is." More and more, "homes" have become "houses," and houses are strictly commodities. Or, as David Harvey puts it, "it turns out that housing finance is not that safe—it was destined to run into trouble" ("Fictional Finance" 40).

6. Horizontal integration, companies merging with or swallowing up other companies, leads most obviously to monopoly—the state all corporations, despite their espousal of the "free market," aspire to. However, government trust-busting is a danger, and vertical integration, the commanding of commodity chains leading to what a company produces, is a way of keeping costs and prices down and controlling the market without "monopolizing" in the horizontal sense. Clare's vertical integration is mentioned by Powers (219).

7. This explains the popular "genre" of whistleblower films that show heroic individuals standing up to the system, such as *Michael Clayton*, *Erin Brockovich*, *The Insider*, and *Silkwood*.

Conclusion

1. As Peter Fleming and André Spicer write in *Contesting the Corporation: Struggle, Power, and Resistance in Organizations*, the "'prison' of corporate power is inextricably linked with the 'play' of resistance" (5). Thus, "such a wholehearted acceptance of corporate power takes the system too seriously," yet "overemphasizing the potential playfulness of corporate life runs the danger of ignoring the fact that . . . systems of control and domination continue to whir on" (4–5).

2. *Life Is Hell*'s main characters are, of course, "crudely drawn" rabbits, as Groening calls them. Yet this is no mere gag but a sort of visual image of the alienation and awkwardness these characters experience. They are confused rabbits in a strange world.

The world of *Dilbert*, however, does *Garfield* one better. The world is "normal," yet the dog can actually talk (Garfield the cat can merely think).

3. *The Simpsons*, of course, has become an industry unto itself and has long since left its creator's ink-stained fingers. *The Simpsons*, also, was chiefly a parody of sitcoms (as when it first appeared as a series of shorts on *The Tracey Ullman Show*) that has since become a self-parody and satirical take on topical issues, while *Life Is Hell* has always kept its critical teeth, whether dealing with AIDS, homosexuality, or various wars.

4. Chris Rock's film *CB4* (1993), however, offers an excellent skewering and exploration of rap music, authenticity, marketing, and the music industry in this light, at one point parodying N.W.A.'s infamous and instigative "Straight Outta Compton" video.

5. It should be noted that the initial germ of *Office Space* came from several animated shorts depicting Milton Waddams's office oppression. Thus, Waddams's rage can be seen as the repressed traumatic kernel of the film, literally and symbolically.

6. There seems to be, however, a possibility of redemption/renewal through mythical cycles as Bell tells his story from a deserted island, similar to Ulysses. David Cowart argues, "Bell is a postmodern Ulysses, returning not to triumph but to the spiritual emptiness of New York before ending up in solitude on a nameless island that would seem to have nothing but its remoteness in common with Ithaca" (610).

7. Art figures in *Americana*, too, through the Jean-Luc Godard–influenced film Bell works on during his road trip. It does not offer transcendence, however. As Cowart argues, Bell's film is itself structurally a closed loop, thus suggesting "the impossibility ... of determining the truly authentic subject among its own proliferating masks" (605). Neither does the failed novel that one character works on in *Personal Days* called *Personal Daze* or the ambiguous satirical send-up of how-to-succeed-in-business books, penned by a fired employee, that is subsequently discovered by the office and called *The Jilliad* succeed as a kind of redemption from corporate life.

8. See especially Foucault's *The Birth of Biopolitics* and *Security, Territory, Population*.

9. In *Biocapital: The Constitution of Postgenomic Life*, Kaushik Sunder Rajan claims that a new phase of capital, "biocapital," has emerged in which "biotechnology and subsequent genomics 'revolutions' are techno-capitalist assemblages that allow analyses, and create types of knowledge, that reconfigure definitions, understandings, even the grammar of 'life itself'" (142). In a similar vein, Melinda Cooper argues in her enlightening *Life as Surplus: Biotechnology and Capitalism in the Neoliberal Era*, that "what neoliberalism seeks to impose is not so much the generalized commodification of daily life—the reduction of the extraeconomic to the demands of exchange value—as its financialization" (10). This can be seen in Cooper's incredible tracing of biotechnology as a post-Fordist, flexible, and speculative mode of scientific production. Cooper writes, "while industrial production depletes the earth's reserves of past organic life (carbon-based fossil fuels), postindustrial bioproduction needs to depotentialize the future possibilities of life, even while putting them to work" (25).

10. Rajan points out how the Indian state willingly allows its population to become a genetic informational database for the biotech industry in order to court foreign investment and to propel its own biotech industry forward (77–103). Cooper, in looking at reproductive technologies (129–151), states, "In the sense that egg markets are increasingly drawing on the underpaid, unregulated labor of various

female underclasses, the difference between human reproductive medicine and the brute commodification of labor and tissues that prevails in the agricultural industry becomes difficult to maintain" (136).

11. The recent Supreme Court decision in *Association for Molecular Pathology v. Myriad Genetics*, which held that "natural" human DNA cannot be patented, demonstrates how the public usually encounters biopolitical issues. They are often highly visible and emotionally charged. However, what seemed like a victory against the commodification of life, which all the major news outlets heralded, was really no such thing. Essentially, the Court decided against Myriad's attempt to patent "natural" DNA in a way that (a) seemingly upheld the sacredness of "life" while, more importantly, (b) allowing "synthetic" DNA to be patented. In short, the decision hinders a (Myriad) monopoly and opens up the capital playing field to more competition in the biotech industry and thus ensures many more DNA patents in the future.

12. Agamben admits that modern biopolitics has its own characteristics but traces its historical origins back much further than does Foucault (who places its birth around the middle of the eighteenth century), all the way to the ancient Greeks via Aristotle's distinction between *zoē* (biological life) and *bios* (political life), which modernity inevitably conflates and confuses. (See *Homo Sacer* 1–12.)

13. Žižek reads the film in a similar way, stressing the biopolitical element, the state of emergency, and the figure of *homo sacer* in an essay on the film's website (as well as in the DVD commentary). See "The Clash of Civilizations at the End of History."

14. Klein explores how neoliberal "shock treatment," as Milton Friedman termed it (Klein 7), was instituted in countries devastated by war, natural disasters, or financial debt, such as Chile, Poland, South Africa, and Russia, among others. In times of crisis, countries "in shock" could be easily compelled by the United States, the World Bank, and the International Monetary Fund to adopt neoliberal economic policy, bypassing any democratic process of legitimation and ignoring counterarguments for economic recovery.

15. As Jeremy Scahill writes in *Blackwater: The Rise of the World's Most Powerful Mercenary Army*, "The rise of Blackwater's private army is nothing short of the embodiment of the ominous scenario prophesied decades ago by President Eisenhower when he warned of the 'grave implications' of the rise of the 'military-industrial complex' and 'misplaced power'" (377).

16. See Peter Pringle's *Food, Inc.*, particularly the case of Canadian farmer Perry Schmeiser (180–183).

17. See Kari Lydersen's "Target: Wal-Mart Lite."

18. The idea of a coming incorporation that I would like to outline here is in reference to Giorgio Agamben's *The Coming Community*, in which Agamben theorizes a novel future community that can never arrive in the sense of reaching a *telos*. This community would be composed of what Agamben calls "whatever being," or "whatever singularity," which "is the figure of pure singularity." It "has no identity, it is not determinate with respect to a concept, but neither is it simply indeterminate; rather it is determined only through its relation to an *idea*, that is, to the totality of its possibilities" (67). "Whatever being" or singularity is always in a state of flux or potentiality and rejects categorization or identification. In this way, "whatever being" constitutes a kind of dis-organized social body or potential community.

19. The multitude, it might be argued, is one interpretation of what Deleuze and Guattari, in *A Thousand Plateaus*, call an "assemblage," in which singularities or "bodies-without-organs" (bodies that dis-organize themselves) experiment with new ways of becoming and resist the logic of identity—come together on a plane of consistency as a collective machine (149–166). But the point here is that both at the level of the individual, now a singularity, and the collective, now an assemblage or multitude, we have an entirely different form of incorporation than the current corporate model offers or indeed can ever offer.

Works Cited

Adorno, T. W. *Aesthetic Theory.* Trans. Robert Hullot-Kentor. Minneapolis: U of Minnesota P, 1997.

———. "The Schema of Mass Culture." *The Culture Industry.* New York: Routledge, 2001. 61–97.

Agamben, Giorgio. *The Coming Community.* Trans. Michael Hardt. Minneapolis: U of Minnesota P, 1993.

———. *Homo Sacer: Sovereign Power and Bare Life.* Trans. Daniel Heller-Roazen. Stanford, CA: Stanford UP, 1998.

———. *State of Exception.* Trans. Kevin Attell. Chicago: U of Chicago P, 2005.

Allinson, Gary D. *Japan's Postwar History.* Ithaca, NY: Cornell UP, 1997.

Althusser, Louis. "Contradiction and Overdetermination." *For Marx.* New York: Verso, 2005. 87–128.

———. "Ideology and Ideological State Apparatuses (Notes toward an Investigation)." *On Ideology.* London: Verso, 2008. 1–60.

Alvaredo, Facundo, Anthony B. Atkinson, Thomas Piketty, and Emmanuel Saez. "The Top 1 Percent in International and Historical Perspective." *Journal of Economic Perspectives* 27.3 (Summer 2013): 3–20.

———. *The World Top Incomes Database.* Web. 27 Dec. 2012. http://topincomes.g-mond.parisschoolofeconomics.eu/.

Anderson, Benedict. *Imagined Communities.* New York: Verso, 1983.

Angell, Marcia. *The Truth about Drug Companies: How They Deceive Us and What to Do about It.* New York: Random House, 2005.

Arrighi, Giovanni. *The Long Twentieth Century: Money, Power, and the Origin of Our Times.* New York: Verso, 1994.

Austenfeld, Thomas. "A Happy Naturalist? Jeremy Bentham and the Cosmic

Morality of *The Octopus.*" *Studies in American Naturalism* 2.1 (Summer 2007): 33–45.
Bakan, Joel. *The Corporation: The Pathological Pursuit of Profit and Power.* New York: Free Press, 2004.
Barbarians at the Gate. Dir. Glenn Jordan. Columbia, 1993.
Baskin, Jonathan Barron, and Paul J. Miranti Jr. *A History of Corporate Finance.* New York: Cambridge UP, 1997.
Baudrillard, Jean. *For a Critique of the Political Economy of the Sign.* Trans. Charles Levin. St. Louis, MO: Telos, 1991.
———. *The Gulf War Did Not Take Place.* Trans. Paul Patton. Bloomington: Indiana UP, 1995.
———. *Simulacra and Simulation.* Trans. Sheila Faria Glaser. Ann Arbor: U of Michigan P, 1994.
———. *Symbolic Exchange and Death.* Trans. Iain Hamilton Grant. Thousand Oaks, CA: Sage, 1993.
Bercovitch, Sacvan. *The American Jeremiad.* Madison: U of Wisconsin P, 1978.
Berstein, Daniel. *Yen! Japan's New Financial Empire and Its Threat to America.* New York: Touchstone, 1988.
Best, Steven, and Douglas Kellner. *The Postmodern Adventure: Science, Technology, and Cultural Studies at the Third Millennium.* New York: Guilford, 2001.
Bey, Hakim. *T.A.Z.: The Temporary Autonomous Zone, Ontological Anarchy, Poetic Terrorism.* 2nd ed. Brooklyn, NY: Autonomedia, 2003.
Big. Dir. Penny Marshall. Gracie Films / 20th Century Fox, 1988.
Bloom, Harold, ed. *Don DeLillo's "White Noise."* Philadelphia: Chelsea House, 2003.
"Blow Out, The." Dir. Tex Avery. Warner, 1936.
Brown, Nicholas. "Cognitive Map, Aesthetic Object, or National Allegory? *Carpenter's Gothic.*" Tabbi and Shavers 151–160.
Castronovo, Russ. "Geo-Aesthetics: Fascism, Globalism, and Frank Norris." *Boundary 2* 30.3 (Fall 2003): 157–184.
CB4. Screenplay by Chris Rock, Nelson George, and Robert LoCase. Dir. Tamra Davis. Universal, 1993.
Chandler, Raymond. *The Long Goodbye.* 1953. New York: Vintage, 1988.
Cheal, David J. *Families in Today's World: A Comparative Approach.* New York: Routledge, 2008.
Children of Men. Dir. Alfonso Cuarón. Universal, 2006.
China Syndrome, The. Dir. James Bridges. IPC Films, 1979.
Clements, Jeffrey D. *Corporations Are Not People: Why They Have More Rights than You Do and What You Can Do about It.* San Francisco: Berrett-Koehler, 2012.
Clune, Michael W. *American Literature and the Free Market, 1945–2000.* New York: Cambridge UP, 2009.
Cohen, Jillian Clare, Patricia Illingworth, and Udo Shuklenk, eds. *The Power of Pills: Social, Ethical, and Legal Issues in Drug Development, Marketing, and Pricing.* London: Pluto, 2006.

Conroy, Mark. "From Tombstone to Tabloid: Authority Figured in *White Noise.*" Bloom 153–168.
Constant Gardener, The. Dir. Fernando Meirelles. Potboiler Productions, 2005.
Coontz, Stephanie. *The Way We Never Were: American Families and the Nostalgia Trap.* New York: Basic Books, 1992.
Cooper, Melinda. *Life as Surplus: Biotechnology and Capitalism in the Neoliberal Era.* Seattle: U of Washington P, 2008.
Court, Jamie. *Corporateering: How Corporate Power Steals Your Personal Freedom and What You Can Do about It.* New York: Putnam, 2003.
Cowart, David. "For Whom the Bell Tolls: Don DeLillo's *Americana.*" *Contemporary Literature* 37 (1996): 602–619.
Crichton, Michael. *Rising Sun.* New York: Knopf, 1992.
Davis, Mike. *Dead Cities.* New York: New Press, 2002.
Day at the Races, A. Dir. Sam Wood. MGM, 1937.
Debord, Guy. *The Society of the Spectacle.* Trans. Donald Nicholson-Smith. New York: Zone Books, 1994.
DeGrandpre, Richard. *The Cult of Pharmacology: How America Became the World's Most Troubled Drug Culture.* Durham, NC: Duke UP, 2006.
Deleuze, Gilles, and Félix Guattari. *Anti-Oedipus: Capitalism and Schizophrenia.* Trans. Robert Hurley, Mark Seem, and Helen R. Lane. Minneapolis: U of Minnesota P, 1983.
———. *A Thousand Plateaus: Capitalism and Schizophrenia.* Trans. Brian Massumi. Minneapolis: U of Minnesota P, 1983.
DeLillo, Don. *Americana.* 1971. Rev. ed. New York: Penguin, 1989.
———. *Cosmopolis.* New York: Scribner, 2003.
———. *White Noise.* New York: Viking, 1985.
Dewey, Joseph. *Understanding Richard Powers.* Columbia: U of South Carolina P, 2002.
Dick, Phillip K. *Do Androids Dream of Electric Sheep?* 1968. New York: Del Rey, 1996.
Donaldson, Thomas. *Corporations and Morality.* Englewood Cliffs, NJ: Prentice Hall, 1982.
Dos Passos, John. *U.S.A.: The 42nd Parallel; 1919; The Big Money.* 1930, 1932, 1936. New York: Library of America, 1996.
Dostoyevsky, Fyodor. *The Possessed.* 1872. Trans. Constance Garnett. New York: Dell, 1959.
Dugdale, John. *Thomas Pynchon: Allusive Parables of Power.* London: Macmillan, 1990.
Dyer, W. Gibb, Jr. *Cultural Change in Family Firms: Anticipating and Managing Business and Family Transitions.* San Francisco: Jossey-Bass, 1986.
Debord, Guy. *The Society of the Spectacle.* Trans. Donald Nicholson-Smith. New York: Zone Books, 1994.

DeGrandpre, Richard. *The Cult of Pharmacology: How America Became the World's Most Troubled Drug Culture*. Durham, NC: Duke UP, 2006.
Deleuze, Gilles, and Félix Guattari. *Anti-Oedipus: Capitalism and Schizophrenia*. Trans. Robert Hurley, Mark Seem, and Helen R. Lane. Minneapolis: U of Minnesota P, 1983.
———. *A Thousand Plateaus: Capitalism and Schizophrenia*. Trans. Brian Massumi. Minneapolis: U of Minnesota P, 1983.
DeLillo, Don. *Americana*. 1971. Rev. ed. New York: Penguin, 1989.
———. *Cosmopolis*. New York: Scribner, 2003.
———. *White Noise*. New York: Viking, 1985.
Dewey, Joseph. *Understanding Richard Powers*. Columbia: U of South Carolina P, 2002.
Dick, Phillip K. *Do Androids Dream of Electric Sheep?* 1968. New York: Del Rey, 1996.
Donaldson, Thomas. *Corporations and Morality*. Englewood Cliffs, NJ: Prentice Hall, 1982.
Dos Passos, John. *U.S.A.: The 42nd Parallel; 1919; The Big Money*. 1930, 1932, 1936. New York: Library of America, 1996.
Dostoyevsky, Fyodor. *The Possessed*. 1872. Trans. Constance Garnett. New York: Dell, 1959.
Dugdale, John. *Thomas Pynchon: Allusive Parables of Power*. London: Macmillan, 1990.
Dyer, W. Gibb, Jr. *Cultural Change in Family Firms: Anticipating and Managing Business and Family Transitions*. San Francisco: Jossey-Bass, 1986.
Eggers, Dave. *A Hologram for the King*. San Francisco: McSweeney's, 2012.
Erera, Pauline Irit. *Family Diversity: Continuity and Change in the Contemporary Family*. Thousand Oaks, CA: Sage, 2002.
Erin Brockovich. Dir. Steven Soderbergh. Jersey Films, 2000.
Escape from New York. Dir. John Carpenter. AVCO Embassy, 1981.
Executive Suite. Dir. Robert Wise. MGM, 1954.
Faulkner, William. *Absalom, Absalom!* 1936. New York: Vintage, 1985.
———. *The Sound and the Fury*. 1929. New York: Vintage, 1985.
Ferris, Joshua. *Then We Came to the End*. New York: Back Bay Books, 2007.
"Financial Legends." *Economist* (U.S. ed.) 15 June 1996: 79.
Fleming, Peter, and André Spicer. *Contesting the Corporation: Struggle, Power, and Resistance in Organizations*. New York: Cambridge UP, 2007.
Foucault, Michel. *The Birth of Biopolitics: Lectures at the Collège de France, 1978–1979*. Ed. Michel Senellart. Trans. Graham Burchell. New York: Picador, 2008.
———. *Discipline and Punish*. Trans. Alan Sheridan. New York: Vintage, 1995.
———. *The History of Sexuality*. Vol. 1. Trans. Robert Hurley. New York: Vintage, 1990.
———. *Security, Territory, Population: Lectures at the Collège de France,*

1977-1978. Ed. Michel Senellart. Trans. Graham Burchell. New York: Picador, 2007.
Friedman, Thomas. *The Lexus and the Olive Tree*. New York: Farrar, Straus and Giroux, 1999.
Frow, John. "The Last Things before the Last: Notes on *White Noise*." Bloom 35-49.
Fucini, Joseph J., and Suzy Fucini. *Working for the Japanese: Inside Mazda's American Auto Plant*. New York: Free Press, 1990.
Fukuyama, Frances. *The End of History and the Last Man*. 1992. New York: Free Press, 2006.
Gaddis, William. *Agapē, Agape*. New York: Viking, 2002.
———. *Carpenter's Gothic*. New York: Penguin, 1985.
———. *J R*. New York: Knopf, 1975.
Gagnier, Regenia. *The Insatiability of Human Wants: Economics and Aesthetics in Market Society*. Chicago: U of Chicago P, 2000.
Gallagher, Catherine. *The Body Economic: Life, Death, and Sensation in Political Economy and the Victorian Novel*. Princeton, NJ: Princeton UP, 2006.
Gauthier, Anne Hélène. *The State and the Family: A Comparative Analysis of Family Policies in Industrialized Countries*. Oxford, UK: Clarendon, 1996.
Ghostbusters. Dir. Ivan Reitman. Black Rhino Productions, 1984.
Gibson, William. *Neuromancer*. New York: Ace, 1984.
Gilbert, Paul. "Family Values and the Nation-State." *Changing Family Values*. Ed. Gill Jagger and Caroline Wright. New York: Routledge, 1999. 136-149.
Glengarry, Glen Ross. Screenplay by David Mamet. Dir. James Foley. GGR, 1992.
Godden, Richard. *Fictions of Capital: The American Novel from James to Mailer*. New York: Cambridge UP, 1990.
Gotham, Kevin Fox. "Tourism Gentrification: The Case of New Orleans' *Vieux Carre* (French Quarter)." *Urban Studies* 42.7 (June 2005): 1099-1121.
Graeber, David. *Debt: The First Five Thousand Years*. Brooklyn, NY: Melville House, 2011.
———. *The Democracy Project: A History, a Crisis, a Movement*. New York: Spiegel and Grau, 2013.
Groening, Matt. *Work Is Hell*. New York: Pantheon, 1986.
Guillory, John. *Cultural Capital: The Problem of Literary Canon Formation*. Chicago: U of Chicago P, 1993.
Gung Ho. Screenplay by Edwin Blum, Lowell Ganz, and Babaloo Mandel. Dir. Ron Howard. Paramount, 1986.
"Gung Ho!" The Story of Carlson's Makin Island Raiders. Dir. Ray Enright. Universal, 1943.
Hammett, Dashiell. *The Maltese Falcon*. 1930. New York: Vintage, 1989.
Hardt, Michael, and Antonio Negri. *Empire*. Cambridge, MA: Harvard UP, 2000.
———. *Multitude: War and Democracy in the Age of Empire*. New York: Penguin, 2004.

Harloe, Michael, Peter Marcuse, and Neil Smith. "Housing for People, Housing for Profits." *Divided Cities: New York and London in the Contemporary World*. Ed. Susan S. Fainstein, Ian Gordon, and Michael Harloe. Cambridge, UK: Blackwell, 1992. 175–202.

Harris, Charles B. "'The Stereo-View': Politics and the Role of the Reader in *Gain*." *Review of Contemporary Fiction* 18.3 (1998): 97–108.

Hartmann, Thom. *Unequal Protection: The Rise of Corporate Dominance and the Theft of Human Rights*. New York: Rodale, 2002.

Harvey, David. *A Brief History of Neoliberalism*. Oxford: Oxford UP, 2005.

———. *The Condition of Postmodernity*. Cambridge, UK: Blackwell, 1990.

———. *The Enigma of Capital and the Crises of Capitalism*. New York: Oxford UP, 2010.

———. "Fictional Finance." Interview. *N+1* 7 (Fall 2008): 38–48.

———. *The Limits to Capital*. New York: Verso, 2006.

———. *The New Imperialism*. Oxford: Oxford UP, 2003.

Heise, Ursula K. "Risk and Narrative in the Contemporary Novel." *American Literature* 74 (2002): 747–778.

Heller, Joseph. *Catch 22*. 1961. London: Corgi, 1979.

———. *Something Happened*. New York: Ballantine, 1975.

Horkheimer, Max, and Theodor W. Adorno. *Dialectic of Enlightenment*. 1944. Trans. John Cumming. New York: Continuum, 1972.

Hussman, Lawrence E. *Harbingers of a Century: The Novels of Frank Norris*. New York: Peter Lang, 1999.

Ingrassia, Paul. *Crash Course: The American Automobile Industry's Road from Glory to Disaster*. New York: Random House, 2010.

Ingrassia, Paul, and Joseph B. White. *Comeback: The Fall and Rise of the American Automobile Industry*. New York: Simon and Schuster, 1994.

Inkster, Ian. *Japanese Industrialization: Historical and Cultural Perspectives*. New York: Routledge, 2001.

Insider, The. Dir. Michael Mann. Blue Lion Entertainment, 1999.

Invisible Committee, The. *The Coming Insurrection*. Los Angeles: Semiotext(e), 2009.

Jagger, Gill, and Caroline Wright, eds. *Changing Family Values*. New York: Routledge, 1999.

———. "Introduction: Changing Family Values." Jagger and Wright, *Changing* 1–16.

Jameson, Fredric. *The Political Unconscious: Narrative as a Socially Symbolic Act*. Ithaca, NY: Cornell UP, 1981.

———. *Postmodernism, or, The Cultural Logic of Late Capitalism*. Durham, NC: Duke UP, 1991.

———. *Signatures of the Visible*. New York: Routledge, 1992.

———. *Valences of the Dialectic*. Brooklyn, NY: Verso, 2009.

Johnston, John. *Carnival of Repetition: Gaddis's "The Recognitions" and Postmodern Theory*. Philadelphia: U of Pennsylvania P, 1990.

———. "Toward the Schizo-Text: Paranoia as Semiotic Regime in *The Crying of Lot 49*." *New Essays on "The Crying of Lot 49."* Ed. Patrick O'Donnell. New York: Cambridge UP, 1991. 7–78.

Jones, Geoffrey. "Multinationals from the 1930s to the 1980s." *Leviathans: Multinational Corporations and the New Global History*. Ed. Alfred D. Chandler Jr. and Bruce Nazlish. New York: Cambridge UP, 2005. 81–103.

Kahn, Herman. *The Emerging Japanese Superstate: Challenge and Response*. Englewood Cliffs, NJ: Prentice Hall, 1970.

Kahn, Herman, and Thomas Pepper. *The Japanese Challenge: The Success and Failure of Economic Success*. New York: Crowell, 1979.

Kaplan, Warren. "Drug Companies as Organizational Hybrids." Cohen, Illingworth, and Shuklenk 41–56.

Keesey, Douglas. *Don DeLillo*. New York: Twayne, 1993.

Keller, Maryann. *Rude Awakening: The Rise, Fall, and Struggle for Recovery of General Motors*. New York: William Morrow, 1989.

Kiel, Paul, and Dan Nguyen. "Bailout Tracker: Tracking Every Dollar and Every Recipient." *ProPublica: Journalism in the Public Interest*. 17 June 2013. http://projects.propublica.org/bailout/.

Kindleberger, Charles P. *Manias, Panics, and Crashes: A History of Financial Crises*. 5th ed. Hoboken, NJ: Wiley, 2005.

Klein, Naomi. *The Shock Doctrine: The Rise of Disaster Capitalism*. New York: Metropolitan Books, 2007.

Knight, Christopher J. *Hints and Guesses: William Gaddis's Fiction of Longing*. Madison: U of Wisconsin P, 1997.

Korten, David C. *When Corporations Rule the World*. 2nd ed. Bloomfield, CT: Kumarian, 2001.

Krippner, Greta R. *Capitalizing on Crisis: The Political Origins of the Rise of Finance*. Cambridge, MA: Harvard UP, 2011.

Krugman, Paul. *End This Depression Now!* New York: Norton, 2012.

———. *The Return of Depression Economics and the Crisis of 2008*. New York: Norton, 2009.

LeClair, Tom. *In the Loop: Don DeLillo and the Systems Novel*. Urbana: U of Illinois P, 1987.

Lentricchia, Frank. "Tales of the Electronic Tribe." Bloom 73–95.

Leonard, Suzanne. "'I Hate My Job, I Hate Everybody Here': Adultery, Boredom, and the 'Working Girl' in Twenty-First Century-American Cinema." *Interrogating Postfeminism: Gender and the Politics of Popular Culture*. Ed. Yvonne Trasker and Diane Negra. Durham, NC: Duke UP, 2007. 100–131.

Lexchin, Joel. "The Pharmaceutical Industry and the Pursuit of Profit." Cohen, Illingworth, and Shuklenk 11–24.

Lydersen, Kari. "Target: Wal-Mart Lite." CorpWatch. 20 Apr. 2006. 4 Apr. 2009. http://www.corpwatch.org/article.php?id=13508.

Mailer, Norman. *The Armies of the Night: History as a Novel, the Novel as History*. 1968. New York: Plume, 1994.

Maliszewski, Paul. "The Business of *Gain*." *Intersections: Essays on Richard Powers*. Ed. Stephen J. Burn and Peter Dempsey. Champaign, IL: Dalkey Archive, 2008. 162–186.

Manchurian Candidate, The. Dir. John Frankenheimer. MGM, 1962.

Manchurian Candidate, The. Dir. Jonathan Demme. Paramount, 2004.

Manhattan. Dir. Woody Allen. Jack Rollins & Charles H. Joffe Productions, 1979.

Marchand, Roland. *Creating the Corporate Soul: The Rise of Public Relations and Corporate Imagery in American Big Business*. Berkeley: U of California P, 1998.

Margin Call. Dir. J. C. Chandor. Before the Door Pictures, 2011.

Marsa, Linda. *Prescription for Profits: How the Pharmaceutical Industry Bankrolled the Unholy Marriage between Science and Business*. New York: Scribner, 1997.

Martin, Randy. *Financialization of Daily Life*. Philadelphia: Temple UP, 2002.

Marx, Karl. *Capital.* Vol. 1. Trans. Ben Fowkes. London: Penguin, 1990.

Marx, Karl, and Friedrich Engels. "Manifesto of the Communist Party." *The Marx-Engels Reader*. 2nd ed. Ed. Robert C. Tucker. New York: Norton, 1978. 469–500.

Matanle, Stephen. H. "Love and Strife in William Gaddis's *J R*." *In Recognition of William Gaddis*. Ed. John Kuehl and Steven Moore. Syracuse, NY: Syracuse UP, 1984. 106–118.

Matray, James I. *Japan's Emergence as a Global Power*. Westport, CT: Greenwood, 2001.

Mattessich, Stefan. *Lines of Flight: Discursive Time and Countercultural Desire in the Work of Thomas Pynchon*. Durham, NC: Duke UP, 2002.

Maynard, Micheline. *The End of Detroit: How the Big Three Lost Their Grip on the American Car Market*. New York: Doubleday, 2003.

McLean, Bethany, and Peter Elkind. *The Smartest Guys in the Room: The Amazing Rise and Scandalous Fall of Enron*. New York: Penguin, 2003.

McQuaid, Kim. *Uneasy Partners: Big Business in American Politics, 1945-1990*. Baltimore: Johns Hopkins UP, 1994.

Melville, Herman. "Bartleby the Scrivener: A Story of Wall-Street." *Great Short Works of Melville*. New York: Harper Perennial, 1969. 39–74.

——. *Moby-Dick; or, The White Whale*. New York: Harper, 1851.

Michael Clayton. Writ. and Dir. Tony Gilroy. Samuels Media, 2007.

Michaels, Walter Benn. "Going Boom." *Bookforum* Feb.–Mar. 2009. http://www.bookforum.com/inprint/015_05/3274.

———. *The Gold Standard and the Logic of Naturalism*. Berkeley: U of California P, 1987.
———. *The Trouble with Diversity*. New York: Metropolitan Books, 2006.
Milkman, Ruth. *Farewell to the Factory: Auto Workers in the Late Twentieth Century*. Berkeley: U of California P, 1997.
Miller, Arthur. *Death of a Salesman*. 1949. New York: Penguin, 1976.
Moore, Steven. *William Gaddis*. Boston: Twayne, 1989.
Moynihan, Ray, and Alan Cassels. *Selling Sickness: How the World's Biggest Pharmaceutical Companies Are Turning Us All into Patients*. New York: Nation Books, 2005.
Mulvey, Laura. "The Myth of Pandora: A Psychoanalytical Approach." *Feminisms in the Cinema*. Ed. Laura Pietropaulo and Ada Testaferri. Bloomington: Indiana UP, 1995. 3–19.
National Geographic. "Portuguese Man-of-War (*Physalia physalis*)." 15 Oct. 2009. http://animals.nationalgeographic.com/animals/invertebrates/portuguese-man-of-war.html.
Network. Screenplay by Paddy Cheyefsky. Dir. Sidney Lumet. MGM, 1976.
Norris, Frank. *McTeague*. 1899. New York: Signet, 1981.
———. *The Octopus*. 1901. New York: Penguin, 1986.
———. *The Pit*. 1903. New York: Penguin Classics, 1994.
Odets, Clifford. *Waiting for Lefty*. *Six Plays of Clifford Odets*. New York: Grove, 1979. 3–31.
Office, The. Writ. and Dir. Stephen Merchant and Ricky Gervais. BBC, 2001–2003.
Office, The. Prod. Greg Daniels et al. NBC, 2005–2013 (USA).
Office Space. Dir. Mike Judge. 20th Century Fox, 1999.
Page, Max. *The City's End: Two Centuries of Fantasies, Fears, and Premonitions of New York's Destruction*. New Haven, CT: Yale UP, 2008.
Park, Ed. *Personal Days*. New York: Random House, 2008.
Pizer, Donald. *The Novels of Frank Norris*. New York: Haskell House, 1973.
Polanyi, Karl. *The Great Transformation: The Political and Economic Origins of Our Time*. 1944. Boston: Beacon, 1947.
Powers, Richard. *Gain*. New York: Picador, 1998.
Pringle, Peter. *Food, Inc.: Mendel to Monsanto—The Promises and Perils of the Biotech Harvest*. New York: Simon and Schuster, 2003.
Pynchon, Thomas. *The Crying of Lot 49*. 1966. New York: Harper Perennial, 2006.
———. "Entropy." *Slow Learner*. 1984. New York: Back Bay Books, 1985. 79–98.
———. *Gravity's Rainbow*. New York: Viking, 1973.
———. *V*. 1963. New York: Harper Perennial, 2005.
———. *Vineland*. 1990. New York: Penguin, 1991.
Rae, John B. *The American Automobile Industry*. Boston: Twayne, 1984.

Rajan, Kaushik Sunder. *Biocapital: The Constitution of Postgenomic Life*. Durham, NC: Duke UP, 2006.

Rand, Ayn. *Atlas Shrugged*. New York: Random House, 1957.

Reed, Naomi C. "The Specter of Wall Street: 'Bartleby, the Scrivener' and the Language of Commodities." *American Literature* 76.2 (2004): 247–273.

Reich, Robert B. *Supercapitalism: The Transformation of Business, Democracy, and Everyday Life*. New York: Vintage, 2007.

Reichl, Alexander J. *Reconstructing Times Square: Politics and Culture in Urban Development*. Lawrence: UP of Kansas, 1999.

"Return of Economic Nationalism, The." *Economist* 7 Feb. 2009: 9–10.

Rilke, Rainer Maria. "The Swan." *Rilke: Selected Poems*. Trans. C. F. MacIntyre. Berkeley: U of California P, 1940. 70–71.

Royster, Paul. "Melville's Economy of Language." *Ideology and Classic American Literature*. Ed. Sacvan Bercovitch and Myra Jehlen. New York: Cambridge, 1986. 313–336.

Saez, Emmanuel, and Thomas Piketty. "Striking It Richer: The Evolution of Top Incomes in the United States (Updated with 2012 Estimates)." Emmanuel Saez's UC-Berkeley webpage. http://elsa.berkeley.edu/~saez/saez-UStopincomes-2012.pdf.

Said, Edward. *Orientalism*. New York: Vintage, 1979.

Sample, Ian. "Leo Sternbach: Chemist Who Invented Librium and Valium, Drugs Whose Uses Are Still Being Explored." *Guardian* 3 Oct. 2005: Obituaries 29.

Sartre, Jean-Paul. "The Humanism of Existentialism." *Essays in Existentialism*. Ed. Wade Baskin. New York: Citadel, 1965. 31–62.

Saval, Nikil. "Birth of the Office." *N+1* 6 (Winter 2008): 109–122.

Savitch, H. V. *Post-Industrial Cities: Politics and Planning in New York, Paris, and London*. Princeton, NJ: Princeton UP, 1988.

Scahill, Jeremy. *Blackwater: The Rise of the World's Most Powerful Mercenary Army*. New York: Nation Books, 2007.

Scarface. Dir. Howard Hawks and Richard Rosson. Caddo, 1932.

Scarface. Dir. Brian De Palma. Universal, 1983.

Schaub, Thomas H. *Pynchon: The Voice of Ambiguity*. Chicago: U of Illinois P, 1981.

Seed, David. *The Fictional Labyrinths of Thomas Pynchon*. London: Macmillan, 1988.

Seventh Seal, The. Dir. Ingmar Bergman. Svensk Filmindustri, 1957.

Shonkwiler, Alison. "Don DeLillo's Financial Sublime." *Contemporary Literature* 51.2 (Summer 2010): 246–282.

Shorter, Edward. *The Making of the Modern Family*. New York: Basic, 1975.

Silkwood. Dir. Mike Nichols. ABC Motion Pictures, 1983.

Sites, William. "Public Action: New York City Policy and the Gentrification of the Lower East Side." *From Urban to East Village: The Battle for New York's*

Lower East Side. Ed. Janet L. Abu-Lughod. Cambridge, UK: Blackwell, 1994. 189–211.

———. *Remaking New York: Primitive Globalization and the Politics of Urban Community*. Minneapolis: U of Minnesota P, 2003.

Sobel, Robert. *Car Wars: The Untold Story*. New York: Dutton, 1984.

Solomon, Norman. *The Trouble with Dilbert*. Monroe, ME: Common Courage, 1997. 21 Oct. 2009. http://web.archive.org/web/20040218235653/http://freespeech.org/normansolomon/dilbert/book/.

"Something This Way Wall-Mart Comes." *South Park*. Season 8, episode 9. Comedy Central. 3 Nov. 2004.

Sontag, Susan. *Illness as Metaphor*. New York: Vintage, 1979.

Spencer, Nicholas. "Critical Mimesis: *J R*'s Transition to Postmodernity." Tabbi and Shavers 137–150.

Stiglitz, Joseph E. *The Price of Inequality: How Today's Divided Society Endangers Our Future*. New York: Norton, 2012.

Superman III. Dir. Richard Lester. Warner Bros., 1983.

Tabb, William K. *The Long Default: New York City and the Urban Fiscal Crisis*. New York: Monthly Review Press, 1982.

Tabbi, Joseph, and Rone Shavers, eds. *Paper Empire: William Gaddis and the World System*. Tuscaloosa: U of Alabama P, 2007.

Taxi Driver. Dir. Martin Scorsese. Bill/Phillips, 1976.

Thorne, Barrie, and Marilyn Yalom. *Rethinking the Family: Some Feminist Questions*. Boston: Northeastern UP, 1992.

Togo, Kazuhko. *Japan's Foreign Policy, 1945–2003: The Quest for a Proactive Policy*. Boston: Brill, 2005.

Tolstoy, Leo. *The Death of Ivan Ilyich*. 1886. Trans. Richard Pevear and Larissa Volokhonsky. New York: Vintage, 2009.

———. *War and Peace*. 1869. Trans. Constance Garnett. New York: Modern Library, 1994.

Tommy Boy. Dir. Peter Segal. Paramount, 1995.

Trachtenberg, Alan. *The Incorporation of America: Culture and Society in the Gilded Age*. New York: Hill and Wang, 1982.

Tratner, Michael. *Deficits and Desires: Economics and Sexuality in Twentieth-Century Literature*. Stanford, CA: Stanford UP, 2001.

Venkatesh, Sudhir Alladi. "Sociology and Katrina." *City and Community* 5.2 (June 2006): 115–118.

Vonnegut, Kurt. *Jailbird*. New York: Dell, 1979.

Wahl, Jean. "The Roots of Existentialism: An Introduction." *Essays in Existentialism*. By Jean-Paul Sartre. Ed. Wade Baskin. New York: Citadel, 1965. 3–28.

Wallerstein, Immanuel. "The ANC and South Africa: The Past and Future of Liberation Movements in the World-System." Wallerstein, *End of the World* 19–33.

———. *The End of the World as We Know It: Social Science for the Twenty-First Century.* Minneapolis: U of Minnesota P, 1999.

———. "The Heritage of Sociology, the Promise of Social Science." Wallerstein, *End of the World* 220–251.

———. *Historical Capitalism with Capitalist Civilization.* New York: Verso, 1998.

———. *World-Systems Analysis: An Introduction.* Durham, NC: Duke UP, 2004.

Warriors, The. Dir. Walter Hill. Paramount, 1979.

Wasserman, Harvey. *America Born and Reborn.* New York: Macmillan, 1983.

Weber, Leonard J. *Profits before People? Ethical Standards and the Marketing of Prescription Drugs.* Bloomington: Indiana UP, 2006.

Weber, Max. *The Protestant Ethic and the "Spirit" of Capitalism and Other Writings.* 1905. New York: Penguin, 2002.

West, Nathaniel. *The Day of the Locust.* 1939. *"Miss Lonelyhearts" and "The Day of the Locust."* New York: New Directions, 1962. 59–185.

Whitman, Walt. "Crossing Brooklyn Ferry." *The Norton Anthology of American Literature.* Vol. B, *1820–1865*. Ed. Nina Baym. 7th ed. New York: Norton, 2007. 2263–2267.

———. *Leaves of Grass: The First (1855) Edition.* Ed. Malcolm Cowley. New York: Penguin, 1959.

Whyte, William H. *The Organization Man.* 1956. Philadelphia: U of Pennsylvania P, 2002.

"Why Toyota Is Afraid of Being Number One." *Business Week* 5 Mar. 2007. 11 Jan. 2008. http://www.businessweek.com/magazine/content/07_10/b4024071.htm.

Wilcox, Leonard. "Baudrillard, DeLillo's *White Noise*, and the End of Heroic Narrative." Bloom 97–115.

Winthrop, John. "A Model of Christian Charity." *The Norton Anthology of American Literature.* Vol. A, *Beginnings to 1820*. Ed. Nina Baym. 7th ed. New York: Norton, 2007. 147–158.

Wolfe, Peter. *A Vision of His Own: The Mind and Art of William Gaddis.* Madison, NJ: Fairleigh Dickinson UP, 1997.

Wood, Adam H. "The Signs and Symbols of the West: Frank Norris, *The Octopus*, and the Naturalization of Market Capitalism." *Twisted from the Ordinary: Essays on American Literary Naturalism.* Ed. Mary E. Papke. Knoxville: U of Tennessee P, 2003. 107–127.

Woodmansee, Martha, and Mark Osteen. *The New Economic Criticism: Studies at the Intersection of Literature and Economics.* New York: Routledge, 1999.

Wright, Caroline, and Gill Jagger. "End of Century, End of Family? Shifting Discourses of Family 'Crisis.'" Jagger and Wright, *Changing* 17–37.

Yates, Brock. *The Decline and Fall of the American Automobile Industry.* New York: Empire, 1993.

Zeiger, John, and Gilbert J. Gall. *American Workers, American Unions.* 3rd ed. Baltimore: Johns Hopkins UP, 2002.

Žižek, Slavoj. "The Clash of Civilizations and the End of History." *Children of Men* website. 29 Nov. 2009. http://www.childrenofmen.net/slavoj.html.

———. *First as Tragedy, Then as Farce.* Brooklyn, NY: Verso, 2009.

———. *In Defense of Lost Causes.* New York: Verso, 2008.

———. *Living in the End Times.* Brooklyn, NY: Verso, 2010.

———. *The Sublime Object of Ideology.* New York: Verso, 1989.

———. *Violence.* New York: Picador, 2008.

———. *Welcome to the Desert of the Real.* New York: Verso, 2002.

Index

Adams, Henry, 165, 170
Adams, Scott, 180–182, 217n2
Adorno, Theodor W., 74, 206, 208n15
Agamben, Giorgio, 4–5, 193–194, 219n12, 219n18
Althusser, Louis, 12–13, 37–38, 43
ambivalence, 3, 127
Angell, Marcia, 131–132
Armies of the Night (Mailer), 169–170
Arrighi, Giovanni, 8
Austenfeld, Thomas, 211n6
automobile industry. *See Gung Ho* (dir. Howard)

Barthelme, Donald, vii
Baudrillard, Jean, 120–123, 125–126, 208n15
Bayh-Dole Act (1980), 128, 215n3
Bercovitch, Sacvan, 88
Berstein, Daniel, 50
Best, Steven, 127
Big (dir. Marshall), 214n5
biopower: overview of, 193–194, 218–219nn9–12; corporations in fiction and, 15–16, 123–124, 159–160, 193–194, 194–195, 205, 219n13; neoliberalism and, 195–196, 219nn14–15
bodies. *See* corporate bodies; individual bodies
boredom, 180–183
Brand, Barry, 132

Camus, Albert, 118
capitalism critiques: corporations in fiction and, 23, 36–37, 48–49, 139; in films, 15, 51, 60, 74–76, 87–88, 106–107, 114, 213n1; in literature, 11–12, 48–49, 208nn15–16; Marx and, 13, 140; multinational corporations and, 51, 60; in popular culture, 15, 48
capitalism/s: and (dis)contents in context of, 3; corporations and, 199–200; corporations in fiction and, 18–19, 22–24, 26, 36–37, 210nn1–2; future of, 17; and historical transitions in fiction, 19, 21, 28–31, 47–48, 136–137, 146–147, 210n3, 210n4, 211n6, 215n2; and influences in fiction, 18–19, 22–24, 26, 36–37, 210nn1–2; living/dead binary in context of, 122; media and, 120–121, 131; multinational corporations and, 3; neoliberalism and, 4, 6, 207n3; as othering, 197; self-perpetuation of, 164–166. *See also* capitalism critiques; future of corporate capitalism
Carter, Jimmy, and administration, 10, 93–94, 215n3
Cassels, Alan, 132, 215n4
Castronovo, Russ, 211n6
CB4 (dir. Rock), 218n4
Cheyefsky, Paddy, 81
Children of Men (dir. Cuarón), 194–195, 219n13

236 / INDEX

China Syndrome, The (dir. Bridges), 99
citizenship, 152, 170, 176. *See also* sovereignty/personhood rights
Citizens United case (2010), 10, 198
class anxieties, 14, 56–57, 59, 72
comic strips, 180–182, 217n2, 218n3
Conroy, Mark, 123, 215n1
Constant Gardener, The (dir. Meirelles), 214n9
consumption/commodification: corporations in context of, 3; corporations in fiction and, 15, 18, 22, 32–33, 127–128, 152, 215n3; corporations in literature and, 209n16; globalization in context of, 5, 71–72; multinational corporations and, 3; neoliberalism in context of, 8; television programs in context of, 75
Coontz, Stephanie, 155–156
Cooper, Melinda, 218nn9–10
corporate bodies: overview of, 3, 13, 17; benevolence of, 107, 144, 146, 147, 215n2; CEO figure in context of, 15, 91–92, 107, 108–110, 144, 146, 147, 215n2; individual bodies in context of, 16, 159–161, 164–165, 166–172, 177–178, 192; as malevolent, 15, 86–87, 91–92, 107, 108–110; neoliberalism and, 8, 208nn10–12; presence of, 3, 12–14, 20–22, 24, 26–27, 31–32, 34–35, 40, 75, 141, 145, 153, 159, 211n7, 216n3. *See also* corporations
corporate takeovers, 28, 76, 93. *See also* mergers
corporation critiques from inside: overview of, 16–17, 180–181; boredom and, 180–183; comic strips and, 180–182, 217n2, 218n3; existentialism and, 180, 183; family discourse in corporations in context of stabilization/embodiment and, 182, 186–192, 218n6; fiction and, 186–192; films and, 183–186, 188, 190, 218n4; future of corporate capitalism and, 190; interchangeable characters and, 182, 186–187; internal contradictions and, 181–182; popular culture and, 181; pseudoreligious side of capitalism and, 189–190, 218nn6–7; resistance as (im)possible and, 180–190, 217nn1–2, 218nn4–5;

television programs and, 16–17, 182–183. *See also* corporations
corporations: ambivalence about, 2–3; benevolence of capitalism and, 10, 14–16, 75–76, 78–85, 88–89, 102–105, 107–112, 114, 142–149, 214n9, 215n2; capitalism and, 199–200; consumption/commodification in context of, 3; (dis)contents with capitalism in context of, 3; as cultural productions, 3, 13; democracy in context of, 3, 200–201; economic criticism and, 12, 48, 208n16; family discourse in corporations in context of stabilization/embodiment and, 182, 186–192, 218n6; financial anxieties and, 3; future incorporation and, 201–206, 219–220nn18–19; gender roles in context of power of, 83, 86–87, 163; history of, 8–11, 208n13; individual bodies in context of, 3, 17, 167, 216nn2–4; internal contradictions and, 15, 75, 80–81, 84–85, 89, 92; late capitalism in context of, 3, 116, 118; limited liability, 9–11, 216n4; malevolent force of capitalism and, 14–15, 74–77, 81–86, 93–96, 98, 100–107, 107–114, 169–170, 213n3, 214n6, 214n9; metaphors and, 8–11, 13, 137; as Other/other, 197; paternalistic power of capitalism and, 16, 142–149, 215n2; power of, 3, 13; privileged position of, 3; resistance as (im)possible and, 3, 175, 217n1; socialism and, 197–201; third-world countries in context of, 60, 94, 113, 128, 196, 214n9. *See also* corporation critiques from inside; future of corporate capitalism; historicization of corporations; multinational corporations
corporations in fiction: biopower and, 15–16, 123–124, 151–152, 154, 159–160, 193–194, 194–195, 205, 219n13; cancer metaphor for corporations and, 169–171, 173; capitalism critiques and, 23, 36–37, 48–49, 139; capital's influences and, 18–19, 22–24, 26, 36–37, 116, 120–122, 127, 131–133, 210nn1–2; CEO figure/corporate bodies benevolence of and, 107, 144, 146, 147, 215n2; consumption/commodification and, 15, 18, 22, 32–33, 127–128, 152,

215n3; corporate bodies in context of individual bodies and, 16, 159–161, 164–165, 166–172, 177–178, 192; corporate bodies' presence in context of, 14, 20–22, 24, 26–27, 31–32, 34–35, 40, 75, 141, 145, 153, 159, 202, 211n7, 216n3; corporate power/capitalism as malevolent and, 169–171, 173; corporate power/capitalism benevolence of and, 14–16, 75–76, 78–85, 88–89, 102–105, 107, 108–112, 114, 140, 142–149, 163, 214n9, 215n2; corporate takeovers and, 148–149; corporate takeovers in, 28; corporation critiques from inside and, 186–192; corporations in context of death and, 15, 116, 118, 127–128, 130–134; corporatization of everyday life/family in, 15–16, 136–137, 142, 144–149, 151–152, 164, 166; culture in postmodern era and, 119–121, 133, 135; death narratives and, 115–120, 134–135, 173, 215n1; democracy and, 30–31, 170; economic criticism in context of, 48–49; existentialism and, 118, 215n2; family discourse in corporations in context of stabilization/embodiment and, 16, 136–137, 139–141, 157, 191, 202, 215n1; family discourse in late capitalist world system/destabilization/embodiment and, 12, 16, 136–142, 149–151, 153–157, 159, 215n2, 216n4; for-profit health care industry in context of neoliberalism and, 174–175, 217n6; future in context of capitalism and, 16, 19, 21, 28–31, 46–48, 159, 161, 163, 165, 171–172, 177–179, 190, 210n3, 210n4, 211n6, 217n5; gender roles in context of corporate power and, 163, 216n1; globalization and, 31, 211n6; historical capitalism transitions and, 19, 21, 28–31, 47–48, 136–137, 146–147, 210n3, 210n4, 211n6, 215n2; historicization of, 18–20, 30, 32–34, 37, 43, 159–160, 169–170, 210n4, 211n5; historicization of corporations and, 12, 159–160, 161–166, 174, 217n6; individual bodies in context of multinational corporations and, 159–160, 164, 176; labor power and, 20, 27, 36–37, 113; late capitalism and, 19, 32–34, 36, 42, 44, 46–48, 116, 118, 120, 127, 135, 159; limited liability corporations and, 165–166, 175, 192; living/dead binary and, 119–123, 135; market in context of death and, 116, 126–128; media's effects on postmodern life and, 15, 115, 119–121, 120–121, 124, 129–132; medicine/medicalization of bodies and, 15, 123–124, 127–129, 133, 166–167, 174–175, 215n3, 215nn3–4; multinational corporations in context of medicines and, 133; neoliberalism/deregulation in context of medicines and, 128–129, 215nn3–4; neoliberalism/destabilization and, 136–137, 149; neoliberalism in context of for-profit health care industry and, 174–175, 217n6; pharmaceutical industry and, 15, 127–133, 166–167; pseudoreligious side of capitalism and, 7–8, 166, 171–174, 208n9; references to past and, 19, 32–34, 36, 42, 44; resistance as (im)possible and, 14, 19–21, 24–30, 32, 35–46, 37, 40–43, 175–177, 176, 205, 211n7, 211n10; science in context of death and, 116, 122–127, 129–130; self-perpetuation of capitalism and, 164–166; sovereignty/personhood rights and, 16, 166–179; technologies and, 116, 119, 127; texts/textual content and, 3, 13; virtuality and, 15, 16, 125–126, 151; wealth distribution and, 30, 33–34. *See also* corporations; *Crying of Lot 49, The* (Pynchon); *Octopus, The* (Norris)
corporations in literature, 11–12, 208n14, 209n16
Cosmopolis (DeLillo), 7–8, 208n9
Cowart, David, 218nn6–7
Crichton, Michael, 50
Crying of Lot 49, The (Pynchon): biopower and, 205; capitalism critiques and, 36–37, 139; consumption/commodification in context of, 32–33, 152; corporate bodies' presence and, 14, 31–32, 34, 40, 141, 153, 211n7, 216n3; future of corporate capitalism and, 46–48, 190, 203–205; historicization of corporations in, 19, 33–34, 37, 43, 160; ISA and, 38–39; late capitalism transitions and, 19, 32–34, 36, 42, 44, 46–48; references to past and, 19, 32–34, 36, 42, 44; resistance as (im)

238 / INDEX

possible and, 14, 19–20, 32, 35–46, 177, 205, 211n7, 211n10; wealth distribution and, 33–34
Cuarón, Alfonso, 194–195, 219n13
cultural antagonisms, 14, 55–56, 59–60, 62–64, 68–69
cultural productions, 3, 13. *See also* popular culture

Dartmouth College v. Woodward (1819), 9
Davis, Mike, 214n6
Day at the Races, A (dir. Wood), 189
Day of the Locust, The (West), 41–42
Debord, Guy, 208n15
DeGrandpre, Richard, 128
Deleuze, Gilles, 156, 208n13, 220n19
DeLillo, Don, 7–8, 188–189; *Americana*, 218n7; *Cosmopolis*, 7–8, 208n9. *See also White Noise* (DeLillo)
Demme, Jonathan, 1–4, 12, 14
democracy (individual rights and freedoms): corporations in fiction and, 30–31, 170; films and, 1; globalization in context of, 5; multinational corporations and, 1–3
Dewey, Joseph, 177–178
Dick, Philip K., 216n2
Dilbert (Adams), 180–182, 217n2
Donaldson, Thomas, 152–153
Dostoyevsky, Fyodor, 138
Dugdale, John, 211n7

economic inequality (wealth distribution). *See* wealth distribution (economic inequality)
"economy of exception", 4–5, 193, 207n5
Eggers, Dave, 6–7
Elkind, Peter, 208n11
Emerson, Ralph Waldo, 30, 46, 190
Empire (Hardt and Negri), 16–17, 65, 151, 201–203
Engels, Friedrich, 13, 142
Enron, 8, 140
Escape from New York (dir. Carpenter), 93
Executive Suite (dir. Wise): comedies and, 76; consumption/commodification and, 77–78, 103–104; corporate power/capitalism as malevolent and, 75–77, 163; corporate power/capitalism benevolence of and, 15, 75–76, 78–80, 163; corporations' internal contradictions and, 80–81, 85, 89; mergers and, 81
existentialism, 180, 183

Faulkner, William, 138
Ferris, Joshua, 16–17, 180–181, 186–192, 202
films: adultery narrative and, 84–85, 87; capitalism critiques in, 15, 51, 60, 74–76, 87–88, 106–107, 114, 213n1; capitalism transitionals and, 91; CEO figure/corporate bodies as malevolent and, 15, 91–92, 107, 108–110; comedies and, 76, 81, 96; consumption/commodification and, 54, 65, 71–72, 77–78, 88–92, 100–101, 103–104, 214n8; corporate bodies as malevolent and, 86–87; corporate power/capitalism as malevolent and, 14–15, 74–77, 81–86, 93–96, 98, 100–107, 107–114, 140, 163, 213n3, 214n6, 214n9; corporate takeovers and, 28, 76, 93; corporation critiques from inside and, 183–186, 188, 190, 218n4; corporations' internal contradictions and, 15, 75, 80–81, 84–85, 89, 92; democracy and, 81–82, 88–89, 91–92, 201; democracy in context of, 1; economic criticism in context of, 48–49; gender roles in context of corporate power and, 83, 86–87, 109–112, 163, 216n1; "just in time" system and, 67–68; late capitalism critiques in, 75–76, 91–93, 112, 114, 213n1; media in context of transnationalism and, 54, 71; minorities and poor/other metaphor in, 96–98, 101, 214nn5–6; multinational corporation as malevolent and, 76, 90; neoliberalism and, 76, 90, 93–94, 99–100, 101–102, 105–106, 150, 203, 213n3; New York City economics in context of, 93–94, 95–99, 213n2, 213n4, 214nn5–6; pseudoreligious side of capitalism and, 56, 60, 68–69, 71, 87–92, 98; satires and, 76, 81; self-understanding in context of consumption and, 74–75; smooth functioning/talking or "systemic violence" and, 54, 67, 71; thrillers and, 76, 113; "true" tales of personal triumph and, 213n1, 217n7; wealth distribution and, 93–94, 98, 101, 213n2, 213n4; world system in, 91–92

INDEX / 239

financial anxieties, 3, 51, 53, 65, 73, 213n11
financial crisis of 2007-2008, 4, 8, 207n1, 208n10
financialization of economy, 6-7, 171, 208nn7-12, 217n5
Fleming, Peter, 217n1
Ford, Gerald, 93
Foucault, Michel, 4, 43, 123, 151, 193-194, 201, 219n12
Frankenheimer, John, 1-2
Friedman, Milton, 5, 219n14
Friedman, Thomas, 5
Fucini, Joseph J., 212n9
Fucini, Suzy, 212n9
Fukuyama, Frances, 5, 91
future of corporate capitalism: capitalism/s and, 17; corporation critiques from inside and, 190; corporations in fiction, 16, 19, 21, 28-31, 46-48, 159, 161, 163, 165, 171-172, 177-179, 190, 210n3, 210n4, 211n6, 217n5; historicization of corporations in context of, 19, 21, 28-31, 46-48, 47-48, 178, 210n3, 210n4, 211n6; multiple reconfigurations and, 11, 201-206, 219-220nn18-19

Gaddis, William. *See J R* (Gaddis)
Gain (Powers): biopower and, 16, 159-160, 193; cancer metaphor for corporations and, 169-171, 173; corporate bodies in context of individual bodies and, 16, 159-161, 164-165, 166-172, 177-178, 192; corporate power/capitalism as malevolent and, 169-171, 173; corporatization of everyday life/family in, 164, 166; democracy in context of corporations and, 170; future of corporate capitalism and, 16, 159, 161, 163, 165, 171-172, 177-179, 190, 217n5; gender roles in context of corporate power and, 163, 216n1; historicization of corporations and, 12, 159-160, 161-166, 174, 217n6; late capitalism and, 159; limited liability corporations and, 175, 192; mergers and, 168-169; multinational corporations and, 161, 170; multinational corporations in context of individual bodies and, 159-160, 164, 176; neoliberalism in context of for-profit health care industry and, 174-175, 217n6; pseudoreligious side of capitalism and, 166, 171-172, 173-174; resistance as (im)possible and, 175-177; self-perpetuation of capitalism, 164-166; sovereignty/personhood rights of corporations and, 16, 158, 166-179; world system of capitalism and, 161, 170
Gauthier, Anne Hélène, 154
Gervais, Ricky, 182
Ghostbusters (dir. Reitman): comedies and, 76, 96; consumption/commodification and, 100-101, 214n8; corporate power/capitalism as malevolent and, 93-96, 98, 100-102, 213n3, 214n6; corporate takeovers and, 93; economic criticism in context of, 48-49; minorities and poor/other metaphor in, 96-98, 101, 214nn5-6; neoliberalism in context of, 76, 93-94, 99-100, 101-102, 213n3; New York City economics in context of, 93-94, 95-99, 213n2, 213n4, 214nn5-6; pseudoreligious side of capitalism/ Protestant work ethic and, 98; wealth distribution and, 93-94, 98, 101, 213n2, 213n4
Gibson, William, 164-165, 216n2
Gilbert, Paul, 154-155
Gilroy, Tony. *See Michael Clayton* (dir. Gilroy)
Glengarry, Glen Ross (dir. Foley), 104
globalization: overview of, 5-7, 146-147, 215n2; consumption/commodification in context of, 5, 71-72; corporations in fiction and, 31, 211n6. *See also* multinational corporations
Godden, Richard, 209n16
Graeber, David, 6, 207n1
Gravity's Rainbow (Pynchon), 38-39, 43
Groening, Matt, 180-182, 217n2, 218n3
Guattari, Félix, 156, 208n13, 220n19
Guillory, John, 11
Gung Ho (dir. Howard): automobile industry history and, 52-55, 61-62, 71, 73, 148, 159-160, 212nn7-9; capitalism critiques and, 51, 60; class anxieties and, 14, 56-57, 59, 72; consumption/ commodification and, 54, 65, 71-72; critiques of, 57, 59, 60-61, 67-68, 70-71; cultural antagonisms and, 14, 55-56, 59-60, 62-64, 68-69; financial anxieties in, 51, 53, 65, 73,

213n11; globalization in context of consumption and, 71–72; "just in time" system and, 67–68; late capitalism and, 51, 54, 60, 70, 73; late capitalism's return to source and, 14, 60; media in context of transnationalism and, 54, 71; multinational automobile industry and, 54–55, 65–70, 186, 212n10; nationalism and, 62–66, 213n11; Other in context of corporation and, 14, 60; pseudoreligious side of capitalism/ Protestant work ethic and, 56, 60, 68–69, 71; smooth functioning/talking or "systemic violence" and, 54, 67, 71; Taylorization of labor and, 60–61; unionization of automobile industry and, 55–59, 61, 66–71, 212nn5–6; white-collar U.S. executives and, 57, 59, 71

Hardt, Michael, 16–17, 65, 151, 201–203
Harris, Charles B., 178
Harvey, David, 6, 146–147, 175, 178, 196, 207n3, 208n12, 215n2, 217n5
Hatch-Waxman Act (1984), 128, 215n3
Hayek, Frederick, 5
Heidegger, Martin, 118, 215n2
Heller, Joseph, 186
Hill, Walter, 93
historicization of corporations: capitalism historical transitions in fiction and, 19, 21, 28–31, 47–48, 210n3, 210n4, 211n6; fictional representations and, 18–20, 30, 32–34, 37, 43, 210n4, 211n5; future of corporate capitalism and, 19, 21, 28–31, 46–48, 178, 210n3, 210n4, 211n6; references to past in fiction and, 19, 32–34, 36, 42, 44. *See also* corporations
Hologram for the King, A (Eggers), 6–7
Horkheimer, Max, 208n15
Howard, Ron. *See Gung Ho* (dir. Howard)
Hussman, Lawrence E., 210n4

individual bodies: corporate bodies in context of, 16, 159–161, 164–165, 166–172, 177–178, 192; corporations in context of, 3, 17, 167, 216nn2–4; multinational corporations in context of, 159–160, 164, 176
industries in literature, 13
Ingrassia, Paul, 61, 212n6
Inkster, Ian, 52, 212n3

Jailbird (Vonnegut), 198–199, 200, 203
Jameson, Fredric, 11, 30, 42, 57, 198, 201, 204–205, 211n5
Japan: automobile industry and, 52–53, 70; class anxieties in context of white-collar executives from, 14, 56–57, 59, 72; cultural antagonisms and, 14, 55–56, 59–60, 62–64, 68–69; economic development of, 51–53, 212n3; joint venture history in automobile industry and, 61, 70, 212n8; multinational corporations and, 51, 54–55, 212n4; nationalism and, 64–65; as threat to U.S. economy, 50–51, 212nn1–2
Jaspers, Karl, 215n2
Johnston, John, 157, 211n7
joint ventures, 61, 70, 212n8. *See also* multinational corporations
J R (Gaddis): biopower and, 15–16, 151–152, 154, 193; CEO figure/ corporate bodies benevolence and, 144, 146, 147, 215n2; consumption/ commodification and, 152; corporate power/capitalism benevolence and, 16, 142–149, 215n2; corporate takeovers and, 148–149; corporatization of everyday life/family in, 15–16, 136–137, 142, 144–149, 151–152, 164, 166; family discourse in corporations in context of stabilization/embodiment and, 16, 136–137, 139–141, 157, 191, 202, 215n1; family discourse in late capitalist world system/destabilization/embodiment and, 12, 16, 136–142, 149–151, 153–157, 159, 215n2, 216n4; historical capitalism transitions and, 136–137, 146–147, 215n2; limited liability corporations and, 165–166; mergers and, 140–141, 149; neoliberalism/destabilization and, 136–137, 149; sovereignty/personhood rights of corporations and, 16; virtuality and, 16, 151
Judge, Mike, 183
"just in time" system, 67–68

Kahn, Herman, 50–51, 212n2
Keller, Maryann, 63
Kellner, Douglas, 127, 134
Keynesian economic policies, 4, 137, 146, 209n16
Kierkegaard, Søren, 118, 134, 215n2

Kindleberger, Charles P., 50
Klein, Naomi, 195
Korten, David C., 10, 165
Krippner, Greta R., 208n7, 208n12
Krugman, Paul, 207n5, 208n10

late capitalism: corporations and, 3, 116, 118; corporations in fiction and, 19, 32–34, 36, 42, 44, 46–48, 116, 118, 120, 127, 135, 159; critiques of, 15, 75–76, 91–93, 112, 114, 213n1; films and, 75–76, 91–93, 112, 114, 213n1; and historical transitions in fiction, 19, 32–34, 36, 42, 44, 46–48; historicization of, 18; multinational corporations and, 2, 51, 54, 60, 70, 73; neoliberalism and, 5, 146–147, 215n2; pharmaceutical industry and, 127; and return to source in context of multinational corporations, 14, 60
LeClair, Tom, 135
Lentricchia, Frank, 118
Leonard, Suzanne, 84
Life Is Hell (Groening), 180–182, 217n2, 218n3
literature, 11–13, 208n14, 209n16. *See also* corporations in fiction
living/dead binary, 119–123, 135
Lumet, Sidney. *See Network* (dir. Lumet)

Mailer, Norman, 169–170
Maliszewski, Paul, 166
Mamet, David, 104
Manchurian Candidate, The (dir. Frankenheimer), 1–2
Manchurian Candidate, The (dir. Demme), 1–4, 12, 14
Manhattan (dir. Allen), 93
Marchand, Roland, 145
Margin Call (dir. Chandor), 7
Marsa, Linda, 128
Marx, Karl, and topics: capitalism as transitional force, 13, 22–24, 26, 91, 210n2; capitalism critiques, 13, 140; capitalism history, 10–13; class identity, 11; corporate bodies, 12; corporations' internal contradictions, 81; ideology critiques, 120; labor power, 36–37, 78, 92; surplus value, 10, 162
Maynard, Micheline, 57, 212n10
McLean, Bethany, 208n11

McQuaid, Kim, 217n5
McTeague (Norris), 30
media, 120–121, 131
Meirelles, Fernando, 214n9
Melville, Herman, 167, 216n4
Merchant, Stephen, 182
mergers, 9–10, 74, 76, 81, 104–107, 140–141, 149, 168–169. *See also* corporate takeovers
Michael Clayton (dir. Gilroy): CEO figure/corporate bodies as malevolent and, 108–110; corporate power/capitalism as malevolent and, 76, 107–114, 214n9; corporate power/capitalism benevolence and, 76, 108–112; gender roles and, 109–112, 163, 216n1; late capitalism critiques and, 112, 114; thrillers and, 76, 113; "true" tales of personal triumph and, 217n7
Michaels, Walter Benn, 11–12, 210n1
Milkman, Ruth, 61, 212n7, 212n9
Moore, Steven, 155, 215n2
Moynihan, Ray, 132, 215n4
multinational corporations: automobile industry and, 54–55, 65–70, 186, 212n10; capitalism and, 3; capitalism critiques and, 51, 60; class anxieties and, 14, 56–57, 59, 72; consumption/commodification in context of, 3; cultural antagonisms and, 14, 55–56, 59–60, 62–64, 68–69; democracy and, 1–3; financial anxieties in context of, 51, 53, 65, 73, 213n11; individual bodies in context of, 159–160, 164, 176; joint ventures and, 61, 70, 212n8; "just in time" system and, 67–68; late capitalism and, 2, 51, 54, 60, 70, 73; late capitalism's return to source and, 14, 60; nationalism and, 62–66, 213n11; Other/other and, 14, 60; Protestant work ethic in context of, 56, 60, 68–69, 71; sovereignty/personhood rights of, 1–2, 176; Taylorization of labor and, 60–61; unionization of automobile industry and, 55–59, 61, 66–71, 212nn5–6; white-collar U.S. executives in automobile industry and, 57, 59, 71; world system and, 3, 91–92, 161, 170. *See also* corporations; globalization; *Gung Ho* (dir. Howard)

nationalism, 62–66, 213n11
Negri, Antonio, 16–17, 65, 151, 201–203
neoliberalism: biopower and, 195–196, 219nn14–15; capitalism/s and, 4, 6, 207n3; consumption/commodification in context of, 8; corporate bodies and, 8, 208nn10–12; destabilization and, 136–137, 149; "economy of exception" and, 4–5, 193, 207n5; financial crisis 2007-2008 and, 4, 8, 207n1, 208n10; financialization of economy and, 6–7, 171, 208nn7–12, 217n5; late capitalism and, 5, 146–147, 215n2; Occupy movements and, 5–6, 203; posthuman in context of, 7–8, 165, 201, 203, 216n1; resistance as (im)possible against, 197; smooth functioning/talking or "systemic violence" and, 54, 67, 71, 113; as utopian project, 6–7; wealth distribution and, 5–6, 11–12, 101, 192–193, 207n6
Network (dir. Lumet): adultery narrative and, 84–85, 87; capitalism critiques in, 87–88; CEO figure/corporate bodies as malevolent and, 91–92; comedy/satires and, 76, 81; consumption/commodification and, 88–92, 100, 104; corporate bodies as malevolent and, 81–87; corporate power/capitalism benevolence and, 81–85, 88–89, 114; corporations' internal contradictions and, 84, 92; democracy in context of corporate power and, 81–82, 88–89, 91–92, 201; gender roles and, 83, 86–87, 163, 216n1; historical capitalism transitions and, 91; late capitalism critiques and, 91–93; multinational corporate capitalism as malevolent and, 76, 90; neoliberalism and, 76, 90, 150, 203; pseudoreligious side of capitalism and, 87–92; world system and, 91–92
Nietzsche, Friedrich Wilhelm, 118
Norris, Frank: *McTeague*, 30; *Pit, The*, 7–8. See also *Octopus, The* (Norris)

Occupy movements, 5–6, 203
Octopus, The (Norris): capitalism critiques and, 23, 139; capital's influences and, 18–19, 22–23, 22–24, 26, 210nn1–2; consumption/commodification and, 18, 22; corporate bodies' presence and, 14, 20–22, 24, 26–27, 34–35, 75, 145, 159, 167–168, 202, 216n3; corporate takeovers and, 28; democracy and, 30–31; future of corporate capitalism and, 19, 21, 28–31, 47–48, 178, 190, 210n3, 210n4, 211n6; globalization and, 31, 211n6; historical capitalism transitions and, 19, 21, 28–31, 47–48, 91, 210n3, 210n4, 211n6; historicization of corporations and, 18, 20, 30, 32, 160, 210n4, 211n5; labor power and, 20, 27, 113; resistance as (im)possible and, 14, 19–21, 24–30, 37, 40–43, 176; wealth distribution and, 33
Odets, Clifford, 212n5
Office, The (television programs in U.S. and UK), 16–17, 182–183
Office Space (dir. Judge), 183–186, 183–188, 190, 218n4, 218nn4–5
Osteen, Mark, 209n16
Other/other/othering, 14, 60, 96–98, 101, 197, 214nn5–6

Page, Max, 94, 96
Park, Ed, 180–181, 186–188, 190, 218n7
Passos, John Dos, 39
Pepper, Thomas, 51
Personal Days (Park), 180–181, 186–188, 190, 218n7
personhood rights/sovereignty. See citizenship; sovereignty/personhood rights
pharmaceutical industry, 15, 127–133, 166–167
Pit, The (Norris), 7–8
Polany, Karl, 7
popular culture, 3, 15, 48, 74, 181, 184, 218n4. See also *Gung Ho* (dir. Howard)
posthuman, 7–8, 165, 201, 203, 216n1. See also neoliberalism
Powers, Richard. See *Gain* (Powers)
Protestant work ethic, 56, 60, 68–69, 71, 98, 166, 172
pseudoreligious side of capitalism: corporation critiques from inside and, 189–190, 218nn6–7; corporations in fiction and, 7–8, 166, 171–174, 208n9; films and, 56, 60, 68–69, 71, 87–92, 98
Pynchon, Thomas: *Gravity's Rainbow*, 38–39, 43; *Vineland*, 46–47, 129–130. See also *Crying of Lot 49, The* (Pynchon)

Rajan, Kaushik Sunder, 218nn9–10
Ramis, Harold, 93
Rand, Ayn, 216n3
Reagan, Ronald, and administration, 6, 10, 46–47, 52, 57, 93–94, 100–101, 128, 156, 181
Reich, Robert B., 144
Reichl, Alexander J., 97–99
Reitman, Ivan. See Ghostbusters (dir. Reitman)
resistance as (im)possible: corporation critiques from inside and, 180–190, 217nn1–2, 218nn4–5; against corporations, 3, 175, 217n1; in fiction, 14, 19–21, 24–30, 32, 35–46, 37, 40–43, 211n7, 211n10; against neoliberalism, 197; in popular culture, 184, 218n4
Rilke, Rainer Maria, 117

Said, Edward, 54
Saval, Nikil, 181
Savitch, H. V., 98
Scarface (dir. De Palma), 184
Scarface (dir. Hawks and Rosson), 184
Scorsese, Martin, 93, 97
Seed, David, 211n10
Segal, Peter. See *Tommy Boy* (dir. Segal)
Seventh Seal, The (dir. Bergman), 119
Shining, The (dir. Kubrik), 57
Shonkwiler, Alison, 208n9
Shorter, Edward, 156
Simpsons, The (television program), 218n3
Sites, William, 94, 97–98, 100
S&L crisis of 1987, 105, 149, 207n3, 213n1, 214n6
Smith, Adam, 80, 91, 141, 152, 162, 176
Sobel, Robert, 62, 67–68, 212n10
Solomon, Norman, 182
Sontag, Susan, 170–171
South Park (television program), 74–75
sovereignty/personhood rights of corporations: corporations in fiction and, 16, 166–179; metaphors and, 8–11, 13, 16; multinational corporations and, 1–2, 176; multiple reconfigurations of capitalism and, 201
Spencer, Nicholas, 215n2
Spicer, André, 217n1
Stereolab, 18
Stiglitz, Joseph E., 207n5

Tabb, William K., 94
Taxi Driver (dir. Scorsese), 93, 97
Taylor, Frederick, 68
Taylorization of labor, 60–61
television news: adultery narrative and, 84–85, 87; capitalism critiques in, 87–88; CEO figure/corporate bodies as malevolent and, 91–92; comedy/satires and, 76, 81; consumption/commodification and, 88–92, 100, 104; corporate bodies as malevolent and, 81–87; corporate power/capitalism benevolence and, 81–85, 88–89, 114; corporations' internal contradictions and, 84, 92; democracy in context of corporate power and, 81–82, 88–89, 91–92, 201; gender roles and, 83, 86–87, 163, 216n1; historical capitalism transitions and, 91; late capitalism critiques and, 91–93; multinational corporate capitalism as malevolent and, 76, 90; neoliberalism and, 76, 90, 150, 203; pseudoreligious side of capitalism and, 87–92; world system and, 91–92
television programs, 16–17, 75, 182–183
Then We Came to the End (Ferris), 16–17, 180–181, 186–192, 202
third-world or developing countries, 60, 94, 113, 128, 196–197, 214n9
Tolstoy, Leo, 115, 138
Tommy Boy (dir. Segal): capitalism critiques in, 106–107; CEO figure/corporate bodies as good/ malevolent and, 107; comedies and, 76; consumption/commodification and, 103–104; corporate power/capitalism as malevolent and, 76, 102–103, 104–107, 140; corporate power/capitalism benevolence and, 76, 102–105, 107, 140, 159–160; mergers and, 104–107, 140–141; neoliberalism and, 105–106
Trachtenberg, Alan, 208n14
transnationalism, 54, 71, 170, 176

United States, and topics: automobile industry, 52–53; blue-collar American workers' class anxieties, 14, 56–57, 59, 72; cultural antagonisms, 14, 55–56, 59–60, 62–64, 68–69; nationalism, 62–63, 66, 213n11; white-collar executives, 57, 59, 71

Vonnegut, Kurt, *Jailbird*, 198–200, 203

Wallerstein, Immanuel, 12, 161
Warriors, The (dir. Hill), 93
Wasserman, Harvey, 9
wealth distribution (economic inequality): corporations in fiction and, 30, 33–34; films and, 93–94, 98, 101, 213n2, 213n4; neoliberalism in context of, 5–6, 11–12, 101, 192–193, 207n6
Weber, Leonard J., 130
Weber, Max, 7, 166, 172
West, Nathaniel, 41–42
White, Joseph B., 61
White Noise (DeLillo): biopower and, 15, 123–124, 193–194; capital's influences and, 116, 120–121, 122, 127, 131–133; consumption/commodification and, 15, 127–128, 215n3; corporations in context of death and, 15, 116, 118, 127–128, 130–134; culture in postmodern era and, 119–121, 133, 135; death narratives and, 115–120, 134–135, 173, 215n1; economic criticism in context of, 48–49; existentialism and, 118, 215n2; late capitalism and, 116, 118, 120, 127, 135, 159; living/dead binary and, 119–123, 135; market in context of death and, 116, 126–128; media's effects on postmodern life and, 15, 115, 119–121, 120–121, 124, 129–132; medicine/medicalization of bodies and, 15, 123–124, 127–129, 133, 166–167, 174–175, 215n3, 215nn3–4; multinational corporations in context of medicines and, 133; neoliberalism/deregulation in context of medicines and, 128–129, 215nn3–4; pharmaceutical industry and, 15, 127–133, 166–167; science in context of death and, 116, 122–127, 129–130; technologies and, 116, 119, 127; virtuality and, 15, 125–126
Whitman, Walt, 30, 87, 172, 177–178, 190
Whyte, William H., 35
Wilcox, Leonard, 117–118
Wise, Robert. *See Executive Suite* (dir. Wise)
Wood, Adam H., 210n1, 211n5
Woodmansee, Martha, 209n16
Work Is Hell (Groening), 180–181

Yates, Brock, 59

Žižek, Slavoj, 2–3, 44–45, 113, 126, 177, 219n13
Zola, Émile, 24, 210n2

About the Author

Ralph Clare is an assistant professor of English at Boise State University, specializing in twentieth- and twenty-first-century American literature. He has published essays on Richard Powers, David Foster Wallace, William Gaddis, and Kurt Vonnegut. This is his first book.

www.ingramcontent.com/pod-product-compliance
Lightning Source LLC
Chambersburg PA
CBHW020114010526
44115CB00008B/826